BOOTLEGGER'S BRIDE

By

Jock Carpenter

Gorman

Gorman

Photos courtesy of Alberta Provincial Archives,
Glenbow Alberta Institute,
Cover photo by Pat Evans
Typesetting and book design by
The Hanna Herald.
Printed and Bound in Canada
Cover photograph courtesy of
the late L. Guzzi, Fernie, British Columbia.

Carpenter, Jock,
Bootlegger's Bride
Includes Index —
ISBN 0-921835-05-1

The publisher gratefully acknowledges the assistance of the Alberta Foundation for the Arts in the publication of this book.

**The Alberta
Foundation
for the Arts**

Canadian Cataloguing in Publication Data

Carpenter, Jock
        Bootlegger's Bride

        ISBN 0-921835-05-1

1. Title.   970.004'97   C77-002183-2
FC109.1.S45C37
F1035

DEDICATION

FOR JOHN PATRICK GILLESE
... AS PROMISED

Piccarilo was a bootlegger for many years and made lots of money. Piccarrilo was a good hearted man, he would always help the poor, but hot tempered, when he heard that his boy was shot, nothing hold him only to revenge.

If he would have stop and think a minute, he might be living today. Many crimes are commited through hot tempered man.

from the diaries of Marie Rose Smith

Courtesy Glenbow Alberta Institute, Calgary, Alberta

CONTENTS

FORWARD

The story you are about to read is my interpretation of the most famous case to emerge in the history of rum running in the West.

In many cases it was difficult to sort fact from fancy, truth from colourful legend. I have chosen to put the book into story form to capture the flavour of the time and have used both truth and legend which I hope is for the betterment of the reader.

The style of the book was chosen to give life to the reams of factual detail regarding the rum runners. The facts of people's lives have been adhered to as closely as possible; the trial sections taken directly from court records and newspapers of the day. My purpose was to write a compassionate book about a true legend with a wealth of little known background.

I wish to recognize the late Charles Anthony Costanzo, uncle of Florence, who gave me many hours of background information on the life of Florence, on his brother Vincenzo, and the family's interpretation of the tragedy.

My deep gratitude to the late Father Fidelis Chicoine who was Florence's spiritual advisor and confessor during her last months on earth. His moving account of those days enhanced and completed the book.

To these two men, for their shared remembrances, I will ever be grateful.

I am indebted to Brian Speirs of the Provincial Archives of Alberta for his time and efforts on my behalf. I am thankful for the research grants provided by Alberta Culture and the Canada Council which enabled me to complete the necessary travel for my research. A general footnote is necessary to cover parts, wordings, verbatim statements and all other information taken from newspapers, the McKinley Cameron papers, Glenbow Alberta Institute; Alberta Provincial Archives, Edmonton, Alberta; as numerous footnoting would impede the chapters.

I owe the impetus to writing the book to Marie Rose Smith, Fifty Dollar Bride, published by Gorman & Gorman, whose diary quotations start and end the book.

To those people who gave me material, interviews, pictures and generously helped with the manuscript but have chosen to remain anonymous, my deepest appreciation.

Writing this book was both a joy and a burden. Although it is not a happy story, it is nevertheless, an integral part of Canadian history. The reader must remember that this is my interpretation only, the true facts having been taken to the grave and the only remaining knowledge cannot come out of the confessional. The reader too, must judge for himself. It is ironic the impact Prohibition had on some people's lives before Alberta voted against it on November 8, 1923.

Jock Carpenter

I

A SILENT
CAGE

A GUSTY WIND blew at the bottom of the day.

Standing by the window, a young Italian girl watched the leaves tumble and roll down the dusty street of Fernie, British Columbia. With a sigh, she slowly raised her arms to pull off her clothes. The late autumn winds blew through the torn screen and ruffled the thin curtain material into a crescendo. The flimsy material caught against her body, clinging to its outline. Her skin absorbed light from the dying day and became luminous, vibrating from deep within. Her body was firm, coupled like a budded rose.

The girl turned reluctantly from the narrow window. In the dusk of the tiny room her eyes caught the reflection of light on the wedding dress which hung on a hook before her. The dress moved ever so gently in the breeze; a delicate, immaculate dress of virginal white. Tomorrow it would become her silent cage. Her name was Philomena Costanzo.

Philomena had been nine years old when her family immigrated to Canada. Closing her eyes she could recall her mother's face the day her father, Vincenzo, came home with the paper. She remembered too, how he burst into the room. His eyes flashed, his mouth trembled and words tumbled forth in half-sentences as he spread the wrinkled paper on the eating table for all to see.

He had been to the Ufficio Informazioni. Now he was swept along on the immigration tide. The advertisement promised opportunity for him in a land of plenty. The land of the midas touch beckoned him and he traced the words on the paper for his skeptical wife. There was work to be had, on farms, in mills and mines.

Philomena remembered vividly the frightened look that had come over her mother's face. The fright was reflected in the room; radiating from its dull walls, bouncing off tiles in the stone floor, and the children, feeling the fear, crept to their mother's side to hold onto her long apron, seeking some small security against the uprooting words of their excited father.

Vincenzo Costanzo, like many others in his day, was responding to the ads, feeling hope start anew in his heart. Poor and unhappy, he saw a chance for a better life and thus sought to leave his homeland. He decided to turn his back on the valleys of his native Italy, to leave its mountains, darkly blue. He ignored his wife's bowed head, averted his eyes when he saw pain flood her face. He applied for immigrant status.

There were many others who joined him. Once their minds were made up, they were undaunted by the differences between the two countries, unswerving in their intent to face the unknown. The men answered the call, adventure and desire in their eyes, hope and courage in their hearts. And when the time came, they took leave of their cobbled villages with sun-flooded terraces; left behind trellised grape arbours and orchards where heavy trees bent down to brood over their bounty. Sons and daughters left aged and sorrowing parents, forcing laughter and gaiety to hide anguish in their hearts. They kidded themselves; after finding a future for themselves and for their children, they would come back. Deep down they knew they would never return.

A good number of immigrants, like the Costanzo family, came from Cosenza, in the Region of Calabria. Many of the immigrants were peasant stock, trying to escape the poverty stricken regions of Southern Italy, the toe of the Italian boot. Others came from the lemon groves of Sicily, the coal mines of Tuscany and Sardinia.

The boat trip to Canada was a nightmare for the young Philomena. Sea-sickness was all around her, food was rancid and the cramped quarters damp and cold. When the ship arrived at the docks the family was apprehensive and melancholy. There they encountered a new and different language, the English tongue. Vincenzo quickly signed up for work with the railway in the west and the family was herded to a special train for immigrants.

Crowded into coach cars, they clung to each other, watched as the great land unfolded — from the pearly haze of dawn till the last light drifted across frost-nipped stubble.

To Philomena, the warm coach car was a welcome relief. Now she was again amid her own people, the dialect the same, the warmth and love of her family was around her. She played with her sister Christina and brother Antonio, and together they coaxed a slight smile back to the face of their mother, Angela. It was like one big picnic as they were fed from the contents of a wicker basket. Sleep came easily at night, bedded down between boxes and crates, lulled by the rocking rhythms of the car. They carried all their possessions with them and watched curiously as their father struggled with the strange bills and coins exchanged for their familiar lira. When the contents of the wicker basket was low Vincenzo worried about leaving the train at infrequent lunch counter stops in the railway stations. Finally the childrens' hunger drove him off and he followed other travellers, watched the exchange of silver and then nodded and pointed to get the same food for his family. When he was gone his wife became very agitated; she pressed her face against the sooty window fretting that her husband might not hear the conductor's hoarse call. The food he brought back was strange and the children yearned for a meal of sausage, a crusty loaf of dark bread, some light wine and a cut of cheese.

Struggling with language problems the immigrant men had no choice but to take the jobs offered to them. They formed a labour force, doing the lowest jobs, doing hard and heavy work that was meaningless to them. They were saddened too, to see their families face discrimination, ignorance and hostility from a population already settled in the land. The children suffered the most; ridiculed and humiliated because of their vast differences in speech, food and clothing. Not only did the immigrants have to master a new language and customs, they had to cope with the change in climate and were unprepared for the snowstorms, high winds and the isolation of a country held tight by the grip of a Canadian winter. Their alienation brought solitude to a people used to the warmth of both kinship and the sun.

There were several ways to get to the west. Single men with no families to take care of chose to work their way west. On the work gangs they toiled twelve hours a day for the sum of two dollars. Some were more fortunate; they received a larger amount but this was again taken from them for their board.

As the work gangs moved towards the west, immigrants dropped from the gangs and settled in small towns and hamlets along the way. They adapted their old country training to the opportunities that presented themselves along the way.

In the larger towns, former farmers became fresh produce peddlers. The venture required no capital; their only expense was the pushcart which they built themselves from rough discarded lumber found in alleys. The men rose in the early dark, buying fruit and vegetables at morning auctions, washing and arranging their display, then spent long hours visiting the homes to find customers. Respite from this hard work was a few minutes taken for lunch, sitting on dusty roadsides near houses where more prosperous people lived, eating warm fruit that oozed juice at the cut of a knife, dreaming over Romano cheese layered between thick hunks of dark moist bread. They lived as cheaply as they could and in time became successful grocers and tradesmen.

Many of the immigrants, including the Costanzo family, found their way to the mountainous towns of the Crow's Nest Pass area in the Northwest Territories that became the Province of British Columbia in 1871 and the Province of Alberta in 1905. Drawn by promises of work in the mines, they settled in small towns that crouched in the Rocky Mountains. Here they found similarities to the land for which they were homesick.

There was something about the squalid little towns sitting in the valleys in a glitter of sunshine, surrounded by wind-worn rocks and water rippling in deep, cold lakes. To these towns the miners brought their families, forming communities that clustered along the main roads, close to the gaping mouths of the mines.

There were several hundred families in this mountainous pass area when Vincenzo Costanzo brought his family to settle in the town of Fernie in the extreme southeastern corner of the province of British Columbia. He found work on the Kettle Valley Railroad as it moved from Revelstoke to Fernie, then took work in a mine.

As the family settled into its own ethnic community, they once again took up their former life style; tight-knit, impenetrable, not caring that other cultures looked on them as backward foreigners. United, the Italian people helped one another, lived below the poverty level to save enough money to own small one or two-roomed houses. They tended their yards, planted gardens of cabbage, onion, turnip and beets, wanting to get close to their adopted soil, to have a feeling of belonging to the land. While the men toiled deep in the damp bowels of the earth their women cooked and cleaned, had their babies, raised the families and made the best of their impoverished lives. Creeping out of bed at the first pallor of day the women went heavily about their tasks until the sky was the colour of deep violet. When the men came home from the mines, the women crossed themselves in thanksgiving. Lack of money for candles or kerosene gave them a much needed rest at dusk.

After years of hard work, Vincenzo too, was able to buy a small, four-roomed house which was crowded by the addition of four more children to the family. The warmth and love in the tiny house was a mantle Philomena drew around her in her growing years. She grew to love too, the small town of Fernie nestled in a valley surrounded by massive, snow-topped blue-gray mountains. The days in winter were short; snow-spotted with spruce trees saw-toothed against thin sunlight. The nights were long with a silver blur of moon playing a symphony of black and white on a mantle of freshly fallen snow.

Spring came late with its smells of sodden grass, tight green buds and wind cleansed in the high country. Curls of woodsmoke hung in the tawny light of evening. Then the rains came; bouncing, battering, rushing, gushing down gutters and through rain spouts, nursing a land which, like an eager lover responded with a lushness to the valley.

Soon there was a luxuriance of succulent plants, meadows of vetch and creeper, a riot of colour. Red and white clover, blue flags, daisies and lemon buttercups appeared. Delicate white blossoms promised a harvest of small, wild strawberries and ruby-clustered raspberries. Queen Anne's lace etched the tall grass with frosty flowers that looked like low-lying mist in the moonlight. Warm shafts of sunlight and high crags of rock around her gave Philomena an exhilarated feeling as she skipped from her home to town on errands for her mother.

Fernie was originally a lumber town. A new town had risen from the ashes of the 1908 fire which nearly destroyed it. The main street, called Victoria Avenue, was dotted with buildings of one or two storeys built with a peaked roof and flat-faced front. Windows were long, narrow and two-framed; the lower slid into the upper to be held up by a bottle or any handy object of the desired height. There were the usual stores of a 1915 mining town; a grocer and drug store, blacksmith, barber, cafe, laundry and hotel. There were a few churches and a schoolhouse, an opera house and post office. Around these were the houses, some owned by the mines and rented to employees. These houses were drab, unpainted, box-like structures. Inside however, the contents were worn and mended, secondhand but immaculately clean. In time these houses were sold to the renters. The single fellows stayed at the hotel or in rented rooms scattered throughout the town.

Many of the houses were one-roomed shanties with additions put on by owners in varying stages of children and wealth. Outside the screened back door a back stoop held a galvanized tub for washing, the wash stand, buckets and

14

pails. Mops hung on the side of the house to dry. The coal shed was close to the back door. A clothes line and chicken pen completed the yard. The chickens ran loose, pecking and scratching in the tiny gardens, returning to lay warm, dark-yolked eggs in the hen house. During rainy days the back yard was a morass of mud; piles of scrapings fell around the shoe scraper attached to the stoop. In later years electricity and water lines came into being but the path to the outhouse was trod for quite some time.

The grocery and dry good store of H. Bentley and Co. was on Victoria Avenue near the hotel. Each morning a clerk, wearing black shirt sleeve protectors from wrist to elbow, came out to sweep the slivery wooden walk. Next to the grocery was a drug store, narrow shelved from the floor to the ceiling and filled with bottles of all sorts; Bendor's Heave Powder, Waterman Blue-Black ideal ink, salt petre. An advertisement for Bovril stood on the counter.

"... Never be without Bovril in the
house. Better than a hot water bottle ... for
the sick ... for a stimulant ...".

In the curved glass fronted showcase, displays of Florida water and scented powder in small round boxes were towered over by tall bottles of Dr. Chase's Syrup of Linseed and Turpentine. Against one wall poultry supplies were piled; hundred pound sacks of Blatchford's Egg Mash, ground oyster shell and bone which sold for five cents a pound.

But it was with the small corner grocers that the Italian community traded. Here they could get staples from their native Italy: dried black olives, pasta of all description and size, tomato paste, cheese in balls the size of a big fist and tied with woven twine for hanging. All were sold in bulk to those with large families. The grocer extended credit to the miners when times were lean and collected when the mines were working. His hand-lettered signs advertised new products, straggling letters reading: — "TomaTos — fresH ToDay". Young boys were sent by their families to work delivering groceries, filling shelves and sweeping floors to pay off mounting grocery bills.

In the dry goods store, immigrant women with rough calloused hands fingered bolts of material, lingered over dainty tea sets. They looked longingly but never bought as the grocer's bill took most of their money. Only the cheapest furnishings were purchased and then only after months of frugal saving.

Down the street was the barber shop, identified by its red and white striped pole. It was a spotless male-dominated cubby hole with a black leather chair which could be swung in any direction. The wall opposite the chair was arrayed with calendars, postcards and pictures for clients to gaze upon. Some of the calendars were daring; burlesqued women in teasing poses and the men laughed, spit at the spittoon, nudged and winked at each other.

"Hey George, don't let the old lady see you looking at that one!"

George would shrug his shoulders as he arranged rows of slender-corked bottles holding sweet aromatic scents. The tools of his trade were arrayed in precision like a dentist. Children in passing heard the hypnotic slap of his razor as he honed it on his strap and they looked in, round-eyed. Their hair was cut on Saturday nights in a warm kitchen by a harried mother with scissors and a bowl.

On a side street was a Chinese cafe and laundry. The single miner or logger came to town to have his clothes washed while he rid his face and head of unwanted hair at the barber shop. The owner of the laundry lived alone; his wife and children were left in China. He went by the name of Sam or Lou, dubbed by a white population unfamiliar with the names of Wong, Wing or Duck.

The cafe, with its advertisements for cigarettes and tobacco, was a busy establishment. There was a choice of seating; a long counter with high stools or small tables surrounded by chairs of twisted metal. In summer the windows were filled with geraniums; in winter the windows wept with steam. The menu was unvaried; beef dishes with rice and potatoes, heavy, filling soups, sandwiches, pie and coffee. Coca-Cola sold for five cents a glass.

On her errands, the meat market was a favorite stopping place for Philomena. The butcher always had a treat for the pig-tailed child with the solemn eyes. The floors were covered with sawdust, freshly raked each morning. It was like playing in the soft dirt of the roadside as she scraped up sawdust piles or drew her name out with the tip of her boot. Most of the immigrant families had their own chickens and pigs and their meat purchases were small; knuckle bones for soup, a bit of sausage meat. When there were no coal orders and the miners laid off, the visits to the meat market were less frequent and the families existed on polenta,[1] and vegetables from the garden.

The main street of Fernie was marked with telephone poles marching down its expanse. A few motor cars were parked in front of the stores. The time was a mixture of transportation; those who could afford the price bought a motor car; those who could not used a horse and buggy. Others walked. In winter when motor cars were useless their owners resorted to shank's pony or a cutter pulled by a horse.

Children of the immigrants were sent to school until they were old enough to work or marry. The school house was set back from the road in a grassy oasis. The yard was green in summer but quickly worn to a frazzle in spring and fall. Desks in the high-ceilinged room were bolted to the oiled floor facing a blackboard with the alphabet printed across the top in capital and small letters. Small boys squirmed in their seats, kicked black boots, hid recess treasures in their desks, spilled the contents of inkwells and shot tightly-wadded paper covered with spit at little girls who disdainfully ignored them. Behind the school were swings and the path to the outhouse.

To Philomena, school was a chore. She dutifully learned to read and write, struggled with her sums. Pushed to the back of the room with the other foreign children she was painfully aware that she was an outsider, branded by her tight braids,

---

1. Polenta — Mush of cornmeal eaten hot or when cold cut in slices and fried.

scuffed boots, dowdy clothes and lunches tied in a bit of flour sack.

Often her teachers, mystified by the dignity of this quiet child, let her have small chores cleaning the blackboards and erasers in exchange for tidbits of paper and pencil stubs. It was one of these kind teachers who called Philomena by her English name, Florence. Florence, said the lady, meant 'flower' and the sensitive child who loved wild flowers quickly adopted the name.

When the end of the school year approached, parents were alerted to the taking of the class picture. Benches were arranged so all children could be photographed in tiers, each showing to an advantage. They arrived clean faced and clean eared, in clothes scrubbed in wash tubs by sweat-beaded mothers with numb backs. Some boys wore suits with matching hats and threatened to punch out the first boy who laughed. The teacher wore her Sunday hat and fumbled shyly with her cameo pin at the neck of a sparkling white blouse. Painfully shy, Florence rarely smiled during the picture taking.

The school yard was used for a variety of community sporting events. The town had baseball, cricket and soccer teams. Horseshoes and dancing were popular. In summer bowling teams scored on the packed clay. In winter, the closest ponds were cleared for shinny and tenderfoot skaters.

The winters went fast for the Costanzo children. Escaping the rigours of the schoolroom, they shouted to each other in their native language as they ploughed through the drifts on their way home, stopping to slide between the hard ruts on the frozen roads. The air was very cold when they at last hurried to a home heavy with the smells of supper. Evenings were spent around a coal stove till an early bedtime. Snuggled down under warm quilts, Florence and Christina talked about the fine ladies they would become and with sleepy eyes watched moonlight outline silvery fronds of frost on the bedroom window.

So Florence Costanzo grew to puberty, mindful of all the

Italian traditions of womanhood. Her sheltered life was relatively uneventful until she attended a baptism in the early spring of 1915. In the Italian community strong and everlasting bonds were formed by the religious liturgicals of the church.

In Florence's community, the birth of an infant was a great event and a cause for celebration. Even greater though was the baptism of the baby. It was a time for all the relatives to come together, to know one another and reinforce the bonds of brotherhood so important to them.

For this particular baptism of a cousin's baby the families gathered on a Sunday after the last Mass of the day.

The day was misty; heavy rains beat down, forming small streams that splashed down from the eaves. The water ran across paths, floated dried grass and twigs down its wider waters. The land had a look of thorough wetness. Then the sun came out; the sky was blue, softly traced with a lattice-work of white. A light wind rippled the grass, the sky became sweet with bird song.

When the light fell full on the small houses enclosed in vine-woven fenced yards, they gathered to greet one another; collarless young men, with jackets unbuttoned over beginning pot bellies, clasped hands in mutual respect, warmth for each other in their greetings. They gave honour to the older members of the families, to the ancient men with skin that hung loose on craggy faces and hands that trembled on their canes. The women were large, dark-eyed and shy beneath fresh-pressed kerchiefs. They kissed one another, offered good wishes to the parents of the new child and presented their growing offspring for inspection. Angela Costanzo's daughters walked primly after her, conscious of the eyes of the young men upon them.

At the appointed time the people gathered near the font in the womb of the church where the infant would be born into the faith. Old women in black scarves crossed themselves and told their beads for the health of the child. The Padrino and

Madrina[2] were the honoured guests for the day. Great care had gone into choosing the godparents; there was more than just a spiritual bond between the child and the godparents. Within the baptism ritual a strong loyalty was welded between two families.

With the Madrina holding the child the ancient rites began. Pride and love shone on her face. The infant slept until the priest touched the baby's lips with a bit of salt. He awoke and his outraged cries echoed through the holy stillness. The Madrina rocked, soothed and he was still. The priest gave the final blessing and it was done.

Later, at the house of the new parents the women prepared to feed the gathering. A fire of pine knots spit in the kitchen stove and coffee was put on to boil. The host put out as much food as his slim purse allowed; he had denied his family much in the weeks preceding the event. A small pig was slaughtered for the occasion and the hams cured. The rest of the meat was made into sausage; the outer layer of skin was cleaned, cut into strips and fried into cracklings for the children. The feet were made into jelly. In kinship the women of the families each brought a contribution to the feast; white beans in a sauce, jars of olives, mushrooms in oil, pickled cucumbers and peppers. The people spilled out of the house into the yard where they sat on the grass, ate a hearty meal and drank wine and beer.

It was a happy day, there was much joviality and whirls of talk which turned to boasting as the levels of the beer barrels dropped. The children jumped and played hide and seek in the shrubbery with the Costanzo children joining in all the games. The nimble-footed Florence won many of the games and her creamy olive skin became flushed with victory. Small tendrils of dark hair escaped the tight braids and curled around her face; her tiny waist showed to advantage in the soft, well-washed dress of dusty pink she wore. Her head was well formed, her cheekbones set high in an oval face. Only her

2. Padrino and Madrina — Godfather and Godmother.

eyes betrayed the sadness of the woman to be; they did not rise boldly, black and flashing, but were deep, downcast.

Angela kept her eyes on her daughters. She was discomfited by the obvious interest of a young man and wondered how he should come to be near every place the young Florence happened to be.

The party lasted well into the night and when the evening moths fluttered around the lamp lights the women and children went home. Somewhere a dog lifted its muzzle and barked at a yellow-minted moon, the sound lingering across the valley. As Florence trudged obediently at her side, Angela put her arm around her daughter, realized that she was a young woman now and wondered when she would be taken from her.

By early morning, when the wind freshened, only the men were left. In the kitchen Vincenzo Costanzo sat at the table. He had more than enough to drink and was staring morosely into his glass.

Vincenzo was unaware of a young man, Carlo Sanfidele, who had watched Florence and her family throughout the day.

The twenty-three year old Italian was a self-assured young man. He came from the town of Solano in the Province of Reggio di Calabria in the Region of Calabria.

Carlo, noticing the older man was drinking heavily, took his chance.

"Vincenzo! There's something you and me should talk about, heh?"

"Anyt'ing Carlo, anyt'ing." The older man's voice was blurred with liquor.

"You know Vincenzo, I am one good workman, eh?"

Carlo's eyes were riveted on the other man. His pudgy face was flushed with excitement and the heat of the room.

"Yeah, Carlo. You a good provider." Vincenzo's voice was soft, slow to come.

"Sua Figlia, Florence, your daughter, Florence, she is needing a husband, no?"

Carlo's eyes through the smoke of the room were hard and

watchful despite his deceptively casual air.

In the crowded kitchen Vincenzo's friends, equally inebriated, caught the drift of conversation. They crowded around the table, gathered together excitedly, sensing the drama to follow, wanting to be part of it. This was unexpected and they eagerly took up the discussion.

"Vincenzo! Carlo, he wants to marry with your pretty daughter, Florence!"

"Yeah, yeah," another man poked Vincenzo with a discoloured finger. "This Carlo, he wants to marry with your little flower!"

The men were in a jovial mood and they chuckled to themselves, delighted with this turn in the conversation.

Carlo waited. He blew thin puffs of smoke into the already pungent smells of the room.

Dazed with wine though he was, Vincenzo felt some sudden protectiveness for his quiet daughter. This Carlo was too forward! This was not how the custom was! Carlo should have come to the house to see the father while Florence kept to another room. Only then would the father and the suitor arrange the dowry and settle on the marriage date. Marriages were parent arranged; the young girl did not see her intended unless properly chaperoned, nor did she listen while the dowry was being resolved. She had no part in any of the discussions; it was all settled between the men.

Vincenzo shook his head to clear it. Still, he reasoned to himself, Florence was of marrying age and there were the other children to support and the mine was not working again. Carlo waited patiently. Outside a mist was drifting in, softening and cooling the night air.

Vincenzo spoke softly, not looking up. The room was still, breath suspended, waiting the answer.

"Yeah, take her. Take her. Sono d'accordo. (I agree)."

Florence's betrothal was sealed.

The next morning, as Florence ate her breakfast mush, Vincenzo told her to bring her school books home. She was to be married.

"But why, padre?"

The girl looked up at him, her face a mask of fright.

"Che...," Vincenzo looked to his wife to help. Angela did not turn from her place at the stove.

"Please, papa...," the girl started weakly in a soft pleading voice.

"Please ... non mi piace (I don't like him).

"Papa, papa?" Her voice rose in alarm. Hot glistening tears started their way down her cheeks. Oh no, she thought, not that man, the one at the party. She remembered the short, stocky man with a touch of meanness about his eyes. Her day crumbled about her feet. Her father was serious, she was to be married to the stranger, to the man who hung around the family at the baptism. She would have to leave her home, leave her sisters and brothers and go with the man. Sleep with him. Her face broke into a feverish blush at the thought.

"He is old ... and fat ...," her brain groped for fitting adjectives to underline his repulsiveness.

At the stove Angela shifted on her feet, wondering just when the explosion would come as she heard the girl argue with her father. The mother knew that her quiet, pensive daughter would never speak to her father in this way unless she was extremely agitated. She had forgotten her place.

Vincenzo dropped his eyes to his plate, turned away from the pinched face before him.

"Non importa! Non fa nulla! (Never mind! It doesn't matter!) Like your mama and me, it is time! Now you marry! Make bambini!"

His fist clenched and unclenched. He got up, knocking the chair backwards and left the room, leaving the rest for the mother to take over.

Angela kept stirring the evening meal of soup made from a pig's knuckle. It was heavy with beans, bought at a reduced price from the grocer, and greens from their small garden. There was very little meat now and the family had been existing on pasta and vegetables.

"It is better." Angela spoke slowly and with finality.

"You a big girl now. Sanfidele, he makes the money. October. In October, you marry."

Her lips were a bloodless line in her face, her heart ached for the girl standing forlornly before her. But the father's decision was final. He had given his word.

Then it was June and the world moved into summertime. It would be the last summer Florence would spend carefree as a child. Her mornings were filled with chores for her mother, her evenings filled with polite calls by Sanfidele while she made infinite stitches in a table covering for her dowry. The afternoons she savoured the most.

When her chores were done she escaped to the nearby fields to walk in brilliant sunshine. There were yeasty clouds around the peaks of the mountains. In the fields she looked for berries, heard the marmot whistle, gathered dandelion seeds in her hand and like a sower of old, scattered them behind her. She walked near the forest and stopped to sit on mossy, lichen-covered rocks, holding a wood violet, perfect and unblemished, cupped in her hand.

As the sun slid behind the mountain tops, and the sky became the colour of banked embers, she ran home. The kettle fizzled and sizzled on the stove, supper was being prepared and her father came home from the mine.

Too soon it was mid-October. The trees were leafless, skeleton-limbed. The wind was sighing in long deep moans, weary of rearranging leaves in the hedges. A harvest moon peered down, stretching small shadows into thick icicles of dark. A fretful Florence walked to the kitchen door, listened to the wind. There was a growing, spreading, sick feeling in the pit of her stomach as she thought of the approaching marriage date; she half turned, her hand rested on the porcelain knob; she debated, contemplating an escape but there was no place to run to, nowhere to go. There was no escape for her. Resignation put soft sadness into the dark eyes. Tomorrow was her wedding day.

A slot-eyed cat jumped down from the wooden railing of the porch and walked sourly into the house, his tail hooked to one side. Florence fed him and turning, took off her apron and left the room.

October 16. Florence woodenly dressed her hair, stepped into the long white dress and looked at herself carefully in the cracked mirror. She turned to search frantically through the dresser drawer and strangely came up with a black-ribboned locket which she tied around her neck. The rusty black of the faded ribbon was an incongruous touch against the stark virginal white of the dress.

Florence would have loved the dress had it not represented the loss of everything she held dear. She liked the sound of her petticoats which rustled as she walked; liked the wide waist band which encircled her slender waist and cut tight underneath young breasts. She caught sight of herself in the mirror and was pleased with the reflection until reality flooded back. With a sigh she picked fitfully at the lace on the sleeves, smoothed the black ribbon at her throat and adjusted the head-dress holding her veil. She savagely skewered the frothy bit of lace into place with long hat pins and was ready when her father called.

The young bride was quiet and composed as she took her father's arm at the door of the Church of the Holy Family. As she entered the romanesque structure of local brick, she saw her relatives and friends waiting with subdued excitement. Waiting also were the bridegroom Carlo and his best man, a stocky, striking Italian who would have stood out anywhere, in any company. His name was Emilio Picariello.

Still in a daze, walking as if asleep, Florence joined her groom. She wanted to beg him, wanted him to release her from her father's promise. The words came to her lips but she could not, would not, utter them. She could not dishonour her father. She felt the cool dampness of the church and a shiver ran up her spine.

Please God, the trembling girl prayed, let it only be a nightmare. I'll wake up any minute ... in my own bed and all this will be gone.

But the hand that reached for hers was real. It was firm,

muscular, a man hand and she dared not pull back. The sweet scent from the roses pinned to her side reached her as she pleaded wordlessly, uselessly.

Oh il mio fidanzato, (oh my fiance), please don't make me marry you. I don't know you and I don't love you. My papa, he would understand. I can make him understand if you would just release me, tell my papa this is all wrong. Let the promise go, please let the promise go. I can make papa understand. I can! I can!

The girl's face reflected her plight and she had a feeling of falling through space. Then a firm hand took her arm and she moved forward again, into the dark recess of the church.

The girl was obediently silent but her face was clouded as she bent her dark head and the veil slipped over her face. Her hand was slim and dry in her father's hand and he matched his step to her small one as they walked to the altar. All around them the wedding music swelled ponderously. With each note of the echoing music the bride felt her life sliding beneath her grasp. The dirge was pulling at her precariously balanced life, forcing and urging her over the side into this union. The white lace covered the thin drawn face and the watchers took her bowed head as shy submission. Only her mother knew the anguish, knew the sorrow locked in the downcast eyes.

As the Roman Catholic ritual of the nuptial mass began, an autumn sun burst through the clouds, lighting the stained glass of the windows, leaving its muted colours on the bowed head of the bride. Above her the vested priest intoned the prayer for divine mercy.

"Kyrie, eleison. Christe, eleison."[3]

Too soon the mass was done and the priest turned to the assembly.

"Dominus vobiscum."

---

3. Kyrie, eleison. Christe, eleison — Lord, have mercy. Christ, have mercy. From the latin version of the Roman Catholic celebration of the Mass.

To which the people answered quietly, "Et cum spiritu tuo."[4]

Now the rituals were over and the people became festive and showered the young couple with grain at the door of the church. Then the wedding party moved in the bronzed light of an October sun to the home of Emilio Picariello.

It was important in the Italian community to make a good showing for a wedding. Parents often went into debt to have impressive marriages to which all the families were invited. The expenses for such a showing were shared by both parents of the bride and groom. Sanfidele, having no parents in Canada, sought the help of his employer and friend, Picariello. Picariello and his wife, Maria, provided their home for the wedding party. In turn, Emilio was chosen to be the best man and witnessed the marriage along with Concetta Colosimo, who was the bride's attendant. Picariello's house, with its sixteen rooms, could easily hold all the guests for the dancing and feasting that was to follow. Sanfidele was pleased with these arrangements, the large Italian was his idol, and he slavishly followed every word he spoke.

Florence and Carlo presided at the marriage breakfast and the bride's cheeks grew rosy with blushes as she listened to the eloquent toasts to her future. She took off her veil, allowed Carlo to take her hand as he led her outside for the taking of pictures.

People crowded into the rooms, sat around the walls as the nuptial couple offered each guest almond cakes and a glass of liquor from a silver tray. The gifts were displayed in one room and as Florence received them, she shyly and sweetly offered the giver a symbolic gift of a small, white egg-shaped candy.

Then into the russet light of the evening came the sounds of vibrating strings. A knowing and subtle smile settled on the faces of the people as the dance was about to begin. The music swelled, giving out its vibrant summons; lilting nostalgic

---

4. Dominus vobiscum — The Lord be with you. Et cum spiritu tuo — And with thy spirit. Latin version of the Roman Catholic clebration of the Mass.

songs from the motherland of Italy. The intimate, passionate music sifted through the rusty light of the dying day. Its rhythms moved the people, reflected in their transported faces. The men put down glasses of gleaming amber liquids and moved into the folk dances of their native land. Their bodies were intense; the music quickened and was over but the men continued the chorus with gruff reedy throats, not wanting to let the sounds die, not wanting to lose them. Again and again the music started, surging echoes of their past, and they danced in exhilaration, totally immersed in the feeling. Sweating and panting, the dancers went to the porch to cool in the night air. Others took their place to whirl into the music. In the corners of the room, old men told roguish stories and filled and refilled their glasses.

While Florence danced, she was aware that upstairs the women were preparing her marriage bed. She wanted the dancing to continue forever. She didn't want to go upstairs.

Florence was afraid of the dance ending, the time when she would have to climb the long steps to the bridal chamber above. She heard again the words of the two women in the pantry, they didn't know she stood at the kitchen sink getting a cool glass of water.

"... and I sat on my trunk, scared stiff ... yeh, an my husband ... he paced around the room, waiting for me!"

"Not me!", interjected the other woman. "I jist wanted to get it over with. All at once! I shut my eyes tight and gritted my teeth. I was so afraid and I hurt, oh how I hurt! But now ...," she laughed and rolled her eyes at her companion, "now we have fourteen bambino, not bad, huh?"

Florence's face was red as she turned blindly from the sink. She knew how a helpless creature felt as it was pinned in a trap. At the door of the room another arm encircled her waist and drew her into the dance.

The bridal couple was expected to spend the night in a specially prepared bed and the groom would resume work the next day. The women prepared the bed with new sheets and blankets that were gifts to the bride. On the coverlet pink and

white covered almond candies were arranged; white streamers and blue rosettes festooned the headboard. The same
candy confetti littered the floor. All was in readiness.

Downstairs, the party was growing noisier as the evening
came to a close. The liquor in the men was giving them a new
boldness.

But there was more. There was Picariello, rising to claim the
tired bride for a dance.

One of the onlookers nudged the other. "I guess the Emperor wants to be the first, heh?"

"Shut up, you old fool!" The other man had sense enough to
whisper.

The first was not to be quietened. He wagged his head
knowingly. "He'll be the first ... you'll see ..."

"Shut you mouth! You idiot!" His friend hissed again, as the
dance came to an end and Picariello bent to touch the girl's
lips. Later, he was to recall that she smelled like violets.

Carlo watched them, blank-faced, his adam's apple working in his throat. Picariello was his boss.

There are people still living today who recall that taut
moment. They remember how the old women nudged their
husbands, urging them to go home. There was trouble brewing here!

They remember the face of the young bride as she looked
from her husband to Emilio Picariello ... not comprehending.

She was not yet fifteen years old.

II

A CHANGE
OF NAME

IN THE WEEKS that followed, Florence's ideas of what a marriage should be were dashed to the ground.

When Carlo took her to his rented room an ugly confrontation took place with his landlady.

Florence was struggling with her traveling bag on the staircase to the second floor of the dingy boarding house when a sour faced woman of medium height appeared in the hall.

"Mr. Sanfidele?"

The voice had a jarring note of accusation to it. Carlo turned to display a toothy smile.

"This here is Florence, my wife. Remember I was telling you about her?"

Florence was embarrassed; she felt cheap and flushed under the other woman's scrutiny.

"She can't stay." The voice was flat, resigned and very firm. "The room, I told you, is too small. I only rent to one person. One person to a room." She repeated herself for emphasis. "Besides, there's one more person to set the table for ... and my back, it ain't what it used to be!" She put her hand on her lower back and rubbed absent-mindedly.

The woman had bright eyes lost in a drab face and they bore into Florence making her fidget on the stairs. The woman was remembering how she, too, had been pretty and soft, like the child face before her. Now her face was lined with years of care and tension. She was not intimidated by the man on the stairs.

"I told you, I told you, don't let me catch you sneaking a

woman in here!"

"If it's more money you want ...", his voice trailed off as he started back down the stairs. He jerked his head at Florence, saying over his shoulder that she should go upstairs.

"Front room, kid, the one at the end of the hall."

The woman had said she couldn't stay but Carlo wanted her upstairs. She escaped to the top of the stairs, sank to the floor and peered through the banister. From below voices floated up to her; angry voices, cajoling voices and she heard for the first time, her husband's plans to leave Canada, to move to the United States to a place she had never heard of, some place in Pennsylvania where he had friends. Now she knew why he insisted her wedding gifts be packed away in cartons.

The floor was hard and cold and her knees hurt. She grasped the railing of the banister, staring fixedly at the scene below, held captive by the outburst.

She rose quickly when Carlo turned to come up the stairs. He took the steps two at a time, whistling through his teeth. His surprise showed when he found her still in the hall.

"Come Flo, go in! It's okay now. Old doll, just wanted more money. We live here for now and then, when we go to the United States we will get a big room, fancy like. You would like that, wouldn't you, Flo?" He was happy, getting his own way.

"But I thought we would have a home where all our friends and family are. Who would we know down there? What would you do? How could we ...", her voice faded away to moth-softness; she coloured at the next words she uttered.

"And a baby, Carlo, I have always loved children. Isn't that what marriage is all about? To have children, have a family like mama and papa?"

There was a small silence. She thought he was listening to her, considering her request and she started in again, sure he would listen. If only he wouldn't look at her so, thoughtful like through narrowed eyes.

"My mother! I would miss my mother. It sounds so far away."

She leaned forward, smiled pleadingly as she tried to take

his hand. She had missed the danger signals; the tightening of his mouth, the cold far-away look in his eyes, the stiff back.

Florence had gone too far. Carlo was incensed. First the woman downstairs with her fretful voice demanding more and now this one. Should all be taught to keep their place, he thought wildly.

He rummaged in a drawer, stripped off his shirt, letting it fall to the floor. He ran his hand over his chin, decided he would not have to shave and pulled another shirt from the dresser.

Florence moved from her chair, coming around to face him. He brushed her from him with a scornful gesture as anger distended his nostrils. His eyes stared boldly at her, made a flush come to her cheeks.

"Be quiet, Flo. There's money to be made down there. Oh, I know. I do for Picariello and he pays me well but not like I get down there. Here you have to work hard for your money." His good looks were darkening with anger.

"The men down there wear big diamond on finger!"

His hand shot out before her to show his naked fingers. He had no thought for her; had given her no diamond ring and only a thin, simple gold band adorned her finger.

"Yeah, and nice shirts, silk, you know." As he talked he smoothed down his cotton shirt and feeling the fibre his face was suffused with rage and the veins in his temples throbbed as they swelled.

Abruptly he sauntered to the old mirror above the wash stand. He peered closely at his reflection and smoothed his hair before he turned to her. His anger was hidden; again he was the proud dandy. It would be better, he thought to himself, if she was agreeable. He would have enough opposition from her family.

Florence stared intently at her husband, at the man she knew so little about. She saw something in his movements and expressions that filled her with apprehension. He was evasive about the truth, twisted it around for his own purpose.

The room echoed her agony.

"But my family, so far away! What will I do? Who will I know?"

Tears spilled down her cheeks. It was bad enough being wrenched away from her home, put in this dreary room, and now, he wanted to take her from the town she knew, from the people she loved and wanted to put her in another place far away, a place filled with strangers.

Carlo was defensive. He came close to her, belched shamelessly and she smelt the stench of alcohol and garlic. She averted her head.

"What's the matter with you, kid?" he hissed.

"You better grow up and soon. You my wife and I can do anything I want with you!"

The girl provoked feelings of uncertainty within him and he lashed out to stop her. He hated the tears, hated the feelings that started within him, feelings he quickly beat down.

"Enough! I telling you! Enough!"

He shook her roughly. "You will go and do as I say!" He slapped her face, his fingers dug into and bruised her arms. The sharp slap was followed by a cry of pain. He panted with exertion, was disgusted with himself as much as he was with her. Grabbing his hat he flung himself from the room.

Florence sobbed as she lay curled into a ball on the tumbled bed. So much had happened to her since her father had given his word. The late sun left the room and the air cooled. She shivered both from cold and shock. The first coating of the shell was formed then, a shell the young girl built around herself for protection from the ugliness into which she was thrust.

And so Florence learned early in her marriage to submit quietly to what she could not avoid. In public with Carlo she smiled and waved gaily; alone with him she became quiet and watchful. She was afraid of him and wondered often how she could get away.

When they arrived at the Pennsylvania town Carlo had chosen, the pattern of their life style slowly emerged. He found the boarding house owned by his friends and told

Florence to move into the middle room on the second floor. The room, as he promised, was larger, gaudier and she was dismayed to find, dirtier.

The boarding house was at the very end of a long street bordering Chinatown. It was a squat looking house of three storeys with a gabled roof. A covered porch, held up by peeling white pillars, ran around three sides of the house. On either side of this abode were vacant lots still in flower-dotted wild grass. The building was situated on a bit of a rise and as it settled with age, the cement steps cracked and tipped ever so slightly giving the house a rakish look. The iron scrolled gates, set in hedges bordering the postage stamp lawns, would not close and stood open all day and night. Instantly, Florence did not like the look of the house.

The girl slept late the next day, rising to dress and fix her hair as the noon hour bell sounded. Carlo introduced her to two men standing in the hall and the girl was uneasy with the looks she received from them. He then took her by the arm, led her through the long hall, up creaking stairs to the third floor. At his knock there was an answer.

An older man opened the door, stood to one side to allow them to enter. With a nasal laugh he offered them a small glass of liquor as he appraised the slender figure before him. Carlo followed his eyes.

There was an uncomfortable silence in the room; the younger man spoke quickly.

"Pretty, isn't she?"

Florence looked up to meet the man's look as his eyes slid over her body and she felt a crawling sensation go over her. She shivered though the room was warm to the point of being stuffy. Florence quickly sat down, although she had not been asked to, crossed her arms over her small breasts, slouched in her chair until she caught Carlo's sneering look of disapproval.

Under their eyes, Florence reddened and looked intently at a spot on the worn carpet. She desperately wanted to leave, to get back to the safety of their dismal room. She was sorry that she had agreed to come with Carlo then realized she had no choice in the matter.

The old man drained his glass and came near her.

"You, you very young, you have bambini?"

The florid man was anxious to draw her into the conversation. He smoothed his small moustache with yellow stained fingers.

Florence looked at Carlo, tried to catch his eye, but the man was cleaning his fingernails with a small pen knife. Turning back to the older man, Florence shook her head and dropped her eyes.

"Ach, what a child. Still," a strange expression came into the hooded eyes, "she is married, she knows."

He wondered about the ugly bruise that stained her left cheek, still visible despite an attempt to cover it. He guessed where she got it and why.

The older man wanted her to work in his 'house', in one of the two back rooms kept for this purpose. She was so young! He wanted her for himself. He urged her to have another drink as he patted the chesterfield beside him, coaxing her to come sit with him. A twinge of loathing went through Florence as the man came over to smooth the back of her hair with a friendly gesture.

A heated discussion between the two men followed and the stubbornness of Carlo surfaced. Carlo had something the owner of the boarding house wanted; it pleased him to have the upper hand.

The older man shrugged, disappointment in his eyes. He deferred to the younger man's wishes; Florence could work but only in the kitchen helping the cook. A sigh of relief came from the girl huddled in the chair.

So Florence spent her days washing burned pots and listening to the cook's gossip about the activities of the house. This older woman, who also did the marketing, was skimming money from the food allowance, serving plain, heavy meals, full of starches and a few vegetables gleaned from the garden at the back gate.

The rooms at the front of the house, rented to the boarders, were cleaned by a woman who came in, did her work, said little and disappeared as quickly as she could. The cook told Florence the woman was working off a debt.

In the two back rooms, the ones right next to Florence's room, two young women received a steady stream of men far into the evening.

In the basement, reached through a cellar door hidden in bushes at the side of the house, came the clink of bottles. Liquor was diluted, coloured and rebottled to be sold at sporting events about the town. There were baseball games, races at the grandstand and a few illicit fighting cock rings. All these involved gambling and drinking and a steady supply of booze flowed from the basement.

Fresh bread wagons, pulled by teams of horses, came to the back door regularly. There was no bread sold here; one of Florence's first jobs in the early morning light was to punch down the bread dough and form the loaves for the second rise.

Carlo had money now and he urged her to buy stylish dresses and slippers, turning her away from the plain frocks she wore. The dresses he chose were of rich coloured fabric designed to outline her tiny waist, the slim hips. He urged her to pile her hair high on her head, bought women's magazines for her to read, then took her to a corner drug store to buy creams and rouges. He delighted in her new appearance and she started to relax. She felt closer to him now and asked small questions about his work, what he did when he went out, where did he go? But he kissed her lightly and told her nothing. He disappeared for days and then she was frightened at being so alone in this house and reaching up felt the wetness of tears on her cheeks.

She lay awake at nights staring vacantly into the blackness of the room. She was haunted by the sounds that came from the back rooms, the drunken laughter and rough bawdy talk, the hoarse grunts heard through the thin walls. She was afraid of the men she passed in the hall, smelled their stale bodies and was repulsed. She would fall into an uneasy sleep, awakened by visions and faces that floated in and out her subconscious. She put a heavy chair against the door, afraid of someone blundering into her room by mistake.

In the very early morning when the house should have been in deep silence, she awoke with a convulsive start at a sound in the hall. She sagged back against her pillow, watching the light define the square windows of the room. Rhythmically the curtains puffed out, then sucked back into the open window. She put out a hesitant hand, feeling the space in the bed beside her. But the bed was cold, Carlo had not come home again.

As the months passed, Carlo had his silk shirts and a small, but real diamond on his finger. He wore new suits, handsome ties and had his nails manicured. He seemed to forget Florence now and she worried about the interest of the older man on the third floor. Carlo was distant and when she spoke to him he watched her through narrowed eyes and she wondered if he had other plans for her. If he had really looked closely at the girl he would have seen a docile person with a face pinched with disquiet, a person who behaved as a marionette.

Florence begged Carlo, again and again, to go home if only for a visit and she wrote tearful letters to her brother Tony, judiciously omitting some parts of the life around her.

Small slivers of sun sank deep into the corners of the room as the wistful girl wrote home. Carlo was out; she knew not where. In the deepening quiet, cuddled into an old wrapper she started a cheery letter home. As always, nostalgia overtook her and the paragraphs grew into silent calls of loneliness, unhappiness and fear. She was dreaming as she wrote, her mind far away in the sweet fields of her childhood and she didn't hear his footsteps in the long hall.

He came into the room and she started in fright, shivered as she remembered his rage when he found one of her letters.

"Hullo, writing again, I see."

His manner was casual, his voice low and gentle, but his underlip was pushed into a pendulous position as he scrutinized the girl. Florence sat quietly, hesitant to cover her paper, to draw attention to what she had written. She returned his steady gaze, unflinching as he walked over and picked up the paper. A flush swept his face. He pounded his fist on the table, then pounded blows, one after another, on the girl. The force of the punishment knocked her to the floor and she cowered in fear as he stumped about the room, railing her with derision, telling her she would end up working in one of the back rooms. Finally, muttering a string of obscenities he marched from the room but not before her letter was savagely torn into a multitude of little pieces.

Florence was relieved when the door slammed behind him. The sharp sound made her start and when she sat up her breath came in small painful bursts of air. Trembling, she pulled herself up, slipped off the wrapper and started to dress. Her arms ached where his fists had rained down the blows. Recently he had been quick to criticize; she did not please him, nothing pleased him, either her dress was not right or her hair not piled high enough. The one thing he didn't censure was the makeup she spread lavishly over her face. She learned to apply the colours, masking her face with rosy cheeks and vivid lips that curled into a seductive smile on command.

Leaving the house she started to walk, passing streets of tall houses crowded closely together. The late sun was warm on her back, the air tangy with a metallic smell from nearby factories. Children played up and down the long blocks. Women with bulging market bags hurried home to start their suppers. She wanted to go into these houses, to be invited in, to see the warmth of the family together and suddenly she was sick as a wave of homesickness washed over her. Florence put out a hand, held the lamp post for support and a child turned to look curiously at her. Shivering and cold, the girl turned back as the sun began to cast long shadows about the street. Houses were dotted with lighted squares, dim beneath lace curtains pulled against the night sky. She wondered idly where Carlo was spending his time, wondered whether his threat was real and wondered, without hope, how she could get home.

Florence was soon to find out. Two burly men waited for her in the parlour. The cook was agitated, caught the girl's arm before she entered the room.

"They asked for him, your husband. Asked a lot of questions, like, where he was from, who he was, you know, all that personal stuff."

Her voice trailed off. She was afraid. Afraid for herself and afraid for the girl. She liked the girl, hated the man. The cook detained Florence, not wanting her to go alone into the parlour. He should face the men, not her. She cowered.

"You know I would help you, if I could." The cook wanted to detach herself from the events to follow. Florence smiled at her, patted her hand and stepped into the room where the men waited.

Strangely she was not afraid of them. They were square jawed men, buttoned into serge overcoats of the same cut. Their eyes were cold and impersonal. They asked for Carlo and she could truthfully tell them she didn't know where he was. This knowledge brought a slight smile to her lips.

"Look here, lady," an angry man growled; he saw the fleeting smile and was not amused by it. "Your man has been unlucky lately." Florence guessed that Carlo had been gambling on his afternoon and evening sojourns.

"He hasn't been around lately, jist up and left."

The same man did all the talking for the two; the other used his eyes intently to stare the victim down.

Florence was somewhat relieved. This was Carlo's problem. Cheerfully she said, "Well now, maybe he will be home soon, why don't you just wait for him?"

"Nah, you tell him, lady, tell him we were here. He has three days to come up with the money. And don't go straying from town."

Florence told Carlo about the two men as soon as he came in. She blurted it out and had the satisfaction of watching the colour drain from his face.

"Do you have the money?"

"Look kid, don't ask questions. Write a letter."

Now he was commanding her to write home. "Tell your mama you coming home."

He pointedly said she was coming home and did not use the plural 'we'. His voice was contemptuous; he liked his life here, liked the money he made and if it hadn't been for a stroke of bad luck, he would never leave. He knew they had to move on and quickly. He knew, too, that the Italian community would know of their arrival and close in to protect and shelter them. Picariello would help, smoothing the waters with his money and the big man would take him back, give him work.

Again Florence did as she was told, wrote a terse note saying she was coming home. She didn't say how, she didn't say when. Carlo had not told her. He noticed that Florence was unnaturally quiet and seemingly unmoved by his decision; secretly she was elated to escape from this evil house and the growing attentions from the man on the third floor.

At a small town near the border between the United States and Canada, the young couple left the train. She was astonished as they started to walk, carrying very little with them. Her stylish slippers were too thin for the rough dirt roads they followed and stones bruised her feet. Still they continued, down roads, angling across fields, always moving towards the unfenced border. They moved at night, sleeping the days away in grassy fields, abandoned buildings, in whatever shelter they could find. They walked in the dusk and at night with the moon and stars shining far above them. Florence was happy now, her face lit by white silver and she tried to tell Carlo her feelings of home. Listening to her sensitive thoughts Carlo stared at her; a scowl came to his face.

They stopped to rest. From his bag he brought cheese and biscuits; they drank water from a stream. On impulse she went to him and slid her arms around his waist from behind, laying her dark tousled head on his back. She whispered of the life she wanted, now that they were going home. He was taking her home and she felt grateful and warm towards him. It was the first time in a long while she had felt any feeling for him. She promised that everything would be beautiful, they could start over, be as a man and woman should be. If he could only turn, maybe this would be the start of their life together, maybe now it could be a true marriage as she dreamed.

He did not turn to her. Instead she felt him stiffen. She found his hand and coming around to face him, looked at him through eyes filled with love. What she found was a sardonic smile that told her nothing would be changed. Carlo would still have his life and she was to be used as he wished.

With sharp words, Carlo shattered her dreams.

"Cut it out, Flo. I want to talk to you. "There is a plan we follow now that we are going back into Canada. Pay attention, you mustn't make a mistake."[1]

Hearing nothing from her he continued.

"Charles Losandro, sounds good, no? You be Florence Losandro, can you remember that?"[2]

He spoke as if to a child. The question was not a question; it was a command and with a sigh the girl acquiesced.

"Benissimo (very well)." She was resigned. She would do as he said.

Florence was silent as she moved back into the shadows where he couldn't see her face. Suddenly he walked over and reached for her. Feeling resistance in her body, he started to coax her softly, teasingly. He wanted her to love him now, but the door was closed to him. She only felt used.

They made the crossing at night, moving stealthily. She followed him in silence; it was to be her pattern for life.

In the days that followed they hitched rides when they could, coming into Fernie late in the evening. He left her at her mother's house; cold, tired and very hungry. He went to find Picariello.

Angela Costanzo was worried about the girl who returned

---

1. There is an indication of illegal entry and a change of name to cover his activities in the United Sttes and some reason to hide in Canada under an assumed name. Sanfidele was later deported to Italy.

2. Sanfidele changed his name to Losandro. There are many spellings throughout the records — Lassandro, Lasandra, Losandra. Author took one of these from a signature believed to be that of Carlo and from a later spelling on a confession belonging to Florence.

so suddenly in the night. All the grime and dust could not hide the expensive clothing she wore nor mask the tired eyes in the tear-stained face. This was not the same sweet innocent girl who left with her husband. The girl that returned was silent, distant, her feelings bundled tightly inside her. She was still gentle and submissive but her manner was hardened by the clothes she wore and the makeup that aged the young face.

Florence had not told anyone of their illegal entry into the country nor did she mention any detail of her life with Sanfidele. Angela watched her pensive daughter as she sat looking into the fire through the opened grate of the coal stove. Although Florence was silent, inwardly she was filled with a strong need to talk; she wanted to tell her mother everything about the house she had recently lived in, about her past and her fears for the future.

Fear is born of uncertainty, anxiety is its sister and even knowing this to be true, Florence could not prevent the feelings of fear rising within her. She was brought up with the fear of displeasing her parents; she had married with the fear of dishonouring her father; now she stayed married to a man she had grown to abhor because of her fear of him. Displeasing Carlo gave her a churning feeling deep within her stomach, a withering look from him put cold fingers down her spine. Again she had the same feelings of being in a trap, helpless, just as she had during the long nights in Pennsylvania and she wanted to forget, blot out the memories, hide them deep underneath the careless attitude she strove hard to adopt. Now there was an inner struggle between her fear of Carlo and the intensity of her need to talk. The need cut through her with violence but the tight feelings would not unravel or unfold.

Angela watched her daughter with speculative eyes and her frown deepened as she looked at Florence's dress of rich plum-coloured velvet with its expensive hand crocheted lace collar. The dress was in sharp discord to the surroundings of the little house; a disparity to the faded cotton dress the mother wore.

The mother's voice broke the stillness, rousing the girl from her morbid depths. The voice was gentle as she searched for the right words to bring out the truth, to help the troubled girl. Florence felt her mother's eyes upon her. The firelight caught and held the glisten of tears.

"Tell me, Philomena, tell me all that happened to you."

"Oh, mama ...," she ran to bury her head in her mother's lap, sought to hide her burning cheeks as the tears ran. Her cry was one of a wounded animal deep in anguish. She was reaching out, clutching for the only peace and comfort she had ever known. The words came out in a violent torrent. The voice, muffled in the folds of her mother's dress told the sordid story.

She blurted out the horrors of those nights, the long nights filled with drunken men in the halls, the debauchery in the rooms next to hers and the threats Carlo made, to put her into the rooms. She told of the men who sidled slyly to her on the stairs, trying to put their hands over her body. Florence was convulsed with sobs and her mother in a tortured voice urged her on.

There was the final impassioned deliverance as her words tumbled out, falling over each other in their rush to bring out the hurt and shame.

Angela heard the story of the evil house, was shocked and repulsed by the corruption and depravity, and her mouth set in a bitter line. She cradled her daughter to her, crooning softly. She loved her deeply, this child of her womb. The girl finally slept, relieved of her ugly burden and her face became as innocent as a child. The mother cried silently into the night.

As Florence rested in the warm shelter of her home, Carlo sought the help of his friend Picariello. The older Italian took him back and gave him a job in one of his many ventures. Picariello also accepted the change of name without question.

"And now I be called Charles Losandro. No Carlo no more!" The younger man took the English equivalent of his Italian name. He was pleased with himself.

There was no answer from the other man. An ugly moment came up when Emilio questioned Carlo about his life in the United States.

"And Philomena, did she like living down there?"

"Call her Florence, will you? Florence Losandro, just like me."

"What did she do?" He spoke hesitantly, not waiting to hear what he suspected.

"She worked in a house down there."

Carlo offered no further explanation; his mouth was dry, he desperately wanted a drink, wanted to get out of the older man's eye.

"A house? A house?"

The question was accusing, cutting.

"Yeah," uncomfortably Carlo started out, "yeah, you know, a boarding house!" The shrug of his shoulders closed the door on the subject.

The older man's face was unmoved as he pondered this information. But if Carlo had watched, looked up from his shame, he would have seen the eyes narrow, anger starting small fires in their depths.

With his future secure it didn't take Carlo long to resume his cockiness. He went to Florence, telling her of his grandiose plans for being Picariello's right hand man. He told her of the money he would make, bootlegging, of course, and of the life she would have with him, now that he would have money again. The girl and her mother sat through the torrent of wind-filled plans as Carlo talked of his ambitions and dreams. Angela Costanzo was bitter; she did not want her daughter to go with him but Carlo was Florence's husband and at his command, she silently got her things.

Picariello was now in charge of their lives; Carlo would follow him blindly. Again, Florence was uncertain about her future.

III

AN AMBITIOUS
IMMIGRANT

AT THE TURN of the century, the immigrant Picariello was living in the city of Toronto, in the province of Ontario. He was a strapping man, five feet, seven inches in height. Although stockily built he moved with dignity and ease. His height was accentuated with a shock of black hair and a sweeping moustache.

Emilio was an ambitious man, young enough to have an unlimited amount of energy, old enough to recognize and seize an opportunity when it came his way. His first few years in Canada were spent in dreary apprenticeship, learning the language and economy of the country. But this was not good enough for the man; he wanted more.

He looked around and found a small store with a reasonable rent. Using his savings he stocked the store with Italian foods and soon did a steady business. He worked diligently, watching with pride as his savings doubled from the returns of the store. But he did not work all the time; he was seen about the community and women watched him covertly. He had a clear eye, a firm ringing voice and the elastic step of youth. In his keen enjoyment of life he was a lively and social figure in the Italian community.

It was at one of the many gatherings held at a local boarding house favoured by his Italian compatriots that Emilio first saw Maria Marucci, the girl he was to marry.[1]

When Maria arrived in the United States from Italy, she

---

1. Maria Marucci — names have been found to differ to Maria or Marian, Marucci or Marucyi.

went to live with her sister Carmello and brother-in-law in Allentown, Pennsylvania. Italian girls of marrying age were scarce and she found she had more than enough suitors wishing to speak for her hand. As was the custom, her brother-in-law took it upon himself to be her appointed guardian in charge of arranging a suitable marriage. This guardian paid no attention to the looks of the man. He was mainly interested in getting the best dowry, choosing an older man with a house and money in the bank. In this tightly regimented style of life, he did not consider the feelings of the comely young girl.

When Maria finally met the man she was to marry, she was appalled. He was thin faced, dour, a widower of undetermined years. Then too, he was stingy, bringing her gifts of over-ripe fruit sold at half price and wilted flowers that were surely picked off the vendor's discards. She saw before her a hard life of submission and child bearing under his tight fist. He obviously did not love her and she could not even like him; she would merely be a servant to see to all his comforts and needs.

Maria had a plan. Every time the man came to call with his bunch of wilted flowers she annoyed him by disappearing to play with the children. She made it obvious that she preferred their childish prattle to his holding forth on his various ailments; his weak stomach and indigestion which could only be cured, he said, by a good cook. He had a terrible combination of complaints, all of which a devoted and dutiful wife would cure. Maria thought to herself ... old man, it's not going to be me! And she set about arranging her own destiny. She wrote to her brother in Toronto and soon she received a reply which made her spin about the room in happiness. She read his reply to her sister.

"You need not marry that man. This is America, not Italy! If he is as you say, stingy and many years older than you, you will not be happy, my sister. Pack your trunks and come to Toronto."

There was more about his plans for her to work in a boarding house but in comparison to the marriage any work looked good to her.

Maria still had to reckon with her brother-in-law. He was very angry, his thin lips white as he raged at her.

"And the dowry? What about the dowry? I will look foolish in front of my friends. You are ungrateful and after I've taken you in, done the best by you, and now, you, a nice Italian girl, you go to some strange place in Canada. And by yourself! Ach! What is the world coming to. Now what your fiance do, huh? All that trouble, to look again. Now who will take care of him, and the men, oh my! oh my! They will laugh at me, can't control a woman!"

Maria put her hands over her ears to shut out his raving. At the railway station she kissed her sister and ignored her brother-in-law. The coal-fired engine took on water for its boiler and sat waiting, making a head of steam. Passengers scurried to the train; there was kissing and waving, some laughter and more than a few tears. With a rocking motion the train started to move.

Travelling for the first time by herself Maria was frightened but determined not to show it. To cover her anxiousness, she was overly prim as she folded her shabby coat, unpinned her hat and placed both in the metal scrolled compartment above her head. As she settled into the plush-covered seat she looked around with excitement at the warm coach with its curved roof done in tongue and groove strapping. Small lights cast strange shadows on interesting passengers around her. A man looked up from his newspaper and smiled at her. The girl's eyes widened, she quickly turned her head and looked out the window. Outside, a softly falling snow was feathering the countryside.

Her brother met her at the station, gave her a once over glance, was satisfied with her looks and propelled her through the door into the street.

"The man, the one you were to marry. Tell me again about him."

Maria's brother was torn between the freedom to choose in a new country and his ethnic upbringing. He had seen too many arranged marriages where a young bride with shining eyes was turned into a dull woman in servitude.

Maria's explanations reassured him. He told her of his plans for her.

"I have a place for you in a boarding house, one of the better ones. No rowdy men here. You work for your board and room and two dollars a week. Do whatever they ask, sweep and clean. Mostly you will wait on tables, serve the food. Do not go into the upstairs rooms alone or when the men are home!"

His tone told her to behave herself. Even if he was not at the house the community grapevine would tell him how she was behaving.

At the house the proprietor looked her over, pursed her lips, saw that she was cleanly though shabbily dressed and showed her to a room she would share with another girl. It was at the back of the house away from the boarder's rooms. "With a grunt the hefty woman said, "Supper's soon. Don't be late. Tomorrow you can serve."

Maria looked around the plainly furnished room. There was a white enamel bed with an old diamond-circle quilt. She bounced on the bed, it was quite soft! Humming to herself, she hung her meagre clothing in the oak wardrobe, catching a glimpse of herself in the bevelled mirror. At the washstand she wiped the train dust from her face and hands, smoothed her dark hair and left the room.

As Maria approached the dining room she was overcome with fright; sounds of men eating, the clink of dishes and the strange dialects coming from the room were enough to make her wish she was back in Allentown. Taking a deep breath, she went in.

The boarding house was full. Five or six men bunked in each room; there was no privacy. It was merely an existence, a transitional point in their lives until they moved on or married.

A motley group of men looked with interest as the slim, dark-haired girl entered the room. Maria looked around the crowded table, dropped her eyes and slid into a seat near the proprietor. Another girl with blond hair pinned tightly at the back of her head came through the swinging door expertly carrying several plates. The girl gave her a shy hesitant smile before she slipped back between the doors.

Maria ate from the plate passed to her. The food was good, well seasoned, and this was undoubtedly why the boarding house was one of the best. Only good food and lots of it would compensate for hard beds and the lack of privacy. She realized she was hungry and attacked the plate as her eyes took in the scene around her.

The men were all immigrants, young, virile and single. They were rough working hulks with hardened, slivered hands, who paid their board out of scanty wages and spent the rest on carousing. There were only three women in the house; the dour housekeeper-cook who was as coarse as a man herself, another servant girl and Maria. Young single girls were scarce and Maria was soon to find that here, too, she would have an ample number of hopeful suitors.

There was one man at the table who didn't belong with the rest. Her eyes took in the cut of his clothes, the manicured hands and well-cut hair. Forgetting her manners she stared at him and Emilio, looking up from his plate, caught her looking and nodded his head in recognition.

Maria's cheeks grew rosy with shame. Emilio, on the other hand, could not take his eyes from the girl. He saw the flushed cheeks and smiled to himself. His gaze wandered boldly over the dark hair which escaped from its rolls and curled in small tendrils about the smooth skin of her neck. He couldn't wait to be introduced.

In the weeks that followed, Picariello haunted the house, hoping to catch a glimpse of the girl as she swept the corridors. Days when she worked in the kitchen and was nowhere to be seen, he despaired and became gloomy. His lucky days were those when he met her in the hall or when she handed him a plate of food. Then he could smile without seeming forward, look into her eyes and imagine there was an answer there.

He was dumfounded to find her gone one day. Inquiring

discreetly, Emilio found out where she was working. Then he took to walking past several times a day.

It was the other girl who lured Maria into a better paying job.

"Come on, you don't need to scrub here now. Come work in the laundry with me. The boss, he likes me, he will take a friend of mine." She urged the doubtful girl on.

"As for me," she rolled her eyes with mock exaggeration, "I don't want to scrub another pot again! I rather scrub clothes!"

This last part was said with defiance and Maria knew her friend had a stepping stone to marriage on her mind. Maria went with her.

Again Maria had to reckon with a man as her brother raved at her. When he found she was determined to go, he quickly found her a room with a respectable Italian family. He kept tighter watch over her now. The century-old laws of their culture were ingrained in both and even in this country she would obey the customs of her native Italy.

Maria scrubbed clothes in the basement laundry. The caustic soap reddened and chapped her hands, her back hurt but she was happy. She made friends with other girls and there was laughter and teasing among them. She saw the stocky Italian pass the laundry several times a day and when the girls saw the faint flush that came to her cheeks when he passed, they teased her. She put her head down over her tub, tried to still the smile that caught the corners of her mouth.

"Ah, Maria," the called, "Chi e quest'uomo? (Who is this man?) He look at you, no?"

They hooted and called teasingly.

"Your brother, he gets angry if he sees!" Amid giggles they scolded her. "Nice Italian girl like you!" They mimicked her brother.

Maria took their teasing with a smug smile and soon was looking with interest as she worked, watching the windows for his passing.

One day just as she looked up, he passed by and seeing her, put his hand to his hat, gave a small bow and their eyes met. Maria put her head down quickly, a ruby flush flooding the olive skin of her neck.

"Maria's got a beau! Maria's got a beau!"

The chant went up. At lunch time she told her friend, "My brother, he would kill me, if he knew. If I smile at Mr. Picariello, he would say I was forward!" They tittered together. Secretly she was happy.

In the back of her mind she worried that her brother would find out and then there would be a confrontation, with her brother seeking the man out to ask his intentions.

At the end of the day she finished work and came from the basement to the street. She breathed deeply the purity of the autumn air, a refreshing smell after the steamy closeness of the basement laundry. The wind carried a chill that crept inside her thin coat to the small of her back and rested deep in the marrow of her bones. She pulled her coat tighter around her and started for home.

At the corner Emilio was waiting. He fell into step beside her.

"Good evening!"

He matched his long stride to her shorter one, felt her stiffen beside him. There was nothing further said and at her gate he tipped his hat and disappeared.

Each day he was waiting, and she began to look forward to the end of the day, fearful he would be at the corner, apprehensive that he would not.

After a few weeks of silence they started to exchange small pleasantries. Maria's brother was away and she wondered how she would tell him about the man when he returned. Still, she tossed her head, she had done no wrong.

Emilio awaited the brother's return. At one small acceptance on the girl's part he would seek her hand in marriage.

Emilio noticed that the girl's hands were gloveless, reddened by her work. She was embarrassed and hid them from sight. He timidly offered her a warm pair of gloves from his store and seeing refusal rise in her eyes, urged her to take them. In the acceptance of the gloves, she accepted him.

Maria wondered about this man with the watchful eyes and

silent temperament; a man who was kind, jovial and generous with what he had. She got to know him as they walked slowly to her home. He gestured as he passed large houses in the immigrant district, houses with sleazy curtains at third-floor attic bedrooms, houses with large verandahs with sagging chairs and bay windows filled with tired plants.

"One day," his arm swept the air from the row of houses to his broad chest, "I own many too!" He was filled with plans for opportunities he saw around him.

Under a bridge, he slowed his pace and she glanced at him nervously.

"Maria...," the word was almost a whisper, a caress. Her eyes widened as he reached for her and she stiffened as he pulled her to him and kissed her.

With a little cry she tore away from him and ran down the street for home, muttering to herself as she ran.

"I nice Italian girl indeed!" She sobbed as she stumbled to the gate. "Now what my brother do with me, what a scene he make with me!" She fled upstairs to her room and locked the door.

Emilio watched the girl as she ran from him, still feeling the shock that had run through his body at her touch. Dazed, he went to find her brother, determined to ask for her hand in marriage.

The wedding that followed on April 16, 1904 was simple; the groom nervous in his celluloid collar and pressed suit; the bride, shy and timid in her tricotine dress with silk braid trim. She wore small kid boots with Louis heels, her old coat and the chamoisette gloves Emilio had given her.

They took up housekeeping in the small back rooms of the grocery store. The bedroom was sparsely furnished with a metal bedstead, a chest of drawers, wooden chair and a small hand-braided rug that covered the cold floor beside the bed. A naked bulb hung from the ceiling. The other room held a table, a couple of wicker chairs with faded flowered chintz-covered cushions, a white washstand with a blue willow pitcher and bowl, a small cook stove and Maria's ancient trunk with its brass studs and worn bindings.

In the early mornings, before she woke him for work, she watched her husband as he slept. With his hair dishevelled he looked vulnerable and lost, a small-boy look arrested on his sleeping face. From deep inside her a need arose; she wanted to feel a child in her arms, a tiny face to look down into with the same stillness. Moving carefully, she touched her swelling belly, growing round despite the flatness of her slat-like body. With a contented sigh, she turned to fit her body close to his; she loved him so much.

When Maria felt her first pains and was gently steered into the bedroom by the mid-wife, Emilio waited the long hours with anticipation. Wet with sweat, his face contorted with each moan that came from the other room. There was the sweet moment of relief as a baby's ragged cry cut the stillness. The tired girl was proud as she lifted his son to him.

"Il mio figlio! Stefano! Mio Figlio!"

He cradled the child jubilantly to his broad chest. It was the second day of November in 1905.

Soon the ambitious Italian was feeling the constraints of working long hours and seeing very little of his savings grow. The rooms behind the store were cramped now with the addition of a daughter to the family.

He talked of moving west. Friends wrote to him, describing in glowing terms the beauty of the mountainous regions in the province of British Columbia. They urged him to come to Fernie where a large community of Italians made their home.

Picariello instantly found himself at ease in the growing town of Fernie. There was no doubt about his ambitions as he started into his small ventures. He was like a young octopus, putting out tendrils, grasping at those likely to make money, rejecting and recoiling from those with very little profit. He was a master mind, always thinking, directing, watching and waiting for opportunities to come. He took a fellow Italian under his wing, made him a confidant and friend and the man, Charles Losandro, returned his gratitude with loyalty, wordlessly pledging his allegiance to the man.

Emilio moved into a large house with an empty macaroni factory across the alley. Picariello put the building to good use. He hired local women to roll small cigars that Losandro sold through the towns of the Crows Nest Pass. Then Picariello dove into the ice cream business, putting wagons on the streets with the best ice cream cones in town. Bare-footed tots waited patiently until they heard the bells on the horse harness, unearthed liquor bottles from their hiding places and ran to wait in the soft dirt of the roadsides for their turn to exchange the bottle for a large, dripping cone of their choice. As the wagon dripped ice cream into the dust of the street, the laughing driver took the bottles held up to him as he scooped the ice cream from the wooden tubs. Two cones for a quart beer bottle! The children thought they were in heaven.

It wasn't long before Picariello's bottle business overshadowed his other ventures and with prohibition, the old macaroni factory took on a new use.

IV

ABOLISH THE BAR!

DURING THE LONG, hot summer of 1915, the people of Alberta had gone to the polls. Months of campaigning by the National Women's Christian Temperance Union did not go unnoticed and after the tabulation of the July 21st vote, the province of Alberta was to be dry. The coal mining towns of the Crow's Nest Pass had voted to keep the province wet but the law passed and prohibition came into force July 1, 1916.

In May and June of that year, newspapers were full of ads offering entire stocks of liquor on sale or by auction.

"Hurry!" read the ads, "only 4 more days and Alberta is DRY!"

In Calgary the entire $50,000.00 worth of stock of the Western Commercial Company Limited was put up for public auction on Friday, June 23 and continued every day until the building was cleared. Rye, scotch, Irish whiskies in bottles and bulk, bourbon, brandies, gin, port and sherry, burgundies, Bass's Ale and Guiness Stout went over the block, sold to an eager public by the bottle or case. Terms cash! Phone M4225! They advertised free delivery to any part of the city.

"Going DRY specials...," the ads told the public. "The liquor act puts a crimp in our business and we are putting an even bigger crimp in our prices!"

One special was Dog's Head Bass Ale, quarts at $3.00, pints at $1.50, and 'nips' for $1.00.

The Diamond Liquor Company gave an extra bonus to their customers. With each purchase of $10.00 they gave, absolutely free, one pint of Mumm's Extra Dry Champagne. Their prices were unbelievable; quarts of quality scotch for 85¢, seven year old rye for 75¢ a quart, imperial quarts of Irish whisky for $1.15 and Wiser flasks, 4 for $1.00.

Where there is money to be made, along comes the schemers! Necessity, they say, is the mother of invention and the Albertans were willing to go to all kinds of trouble to slake their thirst. They found loopholes in the law and when authorities plugged these, others took their place.

With Alberta's neighbour, British Columbia, still wet, it was inevitable that the Pass road between the two provinces would become a bootlegger's trail. Huge profits from illicit sales of liquor were too much for even Picariello to ignore. Unexpectedly, prohibition gave him a very profitable business. Always on the look out for new and lucrative business opportunities, Emilio found his friends in Alberta were eager to buy the whisky he secreted in his car when he came down the Pass on his regular bottle collecting trips. Soon he was coming down each week with a full load of whisky and returning home with a full load of empties to sell back to the distillers.

Money, always an attractive proposal, along with the thrills of daring work, lured Picariello into bootlegging. He could sneer at the penalty when caught; the liquor was confiscated and he had the option of a fine in lieu of imprisonment. Just one load would pay the fine and the rest was pure sweet profit.

The purpose of the act was to prohibit the sale or gift of intoxicating liquor within the province of Alberta, except for other than beverage purposes. It was designed to restrict the consumption of intoxicating liquor within the province itself. Picariello shook his head, looked with distaste at the temperance people and thought, 'Poor suckers, they're beat before they start'.

In reading the act, the population found that the manufacture of liquor by any brewer or distiller was not prohibited; nor did the act prohibit the sale by them to any person outside the province of Alberta, as these privileges were granted to them by Dominion Statute. All that remained was to get the liquor back into Alberta and into the hands of the drinkers.

The act did not prohibit the consumption of liquor in one's own home, provided the liquor was not secured from within Alberta and did not exceed the fixed amount at any one time. If found with a quantity of liquor exceeding the maximum allowed—a quart of whisky and two gallons (one case) of beer—the unlucky person was liable to prosecution under the act. In this way, individual liberty was secured while the liquor trade was restricted. Big deal, thought the drinkers as they started to cache a supply even though they knew they were breaking the law and could be subject to prosecution if caught with an excess.

To legally obtain their supply the imbibers had to bring it in from outside the province. There was no stipulation in the act which limited the amount a person could order from outside the province, yet the householder either kept to his quota by constant ordering or by illegally caching his supply. The penalty when caught was $50.00 and the loss of the right to keep sufficient liquor for his own household needs. Rumours flew back and forth, gathering momentum; people whispered that inspectors were checking sales accounts of wholesale dealers and keeping a tabulation on those who were purchasing heavily. The stories did not stop the purchasers as they cagily stashed their liquor in small amounts in unsuspected places.

The favourite talk in the poolrooms, the cafes or on the back stoop where neighbours sat together in the cool of the evening, was the act and their interpretation of it. They soon found ways to poke it full of holes.

The act provided power to the lieutenant governor to appoint government vendors on fixed salaries to sell liquor to professional men permitted by law to buy it. This select group of men was allowed to resell liquor for medicinal, mechanical, sacramental or scientific purposes but they could not sell liquor for domestic use nor could they make a profit or commission on their sales. The liquor was dispensed upon a sworen statement that it would be used for other than beverage purposes.

Druggists were restricted to 5 gallons at any one time, dentists were limited to 1 pint; doctors could not exceed 2 quarts and the veterinary surgeon, 1 gallon. All were to be dispensed by medical certificate. A clergyman could have 2 gallons of sacramental wine but only if it was not for beverage purpose.

These properly registered professionals had to report each month the quantities disposed of and the balance left in stock. If they neglected to report or did not submit correctly detailed permits, they were liable to fines of $50.00 for the first offence, $200.00 for the second, and $500.00 for the third. Members of these professions who were caught breaking the law would not only be fined or imprisoned but would also be barred from membership in their professional associations and this would automatically disqualify them from doing business in Alberta.

The grounds on which these men could be disqualified were many; failure to send in monthly reports, consumption of liquor on their premises, having more liquor in stock than their quota allowed, or taking forged certificates. Should their employees break any of the rules the unlucky employer was subject to the same disqualification.

Prohibition, said the ads in the papers, was the cure for public drunkenness and social problems arising from the use of liquor. To enforce the act the province was divided into 4 parts, each with a head responsible to the attorney general. This staff was further enhanced by the addition of inspectors and detectives.

Ads also appeared in the newspapers urging people to oppose the liquor act, to read the act and be convinced, it was not prohibition. The ads outlined a lot of loopholes!

Temperance platforms declared liquor to be the root of all evil. It was pure poison! This brought guffaws from the drinkers, who, reading the act, pointed out that liquor was to be used by man and animal for medicinal purposes only. They also noted that the vendors could sell liquor for sacramental purposes on the written request of a minister of the gospel.

How many new ministers were born that night!

Hospitals could sell to the patient but not to the patient's visitors, but... the patient could give his visitors a little nip of hospitality and a nice little room party was underway.

There were many clauses in the act allowing the importation of liquor into the province so the drinkers could have their liquor, it was just not as handy as before.

While the new act took care of the householder, there was a clause forbidding people living in flats or apartments to have any in their dwelling. Not fair, said the apartment dwellers! So they thumbed their nose at the act and ordered whisky anyway.

The express office became a mecca for those who wanted something more! Packards, Fords, horse and buggies, even perambulators collected at the express office, picking up parcels of liquor ordered from wholesale houses over the British Columbia border. Fifty to sixty parcels a day was not an unheard of number. There were four wholesalers in British Columbia; Revelstoke and Golden in the north and Fernie and Natal in the south. All were reaping a rich harvest from thirsty Albertans.

With the law allowing druggists to sell liquor for medicinal purposes, there was a steady stream of new 'sick' with many aches and pains for which only a doctor's prescription would help. The doctors were allowed to prescribe liquor not exceeding a quart at a time. It was noted that a doctor who owned a drug store was handling more liquor than patients.

July 16, 1916 was the hottest day of the year and the 88 degree temperature left a lot of thirsty throats. It was the day the temperance bars opened and throngs of drinkers with expectant faces hurried to the new bars to taste the temperance Chinook Beer. It was a non-intoxicant that looked like beer and was said to be similar in taste and flavour to the regular brew. Prohibition did not seem to be so restrictive as the bars filled with soldiers and citizens.

Along with the opening of the new bars, a newspaper campaign was underway, urging the public to buy the new beer. Edmonton Beer, complying with government regulations, was advertised as the right beverage to build up strength, health and happiness. Calgary Brewing and Malting Co. Ltd. ran ads for Chinook Beer and Chinook Stout.

Also advertised was the best export beer, 'made in Calgary', and ordered from Nat. Bell Liquors Ltd. in Saskatoon. It was touted as the beverage to dine on, work on and sleep on; used with meals it stimulated the appetite and assisted digestion. It imparted strength and energy, and taken on retiring its tonic properties quieted the nerves and guaranteed sound, refreshing sleep.

The brewers must have thought temperance beer was catching on for as the months passed the brewers in Alberta changed their output; they increased the amount of temperance beer brewed and reduced the amount of regular 4% beer for shipment outside the province. They could brew beer for local consumption if the proof spirits did not exceed 2%.

For those people too lazy to order their brew, there were substitute drinks. Newspaper ads urged a product guaranteed to 'break whisky's grip on your loved ones!"

The product, Alcura, would soothe trembling nerves and remove the craving that was ruining homes and stealing otherwise kind husbands and fathers. The $1.00 a box cost had a money back guarantee if the product did not cure or benefit the user.

Alcura 1 was tasteless and could be given secretly in tea, coffee or food. There were few drinkers who threatened their wives just in case they had the idea of using it. Alcura 2 was taken voluntarily by the few who were willing to try curing their addiction.

Another answer to prohibition was called Vin-Ex. It was a non-alcoholic, fruit concentrate which sold for 25¢ a bottle and made 5 different beverages. It was guaranteed to make a sparkling grape champagne, tingling ginger ale, delicious grape punch, rich non-alcoholic grape wine and a non-alcoholic green ginger wine. Needless to say, it was not the most popular drink. It was to be available at all Calgary drugstores after July 1.

In due time, prohibition, which many people took to be a huge joke, turned sour. The drinkers checked their depleted stocks, searched for new outlets, nursed these carefully and when these dried up, turned to newer sources. Up out of all this mess rose the heads of the moonshiners, bootleggers, informers and spies. The age of the big time bootlegger was born. Honest citizens, tempted by money to be made easily after the lean war years, became greedy and deceitful. An act passed by the federal government placed automobiles in the category of common carriers. Several firms loaded their automobiles with liquor, had a correct bill of lading made out consigning the shipment to a customer in the State of Montana and nothing could be done to stop them. Other bootleggers decided to get into the business and the handsome Picariello was one of them. [1]

Picariello was quick to see the demand for liquor in towns throughout the pass where mining was the chief occupation. For the hard drinking men who lived most of their lives in the bowels of the earth, whose lives were gray in the shadows of their work, drink, and the release it brought, was their only extravagance. These men went into the mines in their youth with dreams and ambitions, hoping to make money, good money as a stepping stone to a better life. But the pits took them, played roulette with their lives, made old men of them, and returned them 40 years later, slouched, muscular, squint-eyed.

Every day they came from the pits and returned to the unpainted shacks they called home. They sought relief from boredom, the ugliness of their lives, the excessive harshness where death was a partner in the hole. Drink was their escape. They saw their friends taken, crushed against a cage, run over

---

1. Details on prohibition taken from a variety of newspaper articles of the day. In some cases, wording has been taken verbatim from newspaper articles for effect. Chapter has not been footnoted throughout and only a general footnote is being used as many footnotes would impede the chapter. Newspapers used were Calgary Daily Herald, Calgary Eye Opener, Edmonton Journal, and the Lethbridge Herald.

by mine cars, pinned against walls by loaded cars. Friends were taken from the mines with injuries that would cripple them for the rest of their time on earth. Those were the lucky ones; the unlucky ones died on the bottom, caught in a bump, their lives snuffed out by seeping gas.

When out of the mines the men cast about for a release from reality. Liquor was one release; the company of women the other.

Picariello was more than happy to provide the liquor; the madams in houses that flourished in the red light district provided the other. There was always a choice of girls; the younger ones were the favourites and new ones were always appearing.

The madams were cagey older women, whores whose youth had gone, leaving behind jaded women with spreading figures and tight fists. It was in the alleys behind their houses that Picariello first picked up his empty liquor bottles. Emilio became a familiar figure and many a girl tried to entice the handsome man inside to visit.

Emilio had matured; adding pounds to his frame as he lost some of his youth. But the twinkle of merriment was still in his eyes, his voice was firm, his manner courtly. He attracted women and Maria was jealous of some of the attention paid to him. Her first trip through the red light district reinforced her fears.

The day was warm, the winter drabness cast aside when Emilio took his wife for a drive in the light buggy. As he swung his wife into the buggy her eyes shone with exuberance. Motherhood had not taken her girlish look; she was willowy, her waist waspish under the tightly buttoned serge skirt. Her ecru blouse was set off by a flawless complexion. Two small combs of french ivory held hair coiled high on her head. A gold locket glittered against the trim of her blouse.

They stopped at the grocers and she asked for her order, ticking the items off on her slender fingers. Cream of Wheat flour in a 24 pound bag, 3 pounds of soap chips, a pound of eating figs, a bottle of HP sauce, a case of winter spys (apples) and 2 pounds of Winnipeg ginger snaps. Emilio doled out $4.06 for her purchases and then added a small bag of mixed candy; licorice drops and brightly coloured ribbon candy. Her smile deepened.

At the bakery, a hot and floury baker looked up from his board where he was cutting cookies and came to greet them. He patted his perspiring forehead with a white handkerchief as he leaned against the counter to rest. Soon, a bag of buns, thick with cinnamon and sugar, heavy with raisins and ground brazil nuts, was in her hands.

Emilio turned the horse towards the outskirts of town. Near the brewery was a red light area. The light buggy rolled past some of the larger houses on the fringe and Maria noticed ladies sitting on verandahs brushing and drying their hair in the sun. Others were polishing their nails and sipping tea. They were exquisitely dressed, even overdressed, for an afternoon.

As the buggy moved slowly down the street Maria was astonished to see the girls waving and calling Emilio by name. They were laughing, bent on teasing the Italian who picked up bottles at the back of their homes.

A delicious looking redhead sprang lightly to her feet and strolled to the front gate. She wore a georgette dress of a pretty shade of green with an overblouse of figured minon, traced with gold embroidery. She guessed the woman with Mr. Pic was his wife.

The redhead raised her eyebrows and with a saucy turn of her head called, "Good day, Mr. Pic!" She emphasized every word. Behind her the girls tittered; a faint flush crept up Emilio's neck.

The redhead became bolder; mischief lighting up her china blue eyes.

"When are you coming to see us, Mr. Pic?"

She swung on the gate, her skirts billowed out behind her. Emilio whistled softly under his breath. The sun fell in long rays behind the trees.

Maria turned to him, bewildered.

"Who are these women? What do they do here? And ... they know you? I hear them, they call you Mr. Pic!"

Emilio laughed but remained silent. He stared straight ahead, but Maria persisted quietly, naively.

"They are so pretty, those women. Why are they dressed so, on such an afternoon?"

He turned to her and with a serious a look as he could muster, lied to her virtuously.

"Why ... these ladies are fairies. Yes, that's it, fairies, out here in the woods."

He grasped at the first thing that came into his head. He turned the horses, laughter spilling out his eyes and crinkling the corners of his mouth. Maria frowned; she didn't understand nor did she catch the innuendo in his voice.

With a toss of her head, she folded her arms and sat very straight on the seat.

"What is this thing, fairies? Never do I hear of this. Fairies! Non mi curo molto di questa specie di persone! (I don't much care for that sort of person!)"

She struggled with this information and sounded annoyed and a little suspicious. It was much later when she finally understood.

The handsome Italian was used to attention paid to him by ladies and goodnaturedly put aside his wife's jealousies. This was the only thing that marred their relationship. After one skirmish over a full-lipped customer who was more than attentive to Picariello, Maria was sufficiently annoyed and, waiting until Emilio left town on business, she packed her trunks, gathered the children and took the train to Pennsylvania.

Emilio arrived home late, found the house empty and, guessing where she went, checked with the station agent. The agent confirmed his suspicions. Emilio did not go after her, nor did he contact her. He let her cool her heels since he knew where she was.

In Pennsylvania Maria resisted all efforts by her relatives to get in touch with her husband. She relented only when she found she was pregnant and in time Emilio appeared to take her home. Nothing was said and the couple resumed their lives as if nothing had happened. Maria never left again.

V

NEW USE FOR AN
OLD HOTEL

THE YEAR 1917 was full of surprising changes for the
liquor industry. Prohibition was just not working in the way it
had been intended. Bootlegging had always been a fact of life,
even in the days of the open bar, but now, with bars closed and
stringent control by the authorities, the activities of the
moonshiner and bootlegger grew to astonishing proportions.

With the provinces of Alberta and Saskatchewan dry and
British Columbia and the State of Montana wet, drinkers were
getting nicely settled into routines for importing liquor and no
one was really thirsty. For Picariello, the liquor trade never
looked better; the other ventures of rolling cigars and selling
ice cream vanished.

For some time, preachers in the pulpit had been pointing a
finger at the act, charging it was responsible for the increase in
bootlegging, the manufacture of liquor and all the evils that
went along with this. They were vocal in their welcome of a
new threat to this liquor traffic; the formation of a new police
force March 1, 1917.

The Royal North West Mounted Police persuaded the federal government to change its mandate to include federal
jurisdictions and when Ottawa acted on this, the result was the
termination of provincial police. The provinces were forced to
originate their own provincial police.

The new force, the Alberta Provincial Police, was organized,
and one of its duties was ferreting out illicit liquor activities.

The force divided Alberta into five divisions: A division
located in Edmonton, B division in Red Deer, C division in

Calgary, D division in Lethbridge and E division in Grande Prairie. There were a total of 48 detachments in the province.

The boundaries of D division (Lethbridge) extended east and west to the borders of Saskatchewan and British Columbia and north to Township 18 and south to the United States border. With the Crow's Nest Pass running on one perimeter and the Montana border on the other, it was inevitable that D division would be heavy with liquor offences.

D division was divided into five sub districts with 45 men on strength. Included in this group were 1 inspector, 2 sergeants, 4 corporals, 21 first class constables, 6 second class constables and 2 third class constables. There were 1 detective, 5 stock constables, 2 special constables and 1 employee. In total they had 13 horses, 4 automobiles and 2 dogs. These two were bloodhounds, purchased in the fall of 1921, being a male with the registration number 5 named Badger. The female had a registration number of 6 and was called Tip. The dogs were kennelled at the Coalhurst detachment.

Of all the districts in D division, the one in Blairmore, which included the villages and towns of Coleman, Bellevue, Hillcrest, Frank, Passberg, Burmis and Cowley, covering an area of 720 square miles, was the busiest.

Bellevue, Blairmore and Coleman housed the detachments. This sub district had the highest rate of convictions of all sub districts and a good majority of these involved liquor. Transportation for this sub district included a Dodge automobile, registration number 7 garaged at the Blairmore detachment, and a horse with the registration number 102 stabled at Coleman.

Of all the sub districts of D division, the next one with activity was Claresholm, which included Barons, Vulcan, Nanton and MacLeod. The men in this sub district had their hands full with liquor abuse during the harvest as transients arrived to work in the fields.

The Medicine Hat sub district, including Bow Island, Lomond, Retlaw and Irvine was quieter. The crops poorer and transients fewer; the only major activity in the area came with an attempt to hit oil east of Medicine Hat.

Warner sub district included Manyberries, Foremost, Cardston, Magrath, Coutts and Warner. During the completion of the Canadian Pacific Railway east of Manyberries into Shaunavon, Saskatchewan, an extra constable was posted to cover the area until conditions settled down.

The Lethbridge sub district controlled Taber, Coalhurst, and Pincher Creek. As soon as quarters were completed at Blairmore, Pincher Creek was taken from the Lethbridge sub district and put in with Blairmore. Lethbridge had two cars, both Dodges, with registration number 8 and 11.[1]

When it became evident that the privilege of importing liquor was being abused the government stepped in.

One Saturday morning the express companies were ordered not to deliver any parcels containing more than one quart of spirits or two gallons of beer. The express companies were soon awash with undelivered parcels and the moans and groans of drinkers were heard in the streets. Then, on Sunday morning, word came that put a smile on the faces of those awaiting parcels. The express offices could deliver pending the results of a test case. The flow began again.

Wholesale liquor dealers claimed the act allowed unlimited shipments if these were made legally. Both sides of the controversy agreed to abide by the results of the test case which was to be heard soon. In the meantime liquor flowed easily into Alberta.

When the province of British Columbia adopted its measures of prohibition on July 1, 1917, Picariello was already looking around for a change in scenery. He was sitting on the fringes of the liquor trade, exporting some and bootlegging on a small scale. He could see the vast amounts of money the trade could bring and considered a move to Alberta. He wanted a place that was central to the trade, close to wet Montana but not too far from the stills of British Columbia.

---

1. From Alberta Provincial Police files, Provincial Archives.

When he looked over the Alberta Hotel in Blairmore he instinctively knew it was the building he needed for his operations. From this hotel he was to direct some of the most daring runs in the history of the bootlegger.

Prohibition hit the hotel business, both for the owner and the city treasuries. With their bars closed down, the hotels lost a major source of revenue. They tried to make it up by opening tea rooms and ice cream parlours in the hope of recouping their losses. These ventures did not produce the hoped for revenue and many of the hotels closed; others tried to stay alive with ads promising clean linen, hot water, courteous treatment and well lighted rooms, a home away from home. City treasuries lost funds not only from liquor licences but from taxes as the proprietors made good their cases for a reduction in assessments.

The hotel men, sorely hurt by financial losses, petitioned the government to reopen the bars for the sale of strong beer. Immediately the temperance people came to life, got into their pulpits and held meetings denouncing the request as a bad indication as to the desire of the general public. Those signing such a petition were only the ones who would sign their life away for a beer! The temperance people boasted that the hotel business in Alberta was the best in Canada. The hotel men were quick to disagree. While all this furor was going on, Picariello was making plans for his new hotel.

Pride of ownership settled on Emilio's face as he showed off the hotel to Carlo. The purpose of this trip, he explained carefully, was to see that all space was utilized to best advantage. He started in on the second floor where most of the rooms were rented on a monthly basis.

"We kept the roomers on. The rent not much but we don't need all this room for what we do."

He gave the younger man a large wink.

"You count all the rooms." He had a small notebook in his hands into which he made undecipherable notes.

When Carlo came back with the tally he mentioned several of the back rooms were vacant.

"Good. Save me from tossing anybody out! I need several rooms for drivers. And, lets see, maybe you and Florence take one of the larger rooms. Maybe you like this one overlooking the street, huh?" He thought it might cheer the sad looking girl.

They came down to the main floor of the hotel. There was a large dining room which Emilio inspected carefully.

"The men got to eat somewhere. Might as well be here. I hired a cook. Named Mar Poy." The kitchen was behind a small room opening onto the side street.

"This here cook he wants to have small store, you know, candy, cigarettes and stuff. The little room on the side street good enough. I told him he could, long as men get good meals on time. Should be here soon, to clean the kitchen."

Carlo wandered back into the kitchen, kicked at an old stove, ran a finger over a dirty table. He knew he would eat at Picariello's table.

Picariello was pacing the dining room. He scuffed his toe on the worn linoleum floor, looked carefully at the scarred varnish of the wainscot. The upper walls, papered in a light figured green, were the only feature of the room that pleased him. Stove pipes from a coal heater disappeared through the ceiling at one end of the room. There was a dusty sideboard holding cruet sets, cutlery and table cloths. Near the molded door frame a metal ice box was pushed against the wall. The windows were curtained with rose damask; a wicker geranium holder stood in front. As he walked and thought the man gave clear, concise orders to Carlo. He wanted the floor relaid, the wainscot varnished, the silver polished, new tablecloths and napkins purchased. Carlo was to get the best and Florence could help. Florence, he said, could earn her keep by waiting on tables.

The lobby was minute. A pedestal fern stand, complete with an anaemic looking plant, stood near windows hung with lace curtains. The spittoons, relics from the closed bar, crowded the corners.

"You want to see the house?" Picariello asked.

Another building, quite separate from the hotel but directly behind it, was to house the family.

Emilio was excited about the garage which ran behind the house and connected with the basement of the hotel. Carlo pursed his lips and gave a low whistle. The two men walked through the garage to a basement door at the very end. In the garage cars were hidden from street view; nobody could see what was taken from the cars or put into them. In the basement Picariello made marks in the dirt indicating where long tunnels would be dug. Barrels, boxes, and other junk would cover the entry to the tunnels. Emilio was happy; everything was going as he planned. Even the government played into his hands and brought about changes that put a large smile on the face of the Italian.

After April 1, 1918 liquor shipments into the province of Alberta were to be curtailed; the export business was dead. Now liquor traffic went underground; enter the era of the big time bootlegger and moonshiner. Of these, Picariello intended to be king!

The man started to move quickly. Leaving the running of the hotel to Carlo, Picariello worked intently on building his new venture.

Emilio called on an old friend, a man named Guido. Guido was a middle aged Italian, with no family, who understood the unwritten laws and customs of doing business in an Italian community.

The man was small, slim, with a body as taut as his mouth. He lived his life with fierce determination. Emilio trusted Guido explicitly, and he charged him with finding another driver.

Guido found a young man and brought him to the hotel to be looked over. At the hotel Guido maneuvered the car into the garage and alighting, the two men went through the back entrance into the hotel. The younger man gazed around him with interest, stumbled over his feet; the older man gave him a piercing look.

Emilio rose to meet them, his bulky frame a heavy silhouette against the pale light filtering through the curtained windows. Picariello walked around the boy. Tony smiled and shuffled his feet.

"Come si chiama?" (What is your name?) Antonio Sepi ..."

"What's the difference," the youth shrugged, "Just call me Tony!" The boy waved his hands expansively.

"Wait outside!" was the terse reply.

Guido shot the youth a glance and with a smile on his face, the boy lumbered into the street.

"Well, what do you think? You ask around, seen a few people? He's slow, that boy, slow. Still maybe better he not be too smart."

The heavy Italian grinned to himself, laughing at his little joke.

Guido barely managed a smile, giving just enough to show favour to his boss before he started in on his report.

The boy was part of Guido's 'family', related way down the line through a long forgotten marriage. He had in his favour a good driving record, an innocent but rather blank face and a strong back. His only faults were a bumbling manner and a flirty eye. Picariello ordered a trial run.

Two of the three cars Picariello owned were in the garage and Carlo was fixing the silk roller shade in the back window of one of the cars. He stood back with Emilio, watching as the needle-witted Guido tried to catch the boy, make him look the fool.

Guido dipped a stick into the gas tanks, looked at the mark made. One of the cars was almost empty and he chose this one for their ride. He started to explain the features of the vehicle to Tony but the young man was lost in admiration. He ran his hands over the sleek blue black body and let his fingers slide down the black fenders, gleaming with polish. He sat in the driver's seat, gripped the wheel, excitement in his eyes. He was totally oblivious to the irritated Guido.

Guido swung into the passenger seat. He told the youth to back out and ordered him to drive, picking out streets with rough holes and sharp corners. He gave unexpected orders to which the youth responded with uncanny ease. Soon they ended up at a small hill.

Tony started the car up the hill. The small amount of gas in the tank gave him problems. Running to the back of the tank, the gas was not fed to the motor and the car sputtered, jerked, then came to a stop. It started to roll back down the hill. Tony furrowed his brow. Guido waited.

After a minute Tony brightened, let the car roll back down the hill, turned it around and backed triumphantly up the hill. A huge grin flashed across his face as they came to a stop at the top. Guido crossed his arms in resignation, muttered to himself. He had a feeling he and Tony would be seeing a lot of each other in the future.

With the addition of Tony to the payroll, Picariello had a full complement of drivers. He teamed the new driver with Guido; he himself worked with Carlo or one of the others, Red Jack, Ugo, Benvenuto and a few others who worked at regular jobs but took the occasional run for excitement and extra money.

There were a greater number of vehicles travelling the roads now. Navigating the rough dirt roads was tricky, very few roads were gravelled; most were just rutted, quagmire messes. Driver training was non-existent; the purchaser of a vehicle simply handed his money over to the salesman and took to the roads. Some were natural drivers, understanding fully what the vehicle could do. Others were at a loss, driving nervously and trying to remember the instructions of the salesman. They froze at the wheel, muttering to themselves.

"When you want to stop, shut the gasoline throttle off and engage the clutch. Now, just before you are going to make the stop, put the brake on, leave the clutch in and shut off the ignition. Whoa, whoa, dammit, stop!"

The mesmerized driver hallooed to the car as he drove through a flower garden, across the road into a neighbour's hedge to end up in the back alley.

In winter cars were kept in storage. An advertisement in the Lethbridge Herald noted that cars would be stored in a warehouse for $5.00 a month. This included a battery storage in warm quarters of the Exide Service Station on 3rd avenue south. All interested parties were to call telephone number 2966 Lethbridge.

There was always a lot of movement around a vehicle; greasing, oiling, tightening of bolts. The battery required distilled water fed to it by a syringe. Spark plugs needed to be set and if you were handy and had one thin dime, you could do it yourself. Many automobiles had a tool box bolted to the running board. The careful driver carried a jack for changing a tire, money wrench, a crank, tire tools and a soft cloth. Rattling around the bottom of the box were spare bolts and nuts and an assortment of small tools the owner thought he would need.

The McLaughlin Buick Four was a fast car but Emilio wanted something even better. He traded his cars in, choosing McLaughlin Sixes, capable of high speeds. He had the best cars on the road and to keep them in order hired a mechanic by the name of McAlpine.

McAlpine's job was to keep the cars completely overhauled at all times making a thorough check after each run. To save time, Picariello needed a man who knew the difference between the choke lines and the brakes. He did not want cars that were sluggish; his rules were firm. The cars had to be ready to go at all hours.

McAlpine made no comment to the first order he received. He was to baffle plate larger gas tanks, made to carry full loads of fuel for long runs. With the tanks plated, heavy loads would not tip the vehicles on precarious turns in the high crowned roads.

When one of the automobiles was finished and ready to go, Picariello sent Guido and Tony on one of their first runs together. No two people who were to travel the country could have been as diverse in character as the new team.

Tony was addleheaded; given to giddiness and inattention as he blundered goodnaturedly through life. Guido resembled a hawk. He had the eyes of one and his nose jutted out in a beak like fashion. His whole appearance was one of canny shrewdness, a person not to be trifled with. Working with Tony was to be the bane of his life and although he eventually got around to liking the boy, he would not show it.

Guido and Tony were given one of the back rooms in the hotel, next to one occupied by Carlo and Florence. That the two men were able to share this room was due to a great deal of restraint on the part of the older man. Between runs Tony played his records on a machine he constantly wound and overwound. Guido held his crusty temper in check as he heard over and over again the few cylinder records the boy had. Soon Guido knew all the words to the favorite, 'My Buddy', and could sing along quite well with the Happy Six to 'Time Will Tell'.

Many of the doors along the corridor slammed as the cylinder scratched through its third spin.

Guido preferred to either sleep most of the day, or sit near the window with his cut plug watching with interest the few people who ventured down the alley. He shined his shoes till they gleamed and waited for his runs; Tony's constant fidgeting got on his nerves.

"Dammit, Tony, you're like a fly at the window!", the voice was sarcastic and carried a threat. "Play 'Silver Swanee' once more, just once more, you hear, and I'll bust it over your head!" One more playing of the song would destroy all vestige of his sanity. Tony got the message and ambled from the room.

The small Italian at the window hoped the next run would be better than the last. Emilio had seen the condition of the automobile when it came back in, mud up to the fenders and clumps of grass and muck hanging from the running boards. Guido thought he saw the heavy jowls move in suppressed mirth as Picariello took in the sight of him. Guido had a high water mark on his impeccable trousers and his black patent shoes with their high shine were dulled and dirtied with swamp muck. Emilio didn't ask about the trip but there was the slightest lift of an eyebrow and the ruddy face twitched with a smile. Guido was glad he didn't ask. Hidden under the back seat, gallon bottles of liquor from a still were safely home;

a camouflage of eggs for the hotel dining room sat precariously on top.

Guido's trouble happened on a night run when they were on their way home. Car lights were seen in the distance. Guido ordered Tony to cut his lights and move slowly by the light of a half hidden moon. Both men strained to see the road. Recently, the provincial police watched for car lights pinpointed in the darkness of a prairie night. Pursuing the cars, they questioned the drivers and searched the vehicles.

Crossing the Milk River bridge, they pulled to the side of the road and watched as the lights kept on coming towards them. Guido moved uneasily in his seat. If they were lucky, the lights would turn down another road or into a farm yard.

Tony lit a cigarette with an unshielded match and Guido turned to cuff him, cursing softly. Tony, not having his cigarette to smoke, amused himself by singing.

"... nights are long, when you went away ... I think about you all through the day ... my buddy ... my buddy ... your buddy misses you."

Guido muttered, "Shut up!"; he peered into the gathering dark, his eyes never left the road which stretched before them like brown grosgrain ribbon. The lights had disappeared.

"I think we go now, but slow, dammit, slow! I need to see the road too. Don't put your lights on for a piece up the road!"

They had gone but a mile or so when Tony noticed lights behind them. Tony put on his lights and picked up speed.

"Would you cut that out! Slow down. Non guidare cosi in fretta! (Don't drive so fast!)"

The small man was becoming increasingly annoyed. Their lights were sure to be seen if the other car in front had pulled to the side of the road and sat waiting for them.

"Attento! Cut your lights! Slow down! Watch out!" Guido barked orders. Tony, not too concerned with the gravity of the situation, took Guido's words and lapsed into gibberish with the orders.

He mocked the other man. "Cut my lights, slow my car, watch my foot, cut my foot, light my car, watch my cuts...". He dissolved into gales of mirth at his own cleverness.

Guido barked at the driver again. He felt helpless at times against Tony's rambunctiousness.

"There's a turn in the road, somewheres down around here!" Guido peered through the windshield, found his vision limited and reaching out, pulled the covering from the window so he could poke his head out.

"Somewheres near here is a turn in the road, a pond on one side. You have to watch out for the turn. Go too fast and you won't make the turn! Attenzione! Attenzione!"

He need not say more; nor did he need to put his foot outside the car to know that they sat squarely in the middle of the shallow pond, having missed the road in the dark. Guido muttered inaudible things to himself. Pulling up his pant legs as high as they would go, he looked like a skinny stork as he stiff-legged it to the edge of the pond. Good thing he knew the road, he muttered. There was a farmer down a piece who would bring his team of horses.

Guido and Tony were lucky this time. The farmer got them out of the pond, the automobile was not damaged.

There were only the sounds of muck flying from the tires and undercarriage as the car headed back to the garage.

It took a few months for the two men to develop into a crack team. They had lots of practice.

In 1917 the provincial police had disposed of 127 liquor cases; in 1918 the tally was almost tripled at 347 and the bootleggers had just barely begun.[2]

Helping this along was the start of prohibition for the United States on July 1, 1919. With Montana dry, the bootleggers had more markets than they could fill. After July 1 the river of liquor flowed quite a different way; instead of coming into Alberta from a wet Montana, liquor from stills tucked away in the Alberta mountains flowed back into the now dry Montana. The age old adage, the pendulum that swings, always swings back, was being repeated.

---

2. Ibid.

VI

DEALERS IN WET GOODS!

AS THE BOOZE money started to flow, everyone wanted to get in on the act. Overnight there was frenzied activity; small stills sprang up, wine and beer was made furtively in basements by housewives hoping to add to their pin money and drummers travelled the south country making more money with a suitcase full of bottles than they ever made from their orders of pins and needles. Under the masquerade of a 'dry goods' salesman, many a man stuffed his pockets with fast cash. The amateurs peddled a little here and there and regularly got caught. Their misfortunes taught them more of the fine points of the game but when their efforts were thwarted, they did not dare to complain.

To the big time bootlegger these small peddlers were more of a nuisance than a threat. The big operator sat back safely, paying handsomely for his information on raids and arrests, letting the smaller bootlegger blunder into the arms of the law.

One of these small bootleggers was a drummer from Calgary who travelled to the Crow's Nest Pass early in the week, moved into the south country before returning to his home on a Friday. His wages barely covered the demands of a wife and six children. He was often strapped for cash.

He carried a variety of goods in his cloth covered wooden suitcases. Flinging them open with a flourish he hoped to dazzle the shopkeepers with his array of satin ribbons, fine thread, cards of pins, needles, buttons and fasteners, celluloid collars, and hat trims.

To supplement his income, he started off very small, buying

some heady moonshine which he watered down, rebottled and wrapped in newspaper. He carried the bottles, safe from rattling, in a false bottom of his display case and went merrily about his business.

He worked under a Calgary firm and gave out their card but rarely told anyone his name. He was a man of bulk, his vest buttons straining over a paunch. The flab of his face settled into jowls, made a moon of his face, giving him a contented look. He drove from place to place, eating hearty meals in greasy cafes on his route, talking up his wares — both kinds!

Whenever he was anxious, he betrayed himself, settling and resettling his fedora, fingering the brim with fat fingers.

Across the avenue from Picariello's hotel was the Home Bank and the Club Cafe. One morning the drummer came into Blairmore very early and stopped for breakfast at the cafe. Guido was in Carlo's room which overlooked the avenue. He wanted to borrow polish for his shoes. As Carlo rummaged for the tin, Guido sauntered to the window and stood looking out. A movement below caught his eye; here was the drummer, strolling from the cafe, picking his teeth with a toothpick.

As the drummer stood in the early morning light, an ice wagon moved slowly up the street. The horses arched thick necks, blew and snorted in the cool air, shuffled their feet as the driver flicked the reins over freshly brushed rumps. The drummer hailed the ice man, who paused in his work. Guido watched. He strained to hear the conversation as the ice man gave directions to the drummer, pointing with a long bony arm. Turning, the ice man swung his pick into a cloudy block of ice, bit his tongs into a hunk and moved off the wagon. The weight of the ice bulged his forearms. The drummer, well aware of his flab, was impressed with the performance.

Upstairs, Guido strained to hear what was said. Most of the words were lost to him but enough was heard to make him interested. Just yesterday Guido had seen the fat salesman travelling towards the British Columbia border and wondered why the man was heading out of his sales territory. Guido lost all interest in shining his shoes.

On the street the drummer backed his car up and headed down the road leading out of the Pass. He was confident and happy, he looked the part of a prosperous business man going on a trip.

At the window Guido watched the car until it disappeared from sight. A small whistle escaped his narrow nicotined teeth. The drummer was carrying more than a few buttons today! Guido left the window and went to find Picariello.

For the drummer, it was going to be a nice day. The raw winds of the early morning had suddenly stilled. A night frost, creeping stealthily over the fields was chased back by an early sun. Warm blobs of light moved surely over the fields; reaching for and caressing the tasseled corn, the tomatoes experiencing their first blush. The light rested on maturing pumpkins, warming the large orange globes still finely traced with dark green. Recent rains had delayed the harvest and now the still warm days of an Indian summer allowed farmers back onto the fields. With a self contented smile, the drummer tipped his hat to farmers on grain wagons plodding down roads like slow moving beetles to a feast.

The drummer turned down a rutted road into a small town and stopped in the dust before a store owned by an ancient Chinese named Lou. The salesman chuckled to himself; he had just heard of Lou's arrest.

The story that reached the salesman's ears was hilarious. The police knew there was a bootlegger in town. They set up a watch and saw Lou making more trips to his hen house behind the store, than was necessary for good care of chickens. When Lou left the hen house, one of the policemen tiptoed in, moving carefully so the broody hens would not put up a clatter. Cautiously he ran his hand under a warm sitting hen, receiving a sharp peck in the bargain. His hand slid over a warm freshly laid egg.

Hello, he said to himself, and what is that? His hand gazed a harder object barely buried in the straw. He pushed the protesting hen from her nest and found a bottle. Chickens flew as he went from nest to nest; each nest didn't necessarily have an egg, but each one did have a warm bottle.

Still grinning from his recollections, the drummer settled on a stool at the counter and rummaged in a vest pocket for change.

"Hey Lou, gimme three of those meat pies, a little gravy, some fried potatoes and maybe a bottle of Iron Brew."

Meat pies sold three for 25¢ and the drummer would have to pay an extra 5¢ for the potatoes and gravy. It wasn't much of a lunch but it would have to do. Probably the pastry would be tough, the meat stringy and the soft drink warm. Oh well, he thought, when I deliver this load then, a nice steak, a bit of apple pie, maybe a visit to a girl ... his thoughts drifted off. Lou shuffled off to get the pies. The drummer tipped back his hat and looked around.

It was a typical country store, dingy and dismal from the dusty shelves to the patched linoleum floor. The faded window sign spelled out "Lou's Cafe" but it was more of a general store with a selection of groceries, dry goods and novelties for sale. The window held an assortment of cut glass water sets marked for sale at $4.00. Their pale green sides were dulled by dust and fly specks; the bottoms littered with dead flies. The glass counter behind which Lou sat enthroned held boxes of Princes Pat hairnets, six in a packet for 50¢; pocket mirrors, toothbrush stands, button hooks and shoe lifts. Another shelf held boxes of Dodd's Kidney Pills, Dr. Chase's Nerve Food and Lydia E. Pinkham's Vegetable Compound. Lou was the local drug store too. Behind him within easy reach were the tobaccos, Gold Mine, Old Chateau, Cavendish and Irish Roll.

The drummer finished his meat pies, washing down the last mouthful with his soft drink and strolled to the glass-fronted counter.

"Gimme a pack, the big one."

He laid down 25¢, hunted for another coin, and came up with a dime.

"How's your supply, Lou?" The drummer winked at the shrivelled little man. "A little something for the cold nights ahead, huh?"

The heavy man leaned on the counter and chewed on his toothpick.

"No! No!", the Chinaman was excited. "No good. Cost big money. Police man, he look often! No good!"

He rolled his eyes and threw up his hands, nearly falling off the stool in his excitement.

"Oh well ... I'll be back next week. Maybe then ..."

The drummer wasn't worried. The little oriental had a liking for the stuff and the money it brought.

The cafe owner kept repeating the story, muttering mostly to himself as he lived again through the ordeal with the police. He painfully remembered how it hurt to dig up his savings can in the dead of night and the wrench he felt when he parted with the money to pay his fine.

The drummer was only partly listening; he realized it was talk for his benefit. Likely the crafty little man still had his bottles, now cunningly concealed away from his premises. This old man would never go short and right now some old crock or bottle marked vinegar was hidden in his greasy cluttered kitchen and filled and refilled on stealthy night trips to his cache.

The drummer left the cafe, eased his car out of town and headed down a sparsely travelled road. Dust plumes from his wheels lingered behind him. He reached hilly country; the prairie flatness was left behind and the land spilled into coulee. It was a land of short grass, sage brush and stunted bush. Every pothole cupped moisture from a recent rain. Red-winged blackbirds swayed on tall sedges fringing stagnant sloughs while a frog chorus rose from its cattails. Snags in the pond were shadowed by an overhead sky which laid a filigree pattern of muted silver on its silent surface. Soon a small border town appeared in the distance; the salesman fingered his hat.

The drummer parked his car near a church and set off on foot for his rendezvous. He found his intended purchasers in a cafe; but they curtly and unexpectedly turned thumbs down on this load.

He hastened back to his car and stood beside it, fingering his hat and looking puzzled.

A pretty young woman struggling with many bags and boxes came towards him in a pre-arranged scene. Ever the gallant, the drummer offered to help her with her packages and drove her to her home on the outskirts of the town. With her charms she delayed him, offering him tea and simpering companionship.

While he was being detained, the others followed the pair, stole the car and unloaded the booze. They barely had time to return the car before the drummer came jauntily onto the porch, his ego swelled by flattery.

When he saw the disarray in the car, his contented smile was gone.

Emilio and Carlo laughed when they heard of the drummer's misfortune.

"Poor fellow," they chuckled, "all that booze and he can no tell the cops!"

They chortled back and forth and for days afterward Picariello had a 'contented' smile on his face. Guido wondered about the part Picariello had to play in the adventure, but his boss was not about to tell him. Emilio had other matters on his mind.

Picariello received a telephone call that disturbed him greatly. It concerned his son, Stefano.

Earlier in the summer, after days of heated arguments with Maria about the boy's future, Emilio made arrangements to have his son put into a Calgary school. Maria was against this.

"What he want with fancy learning?" she said contemptuously. "He can work here with us. Learn lots, hey? All that fancy stuff. Non serve! e inutile. (It's no good!) Better you arrange il fidazamento (engagement) to a nice girl!"

Emilio was adamant. He wanted his son to have a formal education, something he had not had. He didn't want his son trapped in the liquor business, better for him to have schooling for an honest profession; Stefano could be a teacher, a bookkeeper or a butcher.

Maria knew Picariello like the back of her hand. He was stubborn to the point of being mulish. But Maria was determined to have a say in her son's future. She looked with affection at her husband, noting the change years had put on his frame.

Emilio won.

In early September he took the boy to Calgary, arranged for his board with an Italian family, enrolled him in school and returned home pleased with himself.

Now he received disturbing reports from the school; Stefano's grades were falling. He was reported to be sneaking out at nights; his antics cut his father to the quick.

"You see, Emilio, you see!" Maria chortled triumphantly. "You bring my son home, here. My Stefano back here where he belong!" She patted the chair beside her happily.

"Certamente no!" (certainly not!) her husband thundered. "Let Carlo get him. The boy no good. I spend lots of money, nice school, new clothes and all those books! Bah!"

Emilio was angry. He reached for a piece of goat's cheese and stuffed it in his mouth. Thinking of his son he mellowed a bit. He remembered the young people, dancing a tarantella to the music of Guido's concertina. Stefano was missed then, the lively boy was always one of the best dancers. It would not do to be soft however, the boy would feel the father's displeasure.

Stefano was happy to be home. Picariello's exasperation with his son's tomfoolery led him to give the boy the most menial jobs about the hotel. But he would never have to go to school again and with this good news, the young boy breathed a sigh of relief.

"You no go to school, you no learn." His father closed the subject flatly as he spread his large palms over the table.

"Now you clean. Like woman, you clean! First the spittoons in the lobby. Lei capisce, non e vero?" (you understand, don't you?)

"Si, capisco," came the reply grudgingly. (I understand.) "But papa, I want to be a driver, like Tony." The boy had an infectious grin.

Looking at his first born, the father weakened. "Forse! Non si sa mai!" (Perhaps! One can never tell!)

But Emilio underestimated his son. The boy did his jobs well, became amenable to his father's wishes, helped out cheerfully in the garage and gradually worked his way into the business. Picariello let him move the cars around, wash them and drive short distances and soon Steve, as he was now called, became an expert in handling the vehicles. He hung around the drivers, keeping very quiet but always listening carefully. Steve knew that it was just a matter of time before he too would take a car out so he watched and listened to his father as he gave instructions and orders to his men.

One lazy afternoon Steve heard the name Mason mentioned and knew enough about the trade to know it was the term used for a moonshiner. He begged his father to be taken along on the visit but Emilio pointed him firmly in the direction of the spittoons and left with Guido.

The swaying sensation of the motor car travelling the road made the large Italian close his eyes and his thoughts drifted to his family; Maria was firmly entrenched in the large house with the children; Carlo was taking care of the hotel and collecting the rents and making plans for the temperance bar that Emilio planned to open.

Carlo had done a good job of the hotel dining room, the room reflected warmth and hospitality. Floral wallpaper covered the walls, new varnish darkened the woodwork. An ornate Franklin stove gave an inviting glow on chilly evenings and soft lamplight gleamed on mahogany chairs, clean linen and sparkling cruet sets. Florence was serving meals in the dining room; Emilio wished the girl was happier, but she was usually very pensive. She and Steve were about the same age and lately they spent time together, sitting in the sun on the steps, laughing and talking. Only with Steve did the girl come alive, lifting her face to the sun. It was then that one heard the girl's soft laugh, heard a melodious lilt to her voice.

As he reflected, Picariello felt a mantle of uneasiness fall around him. He was being very careful now and knew his activities gave him notoriety; it was just a matter of time before he would be caught.

He was making money, a lot of it and his wealth made him proud and defiant. He was aware the provincials were curious about his business, the one behind the facade of hotel keeper. But Picariello had many friends to cover his tracks and they were well rewarded for their efforts. The runs were successful; the only ticket he received was for speeding on the Natal road. The ticket cost him $15.00.

A voice beside him roused the man.

"This Mason, how I get to his place. We're near the town soon. Should be turning off somewheres soon. Better you tell me."

Picariello's voice came slowly, low and weary.

"Make a turn past the feed store, go west. Follow the road into the hills."

Guido started in cautiously, his boss did not seem inclined to conversation.

"How he get that name, Mason, I mean? That's not his real name. What is his real name? Nobody knows."

Picariello grunted. "Must be from the way he put his stuff up. In mason jars, the ones the women use to pickle and stuff. Easy to get, not easy to trace. Every house has dozens of them."

After some difficulty they got to the cabin after leaving the car far down the trail. Walking up the stone littered path Guido was chagrined by his inability to keep up with the hearty robust man walking beside him. Emilio was refreshed from the ride. Guido made a mental note to himself to start working up his muscles tomorrow. Too much sitting in that damn room he thought.

Mason lived in an old log cabin well hidden up a rutted trail. The cabin with its low pitched roof, sat squarely in a stand of pine near a rocky outcrop that served as a lookout. Behind the house were beaver ponds overshadowed by tall pines. The long grass ringing the pools was threaded with the vivid pulsating colours of wild flowers.

Guido was amazed at the lack of cordiality shown by the moonshiner but Picariello seemed not to notice and treated the man with respect. They stood for long moments outside the cabin while chipmunks shrilled and ran over the sun dappled roof. Finally the old man with a nod of his head beckoned them to enter.

The furnishings were scant. A bunk with fresh balsam boughs took up one side of the room. The main feature of the other side was a rusty cook stove with its pipe that disappeared through the dilapidated roof. There was a coffee pot, grease caked fry pan, a rough table and a few stools.

The cabin was dirty; junk, old bottles and other nameless articles littered the corners. Ashes and wood chips were scattered with abandon under the table and trailed to the door. The litter was dappled with an ever changing kaleidoscope of waning light, the patches increasing in density as the light shifted back and forth through the leaves.

A pack rat peered through the early gloom. The remaining light from the dying sun sought and caught the brightness from his beady eyes.

The old man shuffled around, nimble for his years. He cursed and finally found a match to light the lamp. The light was dim; the chimney unwashed and the wick untrimmed.

Mason fed wood into the stove and cut bacon slices from a thick moldy slab. Guido watched with interest as canned fruit, honey, powdered milk and salt appeared on the dingy table. He decided he was hungry when the aroma of biscuits mixed from meal batter came from the black oven. Picariello had not spoken; he sat quietly, seemingly uninterested in his surroundings. The talk would come after the meal. Guido shifted nervously, weary and hungry.

The cook gingerly took his biscuits from the oven, burnt his fingers and cussed. With a sweeping motion he indicated they should eat. Yellow flickers of light from the lamp patterned the table as the men dug into their food.

When the coffee was poured the second time around Emilio cautiously started to talk. The old man cleared his throat, looked pointedly at Guido and Picariello was quick to reassure him. Guido was a trusted man. There was a pregnant silence, the moonshiner's face clouded. His disapproval chilled the air. Emilio motioned Guido out.

The old man was very careful. He had been caught before and it would not happen again if he could help it. He went to the window, rubbed a hole in the dirty pane with a frayed cuff and watched Guido move away from the cabin in the fading light. He fetched a bottle of his own whisky from a hole in one wall and they started to talk. It was a good sign if the moonshiner drank his own brew. Soon the deal was made and Picariello left the cabin to stumble back down the trail. He shook the sleeping Guido and they left the valley for home.

In the week that followed Guido was to meet the man called Mason in a cafe in the town near the valley. It was all arranged; the moonshiner had agreed to meet the slender Italian with details for receiving the load. Guido did not want to go; he had an instant dislike for the old man and felt uneasy. He worried about treading on the old man's toes, then the deal would fall through and Picariello would fume.

Poor Guido was feeling nervous. For several months he and Tony had made good runs. Everything had gone like clock work; they had not been stopped, the loads had gone through. Their luck was too good. Guido felt himself winding tighter and tighter, like the spring of a clock.

Now he sat in the car waiting for Tony to bolt his breakfast. He shifted in his seat, looked critically at his trim finger nails. In annoyance, he abruptly leaned over and honked the horn.

The driver of a passing lorry smiled and waved, thinking Guido was honking at him.

"Nuts! Nuts to you!" said the small man under his breath as he climbed out and slammed the door.

"That asinine boy, why he not talk so much and move faster. Sun will be going down before we get out of town!" He went to hurry Tony along.

Soon the pair were on their way. On the outskirts two children chased horses from under the shade of the trees. The horses, not wanting to be ridden, circled and single-filed back to the trees where they stood droopy-eyed, swishing flies with their tails. The two men settled down for their journey not speaking, each to his own reverie.

When on the high grade, the large automobile picked up speed. It had rained during the night and the water in the ditches alongside the road was wading knee deep. The driver gripped the wheel, knuckles white and kept up his speed. The car headed into a corner, sliding a little on the greasy road. The smaller man glanced nervously at the driver.

"Slow down, will ya." Guido growled, rolling his eyes as the car swayed on another corner and the driver fought to regain control.

"Lentamente, Lentamente!" (Slow, Slow!)

The smaller man wiped his brow even though the air coming into the car was cool.

"Drive like that and you'll have us all in the slammer."

He peered carefully over his shoulder, looking through the half lowered shade on the back window. But the road behind him was clear as far as he could see.

Tony instantly relaxed his foot on the gas pedal, smiled and shrugged his tense shoulders. He grinned a vacant grin. The car settled down from its erratic motions and moved easily along.

"Say Guido, why the old man kick you out?" Tony was curious but Guido was in a foul mood recently and hard to talk to.

"You mean that old coot? The one we's going to see jist now?" Guido set his mouth in a bitter line.

Tony shot a glance at his companion. "Yeah, the guy they call Mason. Carlo, he told me about the time a friend gave him away and the police took him to jail."

Guido squinted as if remembering. "I remember too. I heard the talk. Those mounties, they don't give up. Kept on through the deep snow till they reached the cabin. But Mason was already gone for the winter."

"Must have been a good smart mountie to find it. Which

way now?" They had come to a fork in the road.

Guido pointed to the left.

"You know, that mountie circled the cabin, looking for marks in the snow, trying to see where the paths led. He followed the paths too; one led to a wood pile, another to a frozen stream but one led to a dirt cellar. Imagine, a dirt cellar way out in the brush."

Tony was eager to hear all the story and he prodded Guido on.

"That cellar all nailed up. Nobody do that unless you wants to hide something. He gets out his axe from a pack and chops down the door. Boy, 40 gallons of liquid dynamite! Mason got choice of 6 months or $175.00 fine."

Guido turned, excited by his story, forgetting his own discomfort.

"That old man took the jail term. Yes sir! Spent the whole winter in jail, warm and well fed, all paid for by the government and in the spring he got out, moved up the valley and was in operation the next week. Don't trust anyone now, that one. He is solitary. Oh boy, io ho sete." (I am thirsty.)

They were coming to a small town with one main street and the usual jumble of houses on its outskirts. They pulled up to a cafe with a fly specked window and a hand printed 'waitress wanted' sign. Both the fly specks and the sign had been there for a long time. It wasn't easy to hold a woman to the measly wages of a small town cafe and the girls moved on as soon as they had travelling money. They moved to larger towns where the money and the men were easy pickings.

The men brushed dust from their jackets as they went into the cafe. Tony settled on a stool at the long counter and sniffed the odors of pork and cabbage. He smiled broadly at the sullen waitress. Guido headed for the back house, the rough ride and his nervousness played havoc with his bladder.

While Guido fidgeted at a back table, Tony forgot the reasons why they had come to the small town. Tony couldn't perceive trouble if it lit on his nose. He turned his attentions to the waitress and his food. He was given to giddiness and with the woman he took on a spoony air. He ordered two eggs, once over lightly he said, some slices of pork and then tried to coax a smile from the wide-mouthed girl.

A few travellers appeared in the cafe looking for their supper. Outside shrill children called to each other on their way home from school. A black-stockinged child in a middy dress stopped to put down a penny in exchange for a long strip of paper to which round pastel coloured candies were attached. The cook came from the back and pulled the light cords flooding the embossed squares of tin ceiling. Pools of light from steamy windows splashed on the wooden sidewalk outside.

Guido smoked a cigarette and watched Tony and the girl. This would be Tony's first encounter with a moonshiner. Maybe it would be better if Tony stayed away from the crotchety old man; the boy asked so many questions he might spook the man. Picariello was anxious for this load. It was the last run of the season for this moonshiner and no batches were made during the winter. Too risky. Too much steam and no leaf cover. Guido lit another cigarette.

Tony was getting restless. The waitress was through her shift and the new one was an older woman with a band of dull gold on her left hand. Even Tony was not about to mess with an irate husband.

"Why don't we git going? I ain't going to wait all night for that old coot to show!" Tony shifted from one foot to another, looking to see if his words were making an impression on the other man. There was no response. Guido was immobile. Tony started bravely again.

"Do you think I could drive the girl home?"

He looked with hope at Guido. Tony had hopes of showing off to the girl. Had visions of opening the door to the big car, saw himself taking her arm, helping her inside. He saw her adoring incredulous eyes as he importantly took the wheel, fiddled with the dials and finally, skillfully wheeled the car onto the road. Then he saw himself sitting in front of her house while neighbours peered behind curtains at the shiny car and whispered to themselves. He would casually take her hand, maybe venture a little kiss. Her name was Floss and he wanted to know her better.

Guido hesitated. Picariello wouldn't like it but maybe the business at hand could be accomplished easier and faster with Tony out of the way. Guido waved the young man away. Tony swelled with importance; strutted to the counter and leaned confidentially towards the girl who was struggling into an old coat of suedene.

Now the man known only as Mason came into the cafe. He moved inside noiselessly, looking around. He sat down at Guido's table but gave no greeting to the slim Italian.

Tony was still fussing around the counter with the waitress who started to put on an act of coyness. Guido started up from his chair but the old man put his hand out stopping him.

"Don't bother the monkey," he snorted sarcastically, "the show will last longer."

He grimaced at his own humour. Guido sat down again, signalled the older florid cheeked waitress over and asked for the best of the house for the old man.

The old man ogled the slovenly figure in the tight dress and dirty apron. His rheumy eyes took in the carroty hair, the widening hips. He grunted, 'lots of gravy', and turned back to the table, spooning teaspoons of sugar into his cup. His meal came and he ate in silence. Guido was impatient and decided it was time to test the wind. He spoke cautiously.

"My boss, he sends his regards."

There was a long, long silence. Finally the old man grunted but never raised his eyes. He was intent on the gravy he was sopping up with his bread. Guido had patience. It would not do to rush the man.

Finally the churlish old man looked up from his plate. He looked around the table to see if he had missed anything then gave his attention to the waiting Italian. Guido rubbed his hand over his receding forehead; the cafe was hot and steamy and he wished the man would hurry so he could go home.

"The big fellow, he still wants the run, all of it?"

"Yeah, how many gallons?"

"Forty ... the best I ever run. Clear as spring water."

Old man, thought Guido, every run has been your best. He means the price will be up. Still it wouldn't do to annoy him so Guido kept his mouth shut.

"Where will we pick it up?"

Guido immediately knew as soon as the words were out of his mouth he had jumped the gun.

The old coot glared at him. "I ain't a saying until I sees the stuff." He had the look of a roiled dog.

"I brought the money. I got it here." Guido patted his vest. Inside was a carefully sewn pocket for the money he was entrusted with.

The old man's eyes lit up and his stained goatee twitched nervously. Flatly he said, "how much?"

"What you asked for and more!"

Guido flattered the man, they could then be sure of getting the spring runs too.

"The big man says yours is the best and he sends you an extra gift."

With puckish shyness the man reached for the fat envelope, rifled through the contents in the darkness under the table. His face never changed expression and after a brief moment he said. "The pond below where the moose feeds?"

"Yeah, I know the one." Guido was careful to imprint the instructions in his memory.

"Not the stagnant one but where the moose are seen, feeding in the marsh. You have to pass it before you come to the cabin."

Guido nodded and the old man went on.

"To the side there's a rocky cliff and on the face, there's a den, hidden by trees and deadfall. Lots of good cover. That's the one, tomorrow night."

Guido knew the man would work all night with pack horses, moving his load. He would be out of the valley by dawn. His money would be hidden and should the provincials stumble onto the load, the old man would be far away from his cabin. He would be back when he was sure the load had been moved.

The old man sat back, seemed for a moment to relax.

"There were wolf pups in the den. Three of them born early summer. I seen them once. They's gone now, she has them further down the valley."

The old man had a soft spot for the gray wolf he caught glimpses of as he slipped through the shadows to his still. The den where she had her pups was a good hiding place even if it was littered with bones and dung.

Tony came back into the cafe. He slouched at the counter and the moonshiner rose silently and melted out of the cafe. Nobody seemed to notice him leave. With relief, Guido left the table, slapped Tony on the shoulder.

"Dov'e la donna? (Where is the woman?) He snickered to himself. Back shot the ruffled reply.

"Non ne ho la minima idea." (I haven't the slightest idea.)

He reached for his hat. Guido was quicker, he wanted to have some fun with the boy now that the encounter was over and had gone well.

"Mi permetta ... (allow me) ... come on, get a move on, we can go home now. E'tardi!" (it is late!)

Tony had a red face as he got up from the chair where he lolled dismally on his spine. He looked sheepish and there was the faint mark of a hand on his cheek.

"Not like the others, aye?" Guido remarked wryly.

Tony regarded him contemptuously. The older man heard of some of Tony's conquests and had seen the red scratches on the boy's back. Guido laughed. The boy would learn.

They drove home in the evening light. Cottony clouds puffed the sky and the heat was dense. Hail clouds rose majestically in the north, the sky darkened and rumbled; Tony moved his loose-jointed body in the seat, seeking respite from the heat that dampened his shirt and left large circles of sweat at his armpits. Guido looked at his driver as the boy moved restlessly about. Love was written on the broad face, open and obvious. Tony sure picked funny ones, thought Guido. Take for instance this last one, the waitress with the aquiline nose. Guido couldn't understand Tony's chase of the opposite sex. Never capable of having any deep feelings for others, Guido had never had a girlfriend. He stayed pretty much to himself, never getting emotionally involved, alone even with people.

All Guido had in mind at this moment was a full belly and a good night's sleep. Guido turned up his nose at the Chinaman's fare knowing that meat and zucchini fried in olive oil was waiting at home. His mouth watered as he thought of his favourite, a soft cheese mixed with herbs and bacon bits spread over fresh warm slices of bread. The curtain was off his window and he received a blast of wind in his face, chilled air from the approaching storm. He sucked in the freshness greedily. His nostrils were held high to pick up the scents and smells of his adopted land. Guido sighed audibly. He was home.

Guido planned to sleep late the next day, not rising until the sun was well past the high crags of the mountains. Picariello had other ideas. There was an early morning call for his men. They arose in the early morning to the kissing sounds of birds in the trees. The kitchen was hot, even at this early hour as it was wash day and pots of all descriptions boiled and simmered on the stove.

A blue enamel washbasin of soapy water sat ready for scrubbing sleepy petticoated children. Porridge bubbled, ready to be ladled into flowered china bowls. The wash tubs were in readiness on the porch, the ironing board was in sight.

Pork slabs were frying in a heavy skillet. Picariello arrived in the kitchen, jovial, fresh from a shave. He shook his watch as he spoke to the sleepy Guido.

"L'orologio, si e fermato! Che ora e?" (The watch, it has stopped. What time is it?)

He waited for no reply. Throwing his hands in the air, he rolled his eyes at his drivers, then caught Maria to him.

"Grazia mama! I tell her." A smile came to her face as he hugged her.

"Mi chiami alle sei e mezzo!" (Call me at half past six!)

She escaped from his grasp to save the pork, fried to a golden brown and just now curling at the edges.

Emilio now turned his attention to Tony. He heard of the boy's conquest during a running monologue of the day's events from Guido. He kidded Tony and the boy's round features reddened as he gulped strong coffee from a heavy china mug.

Carlo came into the room and joined the men at the table. The discussion was on the merits of Tony's new girlfriend.

"Well, what she like?" Carlo wanted to hear more, he had an eye for the girls as well.

"Bello!" roared Guido, with unaccustomed fervour.

"Eccellente! Meraviglioso! Magnifico!" Emilio was enjoying himself too. (Excellent! Wonderful! Magnificent!)

Guido got up to mimic the woman's walk. He swung his body with one hand on his hip and the other behind his head.

"Si, Davvero! (Yes. Indeed!)

Now Guido mimicked Tony in the cafe.

"Hello baby, would you like to ...," he peered at the men through half closed eyelids, it was his version of how it should be done," ... have a ride in my car?"

He pushed his hat forward over his eyes and strutted back and forth, dribbling cigarette ashes over the floor.

The men hooted and called. Tony gave them a deprecating smile. He knew the price of his foolishness was the everlasting and repeated recall of his sins by his cohorts. Still, he refused to be baited and enjoyed the show.

At last Picariello grew serious and laid out plans for the evening. Two cars would be taken to the den. Each car would go by a different route. After one car was loaded it would leave and return home another way.

The second car would travel in the opposite direction after it was loaded, circling around the back way to home.

Tony and Guido would travel together; Emilio and Carlo taking the other car. In anticipation the big Italian rubbed his hands together. He turned to his wife.

"Mangero adesso, mama." (I shall eat now, mama.)

VII

A SUMMER
PICNIC

PICARIELLO LAID METICULOUS plans to bring his loads safely to his basement. He knew the country intimately, made it his business to travel all the backroads. When the automobiles arrived at the garage with not a bottle broken, he was immensely proud. He rubbed his hands together, it was just the start.

In 1919 towns in the Crow's Nest Pass were booming. Coal and lumber payrolls ranged from $80,000.00 to $100,000.00 a week. When the economy improved so did the purse of the bootlegger. Into police inspector's reports, all over the province and in D division particularly, went the same story; there was a very large increase in the actual illegal buying and selling of liquor. Back came the reply: find them!

As the mines and mills started working there was a paycheque due to every family and stores stocked to capacity in anticipation of fresh money. People, hardened by their falling level of living over the past months, looked now with new hope to the future.

The booming economy bolstered every business. Shopkeepers breathed a sigh of relief as money flowed into their coffers, old accounts were paid up and merchandise moved from their shelves. Housewives, serving meagre meals during the strike expanded their menus and grocery bills mounted. Credit was again allowed and the necessities of life were quickly snapped up. Women purchased sacks of cornmeal, 10 pounds for 35¢, 5 pounds of white beans for 25¢, and rice, 3 pounds for 20¢. A new brand of flour was introduced — the

Iris Brand, with an introductory price of 75¢ for 24 pounds. The housewives were eager to try it, a welcome change from the war flour[1] they had been using.

To the miners and loggers coming home after a long brutal day of work, the improved economy meant one thing. Their children would have food and the visits to the bootlegger would begin.

These regular visits to the bootlegger meant more work and more money. Picariello scoured the back country, driving long distances, making and sustaining connections so his flow of liquor would be constant. Sometimes he lost a source but a new one would rear to take its place.

With new orders the provincial police combed the country looking for stills. Illicit manufacture of alcoholic beverages was on the increase.

They watched for deserted farms, old abandoned shacks in out of the way places where a still could be set up. Also too, their ears were tuned to gossip and regular reports from informers who thought it was their duty to spy on neighbours.

A sure give away was smoke pouring from a chimney of a deserted farm. The provincials swooped down, took in the evidence and the man paid a fine of $300.00 and costs. Two weeks later, he was back in business. Now the provincials had to find out just where. They should have asked Picariello, he was the first to know.

Sometimes a long watch by the police was futile. They watched a cafe in a small town where known bootleggers made frequent stops. It was suspected the cafe was a rendez-vous. The old cook rented out rooms above the cafe and it was known that travelling women stayed in these rooms when they came to town.

The old cook in the cafe took good care of his business

---

1. War Flour—as written in newspapers, "Mr. Hanna, the food controller, announced beginning January 28, 1918, all mills in Canada commence manufacture of war flour. The new flour was to be one third cheaper but this was not so as it sold in Calgary only 25¢ less than regular flour. Little difference between regular flour and war flour was noticeable; the change was a slight yellowish tint of the war flour loaves."

upstairs. He was disappointed when an older woman turned up to rent a room. His cut of her business could be much less and if they had so much as one strand of gray in their hair he pointed out the benefits of Wyeth's Sage and Sulphur Compound to them. The new compound he said was quick and easy to use.

"No mess, no mess!" the cook told the woman; he nervously ran his fingers through his hair, dark though sparse and one wondered if he too, used the compound.

"Oh yeah," retorted the older whore in a bored voice. "Let's see the stuff." She was irritable, aware of her faded looks, but angry and hostile at having them pointed out by this scrawny man.

"... hm ... only moisten a comb ... drawing through a few strands at a time ... sounds easy ... wonder if it works!"

She muttered to herself, squinting over the directions.

"Let that old fool see me looking this close at the printing then he'll suggest I get glasses next!"

The bottle guaranteed a few applications would produce darkened hair with soft lustre and appearance of abundance that would be attractive to all.

The cook studied her flushed cheeks intently.

"You use? you use?"

The man was anxious, the woman could ruin his liquor business too, drive his customers to the next town.

"We'll see," came the mocking reply. She would use it, needed some form of rejuvenation but wasn't going to let this little runt of a man know it. It was enough that he took a percentage of her earnings for a crummy dirty room.

She must have used the stuff as business was so good that a raid was staged. The frustrated provincials arrested the woman; the liquor was so well concealed that nothing turned up in their search. The woman came before a judge, he fined her $25.00 and costs and ordered her to leave town. She did. Another one quickly took her place.

It was a continuing game of hide and seek. It was a game the unsuspecting Florence would soon be thrust into.

It was now April in Alberta. A soft rain fell. The drops washed dust from tiny cuplets of the lilac flowers, shined the pale mauve petals, darkened the green of the leaves. The drops fell into the dust below, washing and cleansing; there was the fresh smell of damp moist earth. The freshness lay on the land; could be felt on taut dry skins, drawn deep into the lungs, tasted on the tongue.

In the mountain town of Blairmore, windows in the tiny houses were pushed open to capture the freshness although the houses, smelling of dust, mildew, the people smell of lives long lived, could never be freshened. The houses had long ago settled into their characters, like the people who lived in them. Old people, with faces lined like the plaster of their rooms; young people too, with bodies bent and twisted from long hours in the mines, came to the windows seeking the freshness.

From the open window of her room in the hotel Florence listened for a sound. It came gently on the drenched air; the chug of an automobile from behind the building. The sound grew louder as the vehicle rounded the corner. It came to a stop in front of the hotel. From an alley a dog appeared to sniff the tires, then lifted his leg on one.

Florence stirred, then stretched. She sat up, clasped her knees with her arms and looked sleepily towards golden light filtering through long windows of the room. Her thoughts were tranquil until the events of last evening stung her memory. But, there was one consolation in the day to come. And with this thought in mind the girl slipped out of bed and started to dress.

The night before, Picariello, Carlo and Guido sat at the large table in the warmth of a steamy kitchen. The men had worked hard all week, camouflaging loads for distribution. The long moist tunnels cut into the earth in the basement below were filled with bottles of clear amber liquid destined for Montana. All that remained were plans for a safe delivery. The provincials were putting pressure on the bootleggers, watching them closely and deliveries were becoming more dangerous day by day.

Picariello waited for his food. He was morose, lost deep in his own thoughts and his men sat quietly. Maria took the lid from simmering soup and its bouquet filled the air, mingling with the soursweet smell of freshly kneaded bread dough. The children had eaten, their sounds of play squabble were muted by the heavy kitchen door. Maria tidied the kitchen, swept crumbs on the floor. Dust motes swirled into the last lingering light, dancing, twirling about before sinking back to the dark linoleum. She carried on a one-sided dialogue with her husband about the yellowing of her linens, the inevitable ravelling of the children's clothes, about the long seams she had to stitch. He knew she wanted a sewing machine and she would have one he thought. Picariello grunted at appropriate times in the one-sided conversation and she knew he barely heard her. She threw her hands in the air, muttered to herself. She could not reach him now; he was scheming, lost deep in his plans for the load.

She ladled out soup, lifted a heavy pan of pasta, meat, tomatoes and cheese from the oven. The pungent aroma of mingled spices aroused the big man and he looked up.

"You go now, we need to talk, my men and me."

He regarded her fondly and her smile in return crinkled the corners of her eyes. Before she left the room he had already turned his attention to his problem.

"Eat, Eat!" He pushed bread at Guido. Emilio leaned down hungrily over his food, pushing bread into his mouth, burning his tongue on the hot, heavy soup. He finished the bowl, helped himself to a large portion from the pot. He was thinking as fast as he chewed. His hunger sated, he reached for his water glass, drank, swallowed, then wiped the back of his hand over his mouth.

Picariello hit the table with large flat palms. His face was lit with inspiration.

"Yeah, that's what we do!"

He sat back in his chair, looked at the faces of his men with unblinking eyes. His men kept still as they waited to hear the plan. Later there would be time for questions.

"The cops, they watch closely now. Too close. Is dangerous now. We need decoy, yeah, decoy. Something they won't think of and it be right under their nose."

He was pleased with himself. Why didn't he think of this before?

"You got a plan, boss?" Guido was interested in plans that involved stratagem; he loved intrigue and spent his free hours thinking out involved plots.

"Steve will take the load. The boy can drive, drive like a professional."

Talking about his boy, the large Italian's eyes lit up. He was proud of his son now, proud of the interest he took in the business, proud of the way he moved the cars about the garage with sureness, wheeling them in and out, always with ease and a bit of daring.

"Steve?" Carlo was incredulous.

"The boy too young." Guido protested, his brow wrinkled with thought, "he not know the ropes yet." He whistled through his teeth sharply. His smile vanished.

"Both be quiet. Listen to me!" Picariello emphasized the pecking order with a thump on his broad chest. He smiled cheerlessly at the apprehensive men. This was his plan. He was the boss!

"Like I say, Steve, he drive the car. No liquor in it. Just a young man out on a ... how you say it? ... You know ..."

He broke off, looked searching at Carlo, seeking the word.

"You know ... with food in basket."

His face was thoughtful as he searched for the word that would not come. His voice trailed off and he looked from one face to another, seeking help.

"Picnic. You mean picnic." The other man's voice was flat. Carlo had an inkling of what was coming. Suddenly a picture of Florence flashed into his mind.

Florence, standing at the top of the stairs with her hands on slim hips, laughing and crying out to Steve as he came whistling jauntily down the street. Her face was rounded and lit by a light Carlo had never seen. The breeze blew small curls over cheeks caressed by a rosy blush. Her eyes mirrored her soul and were open for all to see. She was intent on teasing Steve and didn't see Carlo at the window, a dark enigmatic expression on his face. Now, Carlo's eyes narrowed and he shot his boss a piercing look daring him to tell him what he suspected. Picariello seized the word.

"Picnic ... yeah, that's it, picnic."

Here it comes, thought Carlo, and Picariello's next words confirmed the man's suspicions.

"Steve, he go on a picnic. Take Florence. They both young. Only, no liquor in the car, just food, lot of it. They get the car through the checkpoint, the one that's been there for a week. Carlo and Tony, they circle the back way with the load. It will be hard and risky, those back roads all bog. Then they meet Steve, swap cars and Steve and Florence, they drive back through the same checkpoint and on to the buyers over the border. Sounds good, no?"

Carlo guessed that Steve was chosen as he and Florence were about the same age. They would be able to pull off the run looking like young lovers. With Carlo, Florence would be withdrawn and silent. The picnic story for lovers would not be possible.

Carlo felt a vague stirring of emotion. He was uneasy with this plan and a small amount of jealousy awakened from dormancy where it lay for the past few years. He knew his boss went about his business, seemingly uninterested in the personal lives of his associates but the man was attuned to any undercurrent in their lives and there was something acutely unsettling about his questions.

Then too, Carlo reasoned, the boy was growing up and Florence had apparently succumbed to Steve's charms the same way that other girls did. The other evening had been the telling.

Steve was flirting with a young girl in the lobby of the hotel. The girl was fair and fragile as a columbine, cool and lovely to look at. She lingered, drawing out the brief meeting with

Steve, hoping that a relationship might develop.

Florence had come down the stairs, moving with deliberate casualness, her perception sharpened by bantering words being flung back and forth between the two below. Carlo watched his wife, saw her eyes drop dejectedly to the floor, saw her face darken with an angered blush. He watched as Florence sauntered to the doorway, watched her pause to let light define her young firm figure. Then she was gone.

Now Carlo wanted to interject, to refuse his wife's help. He wanted to keep her home but it would do no good once Picariello made his plans. As soon as Emilio's mind was made up, he became undaunted with his plans. It would do no good to refuse the man.

Picariello called Florence from the front hall where she played with the children and she came obediently. The girl leaned against the door frame and watched the men gathered around the table, eating, gesturing, arguing and laughing. She looked closely at Emilio, noted the gray that streaked his black hair, still noticeable even after a new haircut cropped his hair close to his head. Her eyes lit lightly on his face, travelling over the lines that appeared on the ruddy skin, noting the bulk that filled out an already robust frame.

Emilio waved a fork at her, gestured for her to sit with them. She filled a china cup with hot coffee from the stove, took the steaming cup to her place at the table. Picariello detailed his plans. Florence heard her part in the run; she was to be the decoy.

Across the table Florence sought her husband's eyes. She wanted him to help, to refuse to let her go. Carlo avoided her eyes, bent his head over the steaming bowl of soup he refilled at the stove. Florence knew she would be forced to go, especially if this would make Carlo look good in the older man's eyes.

Florence's mouth was dry and she fidgeted with her spoon on the tablecloth, crossing and recrossing the checkered cloth. She cleared her throat and started in nervously, using her husband's old name in agitation. He always wanted her to call him Charles.

"Carlo, tomorrow, I was going home, remember?"

Her voice caught, quivered, it had been planned for weeks. She was to take the train early on Saturday afternoon to stay with her family for a few days.

The piercing glance he shot at her told her the whole story. Her trip home was off. His look silenced her into submission. It was the same all over again; she would do as she was told.

There was silence in the kitchen. Florence lifted her cup to trembling lips, then looked at the clock on the wall. It was time to serve dinner in the dining room. The faint sounds of coal, rattling down the metal covered chute into the coal bin below in the cellar of the house, came to her. The men turned their attention back to their food and started to talk of a car problem. She was dismissed.

Florence got up, rinsed her cup and turned to leave the room. As she left Emilio turned from scraping the last bit of sauce from his plate and with his mouth still full, called to her.

"Tomorrow morning, early. You travel with Steve. This be the easiest job in the world. You only need to be ready, ready when we need you."

He turned back to his now empty plate.

The men did not see the eyes that widened in the young girl's face, did not see the light that flickered briefly in them, did not see the softening of her face as she went to the dining room to serve the meal.

All night long rain dripped steadily, running down shingled rooves to fall in beaded curtains of drops, trenching the earth below. It rushed along v-shaped board troughs nailed to the roof edge and ran into the rain barrel standing at the corner of the house. The barrel overflowed, water ran down sides recently cracked with dryness and now swollen with moisture. It flowed over moss growing on the north side of the barrel, moss now intensely and vibrantly velvet green.

The town lay silent until a shaft of early sunlight appeared through a split in the tall peaks. There was the odor of pine and the sound of beak shaped calls. The land was fresh; stirring and whispering in the new light of dawn. In the overflow puddles around the rain barrel, sparrows hopped around taking an early morning bath.

Florence came from her room in the hotel and let herself into the house. Long windows, squared into tiny panes, let muted morning sunlight fall in small squares on the painted stairs.

In the kitchen Florence fixed the picnic basket, deftly slicing bread, mixing hot mustard for the sandwiches. The breakfast dishes on the sideboard told her the men were already in the garage and she hurried to eat, burning her tongue on hot coffee. Steve came into the kitchen and his eyes slipped approvingly over the navy blue poiret twill dress she wore. He was jaunty and festive as he poked his nose into the basket, teased his mother about the food. Florence slipped into her velour coat, adjusted her tam and was ready to go.

The car stood ready, freshly washed and polished. It gleamed in the early sun. The picnic basket very large and conspicuous was on the back seat. There was no liquor in the car.

As the car pulled onto the main street the couple inside contemplated each other with nervous embarrassment. There was a strained reserve about Florence and Steve sensed her discomfort. She sat primly with her hands folded in her lap, her eyes on the road far ahead.

The car picked up speed and Steve cleared his throat, wondered why the girl was so quiet. Usually with him she was a lot of fun.

"Your dress. It looks okay." It was an offhand compliment and she was secretly pleased he noticed.

She murmured her thanks and visibly relaxed. Steve gave her a reassuring nod and started talking about the car. He ran his hands over the satin wood of the steering wheel and pointed out all its features, had her listen to the smoothness of the motor. She was relieved when he started to talk. It gave her a chance to compose herself, to beat down the feelings of excitement that rose to her throat. She breathed deeply and listened indifferently as he chattered away about the difference between the cars in his father's garage. She watched the passing scenery from the open window.

Florence was fond of this part of the Pass, where the forest crowded the road and the sky showed endless blue above. She was always amazed at the suddenness of the prairies. The car slipped through the foothills and there it was — bald, flat, prairie land patchworked into hay meadows and grain fields. There was an instant feeling of bigness.

Now Steve talked about the plan and she reluctantly drew herself from the fields and became instantly alert to his voice. She almost wished the provincials would stop and check them now. They would be clean as a whistle as they rode off down the road.

"Okay, when we drive through the check point, we have to make sure the car is searched. That will be my job. I'll just jump out, leaving the door open and the man will look inside."

She interrupted him, frowning as she tried to get the whole picture safely in her mind.

"Where is the check point? How do you know it will be there today?"

"It's been there for a few days, my father knows these things. He has people who check for him. Maybe they move it up or down the road, but it's still there. My father, he found out, early this morning. They move it around a bit but it's still there, on the other side of Cardston on the road leading to the border."

Florence was amazed at the coolness of his voice. He was like his father, intently serious about the job that was at hand.

"Now, you ask for the best place for a picnic. Flo, make sure they know we're looking for a quiet place to be alone, make them think we're lovers."

Florence winced at the casual words.

Again she must act out a part and she wondered if her whole life would be played in bit parts. Someday surely she would play the major role, important to someone, somewhere, just for being herself. But not with this young man and this realization made her heart throb with dull pain. She remembered the girl who flirted outrageously with Steve in the lobby of the hotel and Florence again felt inferior and dusty in comparison with the blond fairness of the other girl.

Still, she was drawn to Steve though she was bound to Carlo. All her life Florence wanted to belong to someone like Steve, someone tender and loving. She wanted to be able to approach someone, freely and openly, secure in the love she could give, happy with the love she would receive. Trapped in her style of life and her marriage to Carlo she could never hope her dreams would come true. She retained then a separateness, a quietness that drew her apart from the one she sought.

Steve, intent on the check point coming up, spoke quickly.

"The car exchange will take place back in the hills. I know where we have to have our picnic, it's all been arranged. But we have time to kill too! We will have our picnic, we have to wait for the load to come up, might as well enjoy ourselves, make a day of it before we start the run."

There was no anticipation in his voice, no worry about the end of the day when they would try to get the new car through with a full load of whisky hidden cunningly beneath the seats. She nodded, holding back her feelings in their still pool of safety.

"Then we drive through the check point again, only taking the road towards the border. This time we have the load. I hope the car is not searched again. It cannot be searched again, it must not be searched! That will be your job, Flo. You distract the man, make him remember that he searched the car before we had our picnic. You have to distract him, Flo! It's our only chance. I don't want to make a run for it. Can you do it, do you think?"

Now his voice was low and anxious, he was sure of himself, but not so sure of her. Her only answer was a rosy flush to her cheeks.

Steve expertly turned the big car off the main road and took a side road recently graded by a horse drawn blade. The scar of the blade showed on both sides of the road and Florence watched the shadow of the car as it raced beside the road, close but always a little behind.

There was something frightening about a shadow. Real shapes took a distinct form in the sun, were made true by the light; a shadow was the opposite, it was born in a world of half light, a world of twisted shapes, a nether world. A person could get lost in the shadows, swallowed by the grayness. There was no safety in a shadow. Florence shuddered and looked away.

Beside her Steve saw the shiver and wondered if the girl was cold. He took her hand and a soft smile came to her face. He squeezed the slim fingers gently.

"Ready? Are you afraid?"

He hit a muddy hole in the road. Muck flew up on the well polished car. To answer the question in her eyes he said, "The other car, when we get it, will be muddy from the back roads. I thought this one should be a bit muddy too. Just in case."

He was already thinking like his father, scheming and planning, looking ahead at all possibilities for success.

They were nearing the check point. She took a deep breath, smiled and shook her head at him, her eyes lingered to touch and warm him. He smiled back.

They drove into the little town. This one was like all the small towns of the prairies. The only difference was its location and size. The people were much alike, having the same ideals and aspirations. Sleepy looking buildings clustered around railroad tracks; grain elevators were stone-hedged against the sky. Dirt rutted streets, wandering in many directions from the tracks were dotted with various sized lots where children jumped and played in the long grass, hid in the low shrubbery and tore britches and stockings on barb wired fences.

The small towns were a child's delight. Small depressions in the land produced frog ponds after rains where barefooted boys, pants rolled to their knees, caught tadpoles and sailed small pieces of lumber for boats. Most of the girls disdainfully avoided the frog ponds with a squeamish air and tended instead to swings hung from yard trees. They strolled the roads with their doll buggies, made mudpies in jar lids decorated with flower petals and tiny stones, for afternoon pretend tea parties.

The economy of the town depended on the farming community around them. The businesses too were farm related; feed and grain stores, machinery and black smiths were as important as the grocer and gas pump. There was a school house and church. The social structure was rigid with business men being elected to the town board; the school teacher setting forth proper and genteel manners. From there the structure went down the line, ending with the town drunk. Little notice was given to the car that drove slowly down its main street.

To be sure the check point was where his father said it would be. Steve headed down the road and found it. He pulled over to the side of the road, stopped the engine quickly and jumped from the car. He left the door open and stood well back from the door inviting an inspection from the officer walking towards him. Steve's slight smile was very respectful.

The provincial strolled over and stuck his head inside the car. From somewhere inside her Florence found the courage to take on a starry look and sweetly asked where she and her fiance could have a picnic. The man smiled, remembering his own courting days. He went into a long winded description of the various places where two people could be alone and the scenery was grand.

Florence listened carefully to the directions given, picked out a spot on the road that turned to the left. Steve had insisted they turn left.

The girl ignored the man's dialogue on various trysting places in the surrounding country, bringing him back to the spot he mentioned on the left hand road. The provincial's eyes took in the large picnic basket, the obviously empty back seat.

The man stepped back to allow Steve into the driver's seat. With a wave of her hand Florence called gaily to him and they turned left down the road.

As he drove Steve turned to Florence with a look of admiration and relief. Florence smiled back at him; it had been so easy.

She was not worried about the next check point. The only

jolting moment was the thoughts that flooded back; memories she thought were buried deep, memories of when she smiled into the faces of the men in the boarding house. The remembrances brought a tightening to her stomach and to cover these she became at once very merry, joking and laughing over their escapade.

Florence and Steve reached the rendezvous area and turned the car onto a grassy field. They stopped near a slough on the far side of the field and spread a blanket beneath a gnarled pasture tree. Sunlight crept between the leaves tracing ever changing shapes on the ground, splashing hunks of gold into the cool moistness beneath the tree. Florence was to spend one of the happiest times of her life that afternoon, one she would remember and relive over and over during her life.

While Steve checked the tires and fiddled with the gages on the car, Florence spread the contents of the basket on the blanket. She called him to eat and they ate in silence, listening to the plaintive slow notes of a meadowlark. He leaned back against the tree, smiled shyly when she caught his eye. Her face was merry as she broke her sandwich into small pieces and threw them at a wide eyed gopher who promptly disappeared down his hole. She lay on the blanket, counted the clouds, found shapes in them and pointed these out to Steve.

He laughed and playfully tossed an apple to her. She caught it and sank her small teeth into the white crispness, exposing small brown seeded pockets. Steve finished his lunch with a bottle of Cream Soda and sweet crackers from a small wooden box. He called her lazy and pulled her to her feet.

Together they wandered the warm pathways made by the feet of cattle, stopping to sit on an outcrop of granite rock. Idly, Florence traced her fingers over the lichen growing orangely on the rock.

Their feet took them to the other side of the slough where the cut of the plow had not reached. In the long grass day lilies grew and Steve picked a bouquet of them. He turned and with a flourish presented them. Florence laughed and received them with a deep courtesy. He walked close to her and for her, there was no one left in the world but the two of them.

Carefully he chose one of the lilies from the bouquet, lifted her chin with a shaky finger and looked deep into her eyes. Then Steve broke the spell.

There was laughter in his eyes but his hand shook as he held the lily under her chin to see the reflection of the golden centre on her smooth skin. She turned and ran from him. It hurt her to see him make light of so precious a moment.

But he ran after her and they fell together in the soft grass. It was a bittersweet day of enchantment and Florence knew too soon it would have to end. Somewhere a car grunted up a slope. Slowly they walked back to the car.

An identical car drove onto the picnic land. Tony was at the wheel, Carlo at his side. The gregarious Tony was all at once waving and shouting from his window. The heavily loaded car lurched over the uneven ground.

"Save any food for me? I could eat the hind leg off a horse!"

"Yeah," Steve replied evenly, "there might be a few crumbs left in the basket." He turned to Carlo who sat in the car.

"Have any trouble? See anything suspicious? Sure you weren't followed?"

His questions to the smaller man were testy but he was careful not to overstep his position. His father would swat him down if he caused trouble with Carlo. Steve gave the man the respect he earned but there was always the tinge of sarcasm to the younger man's voice. Florence never spoke ill of Carlo but Steve saw hurt in the girl's eyes after cutting remarks made by her husband.

Now Florence waited at Steve's side, not without some uneasiness. As Carlo stepped from the car he turned to address his wife. Florence saw cruelty in his eyes and remembering the days of fear in the United States she shrank from him, turned and walked away to the side of the slough, where the redwings clung to reeds, snipping and slicing the air with their talk.

Carlo started after her then stopped, shrugged his shoulders and turned away.

The cars parted company after the switch was made. The picnic basket bounced in the back over a full load of whisky hidden beneath the seats.

When they were on the main road, nearing the check point, Steve looked sideways at the girl beside him. She had a slight burn of sun on her cheeks and nose. Her hair was windblown and had gone into little curls around her face. She never looked lovelier.

"Hullo, have a nice picnic?"

The man at the barricade, seeing them come back, was at once interested, remembering the very pretty girl who was so attentive to him.

"It was a beautiful spot you picked out," she breathed.

He came close to the car. In her hands she held a bouquet of day lilies and she held them up for him to smell. He nodded to Steve, obviously impressed and waved them on.

The car drove slowly down the street, picked up speed and headed towards the border. Only the terns that skated over roadside ponds heard the laughter from the car.

During the next few years Florence was to travel the country with the bootleggers. Picariello had begun to see his part in the empire was too important for the actual runs. He was the main cog; he began to wean himself from actual transporting of liquor and made sure when he travelled the country, building contacts, finding new sources of moonshine, he carried no bottles in his automobile. He was clean each time the provincials searched his car.

With Florence in the car, the loads had a better chance of getting through. Recently, the police had taken to shoot warning shots at cars that did not obey their commands to stop. Tires had been shot off, radiators pierced.

Picariello was not without a few uneasy twinges at the thought of putting the young girl in such a position but Florence was eager to please, very loyal and completely trustworthy.

VIII

BOOTLEGGER'S CYCLONE

DURING THE WEEKS of June, feverish bottling of spirits went on underneath the hotel. Emilio, dressed in heavy coveralls, emerged from the basement only to eat. Carlo was seen infrequently about the hotel. Both men were getting ready for the July 1 holiday celebration.

There would be a parade, a field day with foot races and baseball game and fireworks to end the evening. On the main street of town a great deal of preparation was made. Merchants were lavish with their window displays, thumb tacking red, white and blue streamers twisted together to frame their windows. Tempting merchandise was arranged to invite sales. Flags were hung on telephone poles.

Excited children ran up and down, outdoing each other in daring feats. A small boy, taunted by his peers, made an exhibitionist walk along a tall fence. He walked the whole length but becoming cocky near the end, lost his balance and fell. Howls of pain accompanied contact with the ground; he turned up at the parade with skinned elbows and knees. The adults too were infected with gaiety, shaking off lethargic feelings of a hot summer. Men swept their walks, polished cars for the parade, tidied their yards, much to their wives' disbelief. The women pressed best dresses, looked at last year's summer hats and took side trips to the milliners to refurbish their hats with new ribbons, bows and cloth flowers.

Early in the day a sea of faces gathered along main street where the parade would march. Women with babies in perambulators waved gaily to their friends. Vendors did a roaring business dispensing ice cream cones and cold pop. Small children in middy blouses and sailor hats carried tiny flags to wave at participants in the parade.

Florence, wearing her coolest dress of sprigged lawn, turned down the offer of a parasol and stood with the children, wiping chins that dribbled ice cream. She turned to wave gaily at the men watching from the upper floor of the hotel. Carlo, Steve, Tony and Guido stood at the front windows, smoked and gossiped about people on the street below. Their work would come later in the day when heat produced thirsty throats.

The town band led the parade which was a bit late in starting. Small boys darted back and forth onto the road; when they spied the band in the distance they called excitedly to everyone watching.

"It's coming! It's coming!"

An expectant murmur ran through the crowd. Playing stirring martial music the band approached. There was a flourish of trumpets, a clash of cymbals, the booming sounds of big drums. Behind them came the veterans and soldiers in full dress uniform with medaled chests held high. They marched with precision, proud of their uniform, proud too of the fact they had lived to return. They remembered comrades who died beside them and it was a sad and sobering thought.

Behind the seasoned veterans the school cadets patterned their ranks in rhythm with the drill of the boots ahead of them. Mothers searched out and pointed to sons. The boys, in front of parents and relatives, held themselves in ramrod precision despite the heat. There was polite applause from crowds knitted into small groups.

One of the returning soldiers brought home a souvenir helmet and uniform. Wearing the ensemble, he acted out the part of the German high command. With a rope tied around his neck, he was led by one of the veterans. The German goose stepped down the street and was roundly booed and hissed. As he passed by, a young boy ran out into the street, trying to kick the 'Kaiser' in the seat of his pants. A mother caught the boy by the ear and sat him down in front of her.

Bringing up the rear were horse and buggies carrying town dignitaries and a few decorated automobiles belonging to merchants. After the parade, the field day started immediately.

Now it was the bootlegger's turn to get busy. Florence was not needed today and she was free to watch the sporting events.

Throughout the day the bootleggers were in demand. Picariello's wares circulated in many ways. Liquor was easy to get, you just had to be in the know. Bottles passed surreptitiously from shanties on the outskirts of town and were quickly snapped up by thirsty men at the edge of the playing field. There was no fumbling for change; patrons knew from long experience the transaction would be quick; they had the correct change ready for their purchase.

As the day passed it was evident some participants of the baseball game had toasted each other more than they should have. Some of the pugnacious supporters argued over an umpire's call, then practiced the noble art on the burnt grass behind the stands. Urged on by equally tipsy friends the sparring partners did more grappling than fisticuffs.

Seeing the crowd a policeman rode up to disperse it and found the inebriated brawlers. The men received tickets for drunkenness in a public place and would appear before a judge along with many others in the morning.

The cafes too were busy feeding the crowds of people who came from nearby towns and farms for the festivities. It was evident that those in the know could get a little more than food from a cafe.

In the fading light of evening, a Salvation Army band gathered on the street corner to play and sing rousing hymns for the passerby.

Women and children strolled to a nearby ice cream parlour buying cardboard boxes of ice cream. They paused, holding their treat by its wire handle, listening to the singing before hurrying home with their melting dessert.

Nearby a screen door slammed and into this peaceful scene a man, happily tipsy, appeared from a nearby cafe and added his voice to the singers. His choice of words was not always the best and he was told to desist by a piqued leader. The band nervously started their song again, tambourines quivering. The drunk started to dance on the gouged boardwalk and did a little cakewalk behind the captain whose rage was purpling the back of his neck.

The drunk, having the audience all to himself, since the band again stopped in mid-note and were staring at him, went into his blurry rendition of "I'm jist blowing blubbles, pretty blubbles in the air ..." He added a few fancy steps before the captain herded his players down the street. The drunk took an exaggerated bow, made a caddish gesture at the back of the retreating captain, then turned back to the cafe to cajole another drink. The fuming captain went straight to the police and the cafe was raided.

When the day was over Emilio met the drivers in the cool of the basement where he counted the take of the day. Tony opened beer for Guido and himself. Carlo, already drinking a beer, swung his legs over a packing case and recounted some of the funny things that happened during the day.

"The best thing I see today was old Scottie from over at Passburg. Don't have the faintest idea of how to bootleg. He wanted to be right out on the street with his stuff."

"Maybe he takes too much taste," Picariello laughed, "fogs up his brain, some of the stuff he peddle could kill!"

"How do you like this guy?" Carlo was enjoying himself. "He put it in a bunch of watermelons. Yeah, you heard me, watermelons!"

The men were curious.

Carlo continued. "He cut the top off the melon, scoop out the inside, fill it with hooch. He put the top on again, and run small pieces of wood around the edge to hold it on. There he was, bold as a brass monkey, hawking juice."

Tony especially was tickled by this adventure. What's wrong with that, he wanted to know.

"It's okay, I guess, excepting you get smart policeman. Looks to see why so many men buying watermelons. Wanders over to see what the attraction is, can't be just the watermelons, maybe wants a cold piece for himself. Then he notices the melons all standing on end, all the same. Old Scottie left his pushcart and all. Beat it down the street and melted into the crowd. Bet he home now, under the bed! Won't do him any good, though, policeman, he know who he is and the old man sure to get a ticket tomorrow. Got the goods too, for evidence. Don't pay to try to be too smart."

Then Picariello spoke up. His words brought a sobering effect to the pleasantries of the day.

"Heard two of the boys from back Fernie way making a run today when they thought everybody tied up with the fun. There were two cars in convoy. Rather than have police catch the load, the boy run it into the lake. The other car, no liquor, he pull over and the police real mad. Made them so mad he got every ticket they could think of."

The drivers were really interested in this news. "Do you think the car can be pulled out?" They were thinking of some quick money.

"No!" Emilio's voice was flat. "That lake real deep. Some says it has no bottom. Okay if the car on a ledge but I no go in after it. I no go in Crowsnest Lake!"

The set of his shoulders and his tone, bespoke some of the worries he anticipated.

Tony was annoyed. "What could they get him for?"

"Well, for one thing, speeding in excess of fifty miles an hour, not stopping for police." Emilio ticked items off on his finger. "Then obstructing police in their duty. That's three big fines and costs."

"They have to work harder to make up the fines. But the car ..." Tony saw the brooding look in Picariello's eyes. There were more and more arrests.

Picariello applied for a permit to carry a gun. Magistrate Gresham issued the permit; he could carry a 38 revolver for business reasons. He carried large amounts of cash with him and was afraid of robbery. Then too, disturbing news came through the grapevine; three cars were travelling from Calgary towards the border. The first two vehicles were loaded with whisky, the last car was a decoy. Near Macleod a car passed and went on down the road. The bootleggers kept on travelling not knowing the car far in front was the Alberta Provincial Police.

At a turn in the road, the police stopped to halt the approaching vehicles. The cars picked up speed and got past, all except the last one. The police shot, hit the radiator; one shot winged a tire and the driver was forced to pull over. The other two cars got away.

The police searched the third car to no avail. There was no whisky. They laid every charge they could against the driver who merely smiled.

Picariello had plans for one car to leave tomorrow. He discussed the run with Tony and Guido. Florence too would be taken along for the ride.

As they left the town of Blairmore their headlights cut a beam of light through the early morning dawn. A rising sun cast shadows on dust coated weeds lining the roadside.

They moved with no trouble through the foothill towns. Tony was driving. Guido dozed in the seat beside him. Florence was cramped in the back sitting amid sacks of corn feed.

Tony pulled his cap down over his eyes and looked at Guido beside him. He finally spoke.

"Why don't you take a little whisky, just to bring up your spirits?" They were running a road about seven miles west of Macleod. The air carried the aroma of freshly cut hay. Tony turned onto a narrow road with a high grade.

Tony tried again. "Rained here last night," he said companionably. He wanted to draw Florence or the smaller man into conversation.

"The road's greasy, watch your speed!" was the only reply he received.

The high crowned road was slippery from rain. Tony laughed and picked up his speed to annoy and tease the other man. It was an error in judgment on his part and on a turn he struggled with the wheel, finally losing control. The car went through the ditch and into the field where it turned over on its side. The sounds of metal rattling was heard, the tool box was forced open and the contents scattered over the ground. The bumper caught and was bent in two. A smothered shriek was heard from the back seat. As the car turned over the people inside were enveloped with dust from the floorboards.

There was silence inside the vehicle.

With one hand holding his neck Guido climbed out. On his hands and knees he laboured to the back window, peered inside for Florence. From her crumpled form he evoked a small response. He helped her out and she sat on the ground, wiping dust from her face.

Guido looked around at the mess, sacks were everywhere, flung like rag dolls from a carriage. Tony was dazed and Guido and Florence had to pull and tug to get him from the vehicle. They propped him up against a sack. From nearby came the asthmatic sounds of a tractor.

The swarthy face of the small Italian was pale as he sat with his head in his hands trying to think. He looked at the car. It was Picariello's own, a cream coloured license plate lettered Alberta 1740 in black, was clumped and buckled with mud.

Guido shook his head, started the shaky Florence down the road towards the tractor sounds.

In the farm yard Florence waved a bill under the nose of the farmer who was startled to see the well dressed woman covered with dust walking up his driveway. He agreed to bring the tractor to upright the car.

Florence pleaded with the farmer to hurry and started back down the road, half running in her haste to get the car righted. She wasn't even sure it would run.

Nearby, several roads over, two provincial police were on early morning patrol. They saw fresh tire tracks in the muddy side road and turned their vehicle around to follow them.

"Hey, look at that!" A wiry provincial pointed to the car in the field. "Bet someone's hurt in that wreck!"

One of the provincials quickly went to the assistance of Tony. Speaking to Guido he said, "We'll have to get this man to a doctor quickly. He's hearing cuckoo birds!"

Guido ignored the man, shrugged his shoulders and moved away to the other side of the car.

The other policeman sat down on one of the sacks and started to make out a report. He pulled out his pad and pencil and asked Guido a lot of questions. He wrote the details down, the names and addresses of the people in the car, the licence number and description of the vehicle.

"Alberta one ... seven ...", he wrote, then stopped. He looked up and frowned.

"Say Harrold," he said as he stood up, "my ass is all wet!"

His partner laughed. "Your ass is always wet!" He teased the younger man; he was new to the force and very excitable.

"No!" the other one was definite. "These sacks aren't wet and yet my pants are!" He looked puzzled. Guido whistled a small tune under his breath.

"Maybe you peed them with excitement." The other man guffawed good naturedly at his own joke.

The standing constable still looked puzzled. He wiped his hand over the seat of his pants, felt his hand, then smelled it. Realization flooded his face.

"Well ... I'll be dammed ..." he said.

Just then Florence came over a small rise in the road. She spotted the other car, guessed who the men in the field were. She stopped the farmer and bribed him to take her to the closest town. She had to get in touch with Picariello!

The grim faced Guido and Tony were taken in along with the evidence. It would mean a morning call before the magistrate, a heavy fine and costly repairs to the vehicle.

But Guido and Tony weren't the only ones to spend an occasional night in jail. The liquor traffic was like a weeping wall; as soon as one hole was plugged, three or four others opened up and the police were kept busy trying to staunch the flow.

For Picariello, liquor trickled into the hotel from many

places. Some of it came to him by train from British Columbia, dropped off in various places by train crews to well paid station agents along the line. Many a man went home, a bottle in his lunch box, pleased with his take and oblivious to what he saw on the way.

In time the amounts shipped grew from a few cases to a carload as the bootleggers got bolder. Even with Picariello striving to keep everyone happy the loads at times backfired.

In the Pincher Creek station, a disgruntled baggage clerk reported for work. He pulled on his sleeve protectors and adjusted green eyeshades. He sat on a high stool with a booted foot tucked into the rung, hitched a thumb in his suspenders and brooded, another load was coming through, maybe on this next freight. Sometimes the seal was broken, the sacks put inside the baggage car or the liquor concealed in lumber or coal cars. [1] The drivers followed the train by car hoping the train would stop at a convenient spot where they could get the goods off undetected. The baggage clerk was to close his eyes to the broken seal in return for a few bottles.

Now instead of shipping a few cases, the bootleggers were getting greedy and the last shipment had widened the eyes of the clerk; 45 barrels of whisky, all hidden under soft drinks which camouflaged the top. And his take was only a few measly bottles!

Annoyed, he placed a furtive call to the Alberta Provincial Police and the shipment was picked up when the train pulled into the station. Bitterly, Tony turned the car and headed for home. At times Picariello put him, dressed as a tramp, on the train to look out for a shipment. Tony was glad he wasn't aboard today!

---

1. Alberta Provincial Police reports, Provincial Archives, state "The bootleggers now resort to shipping by railway on freight trains, concealing the liquor in lumber, coal etc. and it is extremely difficult to detect. Two large shipments were seized while in transit. The liquor was not claimed although we knew who owned it. The C.P.R. officials have given us every assistance with regard to illegal shipments of liquor. The fines imposed under the act amounted to $111,629.00; estimated value of liquor sent to Vendor, $29,320.00; estimated value of liquor sent to Hospitals, $500.00; estimated value of liquor destroyed, $16,355.00. The latter was mostly composed of beer and bootleg whiskey. There were 113 jail sentences."

Little by little, Florence found herself thrust into the eye of the bootlegger's cyclone. She no longer waited on tables in the dining room, barely had time to play with the children. Her days were taken up travelling with Picariello or on trips with the drivers. In her spare time she fixed her hair, took care of the clothes she wore about the country on the runs. Other times she fell asleep in her clothes, tired from the heat and the length of the long trips.

Whenever she could, she escaped from this life and took the train home to Fernie. Hurrying down the familiar streets, Florence would burst into the house crying, "Mama, I'm home, I'm home."

IX

THE
GODFATHER

THE STRAIN OF running a large bootlegging empire was beginning to show on the Italian. Now in his fortieth year, his ambitions dwindled and he looked with interest at easier ventures.

On the first Monday of the year 1921, Picariello rose early. In the kitchen Maria was pressing his shirt and the sweet sounds of her singing came to him. Usually the tender ballad, 'Come back to Sorrento' soothed him but not today. He walked around the house, looked at things absentmindedly. Maria helped him into his shirt, warm and sweet smelling from the wash. Taking a brush she went over his coat, picking off minute particles of lint, then stood back to look at him. She was proud, felt a toast was in order.

"Beve un bicchiere di vino?" (Will you have a glass of wine?)

She looked at him fondly, he was, as she said 'di buon aspetto'. (good looking)

Guido came in to eat. He too, felt a lift, taking pleasure in his boss. Picariello had been elected to the town council and today was the first meeting. Guido swelled with pride.

As required by the Town Act, the council was charged with having a meeting on the first Monday of the new year. Into the council chambers filed an assortment of men, each voted to this honour at a recent election. Archie McLeod, the Mayor of the town was at the head of the table; around him sat the councillors. J.E. Gillis, J.A. McDonald, Joseph Montalbetti, Emilio Picariello and William McVey.

It was strange Picariello aspired to run for a seat on council.

But there was two sides to the man; one was the notorious bootlegger with all the cunning transactions made to keep his crown as 'Emperor' of the whisky running business. Another was that of the business man, deftly running his many enterprises with a firm hand. Mingling both sides was the family man, head of the family he loved.

Emilio was settling into an image of the benevolent godfather. He was influential in the community. The immigrants in recent elections voted solidly for him. The Italian population concentrated in Pass towns grew larger each year as new immigrants arrived. The newcomers had education and language problems and worked for measly wages. To them, Picariello, once an immigrant too, had risen to a lofty position above them. This success earned prestige and respect accordingly.

Picariello brought his own touch of luck to a situation where there was fast money, easy work and a bit of daring. That he was breaking the law was of no account to his fellow man as they too skirted the law when there was no other way.

There were others in the towns that hated him. Some had had unsuccessful business dealings with him. The majority of his compatriots at some time or another had known his compassionate help.

Emilio's life style was likened to that of the town Robin Hood. He knew the road immigrants faced, he had walked down it himself. He knew what it was like to feel around in a purse for a few coins to feed his family and come up with an empty hand.

While Emilio reveled in luxury his wealth gave him, it was not his nature to be greedy and he sought to share his fortune generously with others. He was not however a dupe, a man to be taken lightly or trifled with. He could turn with cunning revenge on an attacker and his fury held a quiet dread. There were not many who dared cross him.

Picariello often boasted of his resources. Those around him knew he could put his hands on thousands of dollars at a moment's notice and he often did, taking money from a sweaty hat band, from under a pile of greasy rags in the back seat of his car or from an inside pocket. In their time of need the poor came to him and he turned no one away.

Winter time seemed to be the worst for the poverty stricken. When food from gardens was scarce and the winter winds made sickness prevalent, the unemployed came steadily to his door.

A man appeared cold and hungry. Maria asked him to come in and he stepped from the stamped down snow of the steps into a warm kitchen. The man's feet, in worn and torn galoshes, left wet marks on the dark linoleum, snow clots fell from his hat. His eyes fixed on the table of food and Picariello, already seated at the table, asked him to sit down. The man sat, watched as Emilio piled his plate high with food, then ate with restrained and obvious relish. The children, rosy-cheeked from a play in the snow, swung short legs from their chairs as they ate a dessert of currant bread spread with thick jam and drank hot milk heaped with teaspoons of Baker's Cocoa and sugar.

At the Hoosier kitchen cabinet Maria turned the sifter and flour fell from the glass fronted bin into a bowl below. There were clanking sounds from the furnace pipes and the children, gradually warming, took off layers of sweaters. In silence the men ate.

Maria washed the dishes and hung the dish towel on a peg where it dried to a gray stiffness. She herded the children from the room; Emilio turned to the man and rocking slowly back and forth, arms across his big chest, heard what he had heard so many times before.

"My wife and bambino sick," the man said. "No work for long time, no money for doctor, no money for food. Don't know what I do."

His begging left a raw and angry wound in his eyes. The bootlegger was quick to see the suffering and rose quickly.

"You need a loan." They both knew it was called a loan to save face for the poorer man and both knew it would never be repaid.

"Lots of food you need, bread, meat for the broth, pasta and milk, oxo cubes too, helps those who sick."

He scratched his head, thinking of what the man needed.

"The house, she is cold, need coal too. I send it to you. Lots of tons."

He fished around in his pockets, bringing out more money and added these to the pile already on the table.

"Go now, you need more, come back."

The man squared his shoulders, grasped the hand offered to him and left. Emilio poured more coffee and sat down to think. He pulled a small book from his pocket, it was nearly full of notations, money he had given to people, money he had advanced to those who were willing to turn their eyes away from his activities. It was time to make a different trip.

In the morning Emilio walked across the street to the train station. As he waited for the passenger train to come in, the unpredictable Italian paced the rough planking of the station floor. At the last moment, instead of taking his place in the passenger coach he waited and swung himself up the steps into the crummy at the end. The large amount of cash Picariello was carrying had to go into the right hands. In a few days Carlo would meet the train at Macleod and drive his boss back to the hotel. Nobody would guess where he had been.

Spring was coming now and the runs would soon start. This realization put a hard lump in Florence's throat and nightmares shattered her fitful sleep. She felt a weariness in her body as she slid on silk hose and pulled on a warm dress of wool in a waterfall green colour. Opting for shoes instead of the winter overshoes she hated, she slipped her feet into her newest pair. They had been costly, a strap pump in black patent leather with a new flapper heel.

Carlo took Florence along with him when he drove the muddy thawing roads to Macleod to pick up his boss. In the town the car came to an abrupt stop at the side of the road where Carlo could watch for the train. Florence shivered and huddled deeper into her coat.

During the night a spring snow had fallen and behind them

the mountains were dusted with white. A low mist lay close to the land and the warm sun that rose crept over the clouds, outlining the frost whiskered grass, casting sooty shadows on the snow. Long grass bordering the sloughs was matted under the weight of the snow. The hardier stalks held up under its weight but the weaker grass bent and folded under.

It's like my life, Florence decided. She was a weaker stalk, one failed in life, crouched under the cold, defeated and miserable, unable to help herself.

"Looks like we shouldn't wait. Too cold, maybe we should go. He's not coming."

Her voice trailed off.

"Maybe we missed the train." She looked to her husband, hoping to convince him.

Losandro tried to keep an edge of contempt out of his voice. "No! Pic said we should wait. We wait!"

There was a finality in his tone. She sighed and turned her attention again to the landscape. Her thoughts lost themselves in a tumble as she watched the sun's rays skitter across the skim ice of a ditchside pond. The ice was the kind she liked to step on, it lay like loosely crinkled cellophane, barely lying on the surface, fragile, crystalline.

In the distance a train moved towards the town, beside her Losandro straightened in his seat. She looked sideways at the man, wondering when she could again approach the subject of their leaving Picariello.

For the most part Florence was a natural diplomat, avoiding any subject that would bring about a quarrel. When Carlo was happy and relaxed with her she was buoyed with hope and sometimes found the courage to beg him to leave their style of life.

Back at the hotel, cold and stiff from the day's ride she tried again. Her cries were unheard as Carlo mocked her cynically. She dared to go against the whole force of his rising anger as she coaxed him to think about starting over some place else. She had not yet come to the point of total disillusionment with her marriage.

"I want to leave," she cried, "please Carlo, let's go some place, far away, far from the big one's shadow."

Her face was pathetic, her manner anxious, her voice husky. "Please Carlo, oh please."

She reached out to touch him, cheeks burning a dusky rose against the olive of her skin. It was against her nature to beg this way. She felt humiliated but would have done whatever he asked if only he would take her away.

Again, as she observed so many times before, she saw her husband's complete and utter devotion to his employer. It was a loyalty she would never have, a barrier she could never hope to penetrate.

As usual he turned away from her, uttered an oath. The movements of his stocky body bore the anger he felt and his voice, when it came through the petulant lips was defensive.

"You!", the voice was stabbing, "Why you want to do this? Look at your life, how ungrateful you are. Picariello, he is good no? You have warm room, lots of good food, not just beans like at your home. Look at your silk stockings! You think you have those on miner's wage! Ha! Think again!"

To this she commented coolly, "But I don't need them. I need other things."

He was unaware of what she referred to.

Florence was unsure of her voice but surprised at the tranquility she was able to muster. There was only a small vestige of hope left in the girl. A strong sense of duty prevailed upon her to try for the last time. It would be the last time she had to humiliate herself.

In order to have a real marriage, to raise the family she wanted, to build a future, Carlo would have to leave this life. The choice was his, it was all in his hands.

Florence was willing to do her duty to complete her marriage, regardless of the costs. Sadly she thought of the small shards of happiness she had during the summer months.

"You," again Carlo shook his finger in her face, "you could do something in return for what you get, you could do as you are told. Leave the planning to us, to the men!" His voice snarled, caught on the jagged notes of anger.

"But I do, I do!" she cried defensively.

It was no use, Carlo left the room quickly, escaping the argument. The room was empty and so was she. All that was left was defeat and a strange brooding look that never died in the dark eyes. She shrank back in her chair to sort out her life, to gather some sensibility from which she could make her way.

To Florence the day was parallel to the day Carlo told her about the move to the United States. She was trapped in the same way. She could not leave, her marriage was a permanent tie unto death; but there was one thing the girl could do. ,

With the relationship openly strained Florence left Carlo's room in the hotel. It happened innocently enough, when one of the babies was sick, Florence moved to a room in the house to help. She stayed in the children's room and nothing was said. Carlo paid little attention to the girl and the family knew she was lonely. Picariello let her stay.

Now Florence became more involved with the bootleggers than she had ever been before. She rode with Picariello on his foraging trips and became his confidante.

Slowly the girl changed. Once she was a timid shy girl who could barely meet another person eye to eye. Now she could hold her own. To the drivers she appeared as a knowledgeable young woman who was amicable company on trips and not afraid to do her part. The men did not see the girl as she really was, did not see through the impenetrable barrier she drew around herself.

Florence was well aware of cold stares on the street, well aware of the remarks made when she rode by in the bootlegger's car. But she looked for the most in life, some of the trips could be fun after the seriousness of the delivery. With Tony and Steve she enjoyed herself; with Guido or Carlo along the trips were dull and uninteresting.

On the way home from one trip the car passed over a small bridge at Shank's Creek on the road back from Montana. A summer shower overtook them by surprise and Steve, wheeling expertly, hit for open country, mowing down weeds and leaving a trail of crushed grass.

Florence laughed in exhilaration as she tried to get the window flap up, tried to stop the wind blown drops that hit her face. Steve, in fun, wheeled the big car around and around in circles, laughing as the car rocked over the uneven ground.

Tony had been asleep in the back, now he fell from the seat to the floorboards and lay giggling weakly as the car went round and round.

"Stop, Stop," she laughed. "I'm getting all wet!" She collapsed into laughter.

"Look, there's a barn. Come on, Steve, I'll race you to it."

A deserted barn stood in the fenced field. She lifted the wires, slipped through the opening and ran. There was a splattering of large drops. She was again running as carried by the wind, running through the fields of her youth.

In the barn their symphony was the beating of the rain on the rusted tin roof, the drip drops forming around the window frames, and the splendour of the rainbow after the storm was spent. She felt Steve close to her as they walked back to the car, passing through an old garden where a house once stood. The garden was wild, sown and resown with prolific seeds. At its borders fox glove grew and stunted hollyhocks wore rain drops prismed by the emerging sun.

"Che bel giardino!" Florence clapped her hands happily.

Back at the car Tony lumbered around wiping the windshield. He watched them come, squinting into the sun.

"Lunch time, I'm hungry!"

The sun was warm as she sat on a half rotted stump and pulled long grass growing at her feet. Overhead a hawk creased the blueness of an infinite sky. The brown gray body traced lazy loops in precision as he covered the land in his hunt for food.

Tony coughed and sneezed with a summer cold. Florence told him of her childhood winters when coughs and colds racked the children. Her mother made her own remedy, she could not afford a store bought medicine.

She doled out a few nickels from her slim purse to buy a two ounce bottle of Pinex which was poured into a whisky bottle. The bottle was filled with cornsyrup, molasses or honey, whatever was at hand. The potion fed the family's coughs all winter. Florence promised to get him some of the mixture on her next trip home.

She turned away from Tony, turned to look at Steve stretched out beneath a tree on the sun patterned grass. It was peaceful here, a delicate balance of warmth and cool beneath leaves of lucent green. She thought she knew the boy well but he would remain a stranger to her in many ways.

I could love someone like you, her silent thoughts went out to him. Someone who would care deeply for me. Someone who would take my love and give it back to me.

She turned abruptly away. She had been imbued with a feeling of peace and now it was slipping away. Savagely and almost brusquely she threw the stick she had been peeling. Steve wondered what had caused the abrupt change.

"Flo?"

To Florence it was more than a question, it was a caress of her name. She turned to him again, gathered all the warmth she could from his eyes. Lightly she arose, smoothed her skirt and looked quickly away.

"Time to go!" was all she said. She was again the brisk bootlegger's confidante. The mask had slipped in place.

Florence had an infinite capacity to express love, but there was no one she could give to, no one to receive it. She had no identity in her marriage to Carlo, it was merely a shell; she was a convenience to him.

The young girl had a gentle gift of love to bestow and in her loneliness Carlo could have made her a complete person. But that was a long time ago. Now the shell was formed, hardened and scarred from the years of her marriage. Florence took one day at a time, taking what was meted out to her.

Even with the increasing dangers she was facing, the runs were an escape, an escape from Carlo and the ugliness of her life and the reality of what she had become. And while she was consciously railing against such a future, she was unconsciously being pulled in exactly that direction by the cares and feelings growing in the maturing woman.

milio Picariello, 1922
urtesy Glenbow - Alberta Institute, Calgary, Alberta

Florence and Maria Picariello
Courtesy R. Lento

Emilio Picariello and family, 1915
Courtesy Glenbow - Alberta Institute, Calgary, Alberta

Stephen O. Lawson, Alberta
Provincial Police, Sept. 18, 1922
Courtesy Glenbow - Alberta Institute, Calgary, Alberta

Constable Michael Moriarty, Alberta
Provincial Police, 1920's
Courtesy Glenbow - Alberta Institute, Calgary, Alberta

J. McKinley Cameron, lawyer for the
defense
Courtesy Glenbow - Alberta Institute, Calgary, Alberta

John E. Brownlee, Attorney
General of Alberta
Courtesy Glenbow - Alberta Institute, Calgary, Alberta

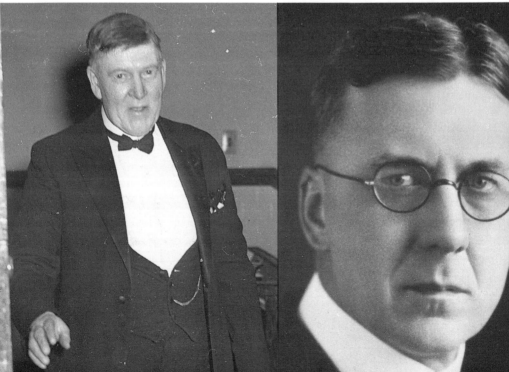

...on mountain pass where the bootleggers travelled - Crowsnest Pass area
esy Glenbow - Alberta Institute, Calgary, Alberta

...en Oldacres Lawson, Alberta Provincial Police. 1912
esy Glenbow - Alberta Institute, Calgary, Alberta

Illicit still seized near Cardston, Alberta
Alberta Provincial Police, 1920.
Courtesy Glenbow - Alberta Institute, Calgary, Alber

Emilio Picariello (right) and Charles Losandro. Fernie, old macaroni factory at left.
Courtesy Glenbow - Alberta Institute, Calgary, Alberta

WANTED! *By LIQUOR TRAFFIC*

☙ Ten Thousand New Canadian Fathers and Sons

☙ Ten Thousand New Canadian Men and Boys

TO TAKE THE PLACE OF

Ten Thousand Drunkards Dead!

ABOLISH THE BAR

ESDALE PRESS EDMONTON ALTA

Poster used by National Women's Christian Temperance Union for the anti-liquor campaign.

Courtesy Glenbow - Alberta Institute, Calgary, Alberta

Poster used by National Women's Christian Temperance Union
Courtesy Glenbow - Alberta Institute, Calgary, Alberta

BEER AS FOOD

If beer is a food why do you so often see a man begging for something to eat after he has been on a three days' drunk.

Water is the strongest drink; lions and horses use it, and Samson never drank anything else.

THE
LIQUOR TRAFFIC
MUST GO

THE REVENUE IS SMALL COMPARED
WITH THE COST

IT CAUSES
Poverty, Misery
and Crime

THE REMEDY

NATIONAL CONSTITUTIONAL PROHIBITION

NATIONAL WOMAN'S CHRISTIAN TEMPERANCE UNION
EVANSTON ILLINOIS

Poster used by National Women's Christian Temperance Union for anti-liquor campaign.

*onstable R. M. Dey, Alberta Provincial
olice.*
urtesy Glenbow - Alberta Institute, Calgary, Alberta

*Bloodhounds, Tip and Badger, Alberta
Provincial Police.*
Courtesy Glenbow - Alberta Institute, Calgary, Alberta

berta Provincial Police, in motorcycle and side car. 1923.
urtesy Provincial Archives of Alberta, Edmonton, Alberta

Alberta Provincial Police Patrol Car 1931.
Courtesy Provincial Archives of Alberta, Edmonton, Alberta

View of Coleman, Alberta. May 17, 1913.
Courtesy Glenbow - Alberta Institute, Calgary, Alberta

emale cell, Police Jail, Calgary, Alberta
ourtesy Glenbow - Alberta Institute, Calgary, Alberta

Father Fidelis Chicoine, O.F.M., who was Florence's spiritual advisor as she awaited her execution and the author Montreal, 1979.

lorence, awaiting her execution, 1922.
ourtesy Glenbow - Alberta Institute, Calgary, Alberta

*Seizure of liquor at Crowsnest Pass by Alberta Provincial Police.
L to R: (sitting) Constable Coombs, Sgt. Scott, Constable Dey (standing) Detective Pass, Sgt. Harrison.*
Courtesy Glenbow - Alberta Institute, Calgary, Alberta

Car in process of search by Sergeant Scott, during chase after the son of P. cariello. 1922.
Courtesy Glenbow - Alberta Institute, Calgary, Alberta

Seven carcasses of hogs containing contraband liquor.
Courtesy Glenbow - Alberta Institute, Calgary, Alberta

ellevue Detachment, Alberta Provincial Police, 1920's.
urtesy Glenbow - Alberta Institute, Calgary, Alberta

lberta Provincial Police Detachment, Blairmore, Alberta, 1920.
urtesy Glenbow - Alberta Institute, Calgary, Alberta

The Alberta Hotel, Blairmore, Alberta.
Courtesy Glenbow - Alberta Institute, Calgary, Alberta

Street in Coleman, Alberta, ca. 1912.
Courtesy Glenbow - Alberta Institute, Calgary, Alberta

Lethbridge Court House, Alberta Provincial Police cells in basement, note bars on windows.
Courtesy Galt Museum and Archives, Lethbridge, Alberta

Court House in Blairmore, Alberta, 1920.
Courtesy Glenbow - Alberta Institute, Calgary, Alberta

House
rmore, Alta.

Victoria Avenue, Fernie, British Columbia
Left to right: H. Bentley and Co. (dry goods, groceries) Fernie Drug Co., Victoria
Hotel.
Courtesy Glenbow - Alberta Institute, Calgary, Alberta

Fernie, British Columbia, ca. 1912.
Courtesy Glenbow - Alberta Institute, Calgary, Alberta

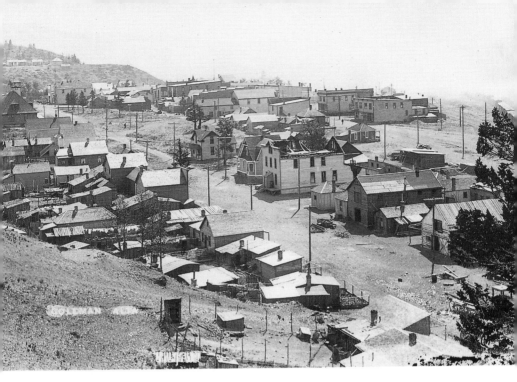

View of Coleman, Alberta, ca. 1912.
Courtesy Glenbow - Alberta Institute, Calgary, Alberta

Railway station at Blairmore, Alberta, ca. 1906.
Courtesy Glenbow - Alberta Institute, Calgary, Alberta

View of Government Street, Fort Saskatchewan, ca. 1906.
Courtesy Glenbow - Alberta Institute, Calgary, Alberta

Canadian Northern Railway Station, Fort Saskatchewan, Alberta
Courtesy Glenbow - Alberta Institute, Calgary, Alberta

X

A PASS
CHRISTMAS

THE NEXT TWO years were about to bring some startling changes for Picariello and his extended family.

When the rising heat of a July morning threatened to smother the man lying in the upstairs bedroom, he awoke, swung his stiffened limbs over the side of the bed and yawned.

Advancing to the mirror Emilio peered at his grey streaked hair, rubbed his hand over the heaviness settled in his face. Ah, Emilio, he thought to himself, you are growing old. But not yet, he mused, aware he had many things in his favour; a clear eye, springy step despite some stiffness in his joints, a firm voice and keen wit. He had enormous energy and a sharp interest in the world around him. Each season of man, like nature, has its own beauty and comforts and Emilio was well aware of his.

Maria came into the humid room, threw back the curtains, allowing the sun to creep into all corners. She was in her fifth month of pregnancy and he looked at her, aware of an over-powering feeling of protectiveness building inside him.

"The bambino, he still makes you sick?"

Every child had brought retching and hearing her, he felt the sickness come to his throat.

"He? Who say it be he? Boy? Maybe a girl, with fat cheeks and curls, huh?"

She liked to dress the babies; had a penchant for long dresses with crocheted edges.

Today was laundry day and she waited impatiently for the bedclothes. He hurried to dress. She would want to get the clothes washed and pinned to the clothes line before the heat of the day. Emilio was ready for breakfast but still Maria fiddled with the combs and brushes on the dresser.

"Coming, mama? I think it too hot to eat. Just a roll and some coffee."

Emilio turned to leave the room, the stairs creaked under his bulk.

Maria followed him to the kitchen. A small breeze came through the screen and the man moved his chair.

"You see the man today? The one who wants the store?"

"Yeah, this afternoon." He wiped his forehead with the back of his hand.

"You know him? He was one of them wasn't he?"

She knew the man had been a provincial police officer and thought it unwise her man should deal with him.

"He resigned, now is finished. Now he is businessman, like me. Just ordinary man, like me, mama."

He tried to soothe her, wanted her to leaving the planning to him. She usually did, except this time.

The woman was unhappy. Still, if Emilio went into other ventures then the bootlegging could stop. She had begged him to quit, the dangers grew year after year. Now her son was enmeshed in the business and Florence was being drawn in deeper every day.

It was late afternoon before Picariello had his meeting with John Bannatyne Risk.[1] Emilio knew the 43 year old man had spent 8 years with the Royal North West Mounted Police, had been a guard on Parliament Hill.

The meeting was short; the outcome simple. Emilio financed the business to the tune of $11,000.00 and left the running of the store to Risk. Their arrangement was straightforward: the managing of the store would fall on the shoulders

---

1. John Bannatyne Risk joined the Alberta Provincial Police as a first class constable Reg #21, February 22, 1917 and rose from corporal to sergeant. On June 13, 1918 he was made Acting Inspector of D Division at Lethbridge. He resigned from his post June 15, 1921. He was a dark complexioned man with black hair and cool grey green eyes, born 1874 in LainBlash, Scotland.

of Risk. After wages and other expenses were deducted, 50% of the profit would go to Picariello, 50% to Risk. They shook hands on the deal. The Pass Clothing Company was in business. [2]

Risk alone took responsibility for ordering stock for the new store. He stocked the shelves with items from the Hamilton Hosiery Company, Liberty Waist Company of Montreal, Niagara Neckwear Company and Acme Glove Works. Peddlers from the Tobin Shoe Company and Cooper Cap Company paid calls. Emilio came daily, looked around, nodded his approval and turned his attention to his bootlegging empire.

For Florence there was no change, the young girl spent the long summer travelling with Picariello and his men. She developed a warm camaraderie with the drivers as she took the runs. She closed her eyes to the ugly side of the trips and instead looked to beauty surrounding her. She grew to know the south country of Alberta; the flat lands and deserted roads of the back country. She saw feverish blotches of colour of the devil's paintbrush growing beside the road, ate her lunch beside a small pond in the ridge country where the rising wind kneaded the waves into lather, froth scumming the shore. The cars left in lantern light and returned to the mountains when clouds were adrift in a heliotrope sky.

For the girl there was no turning back, she couldn't change her world, so she accepted the life she had to lead. Beneath the false facade, only she and her mother knew the difference.

As the long hot summer wound into fall Picariello attended to another project. He hired men to dig and level the ground where a crossing was made from one side of the street to the other. It was muddy, he said, for his Maria to cross to the shops. Maria, heavy with child, merely smiled.

Children gathered to watch as gravel was spread over the ground and a hand-turned cement mixer went into production.

---

2. From papers, the Examination of Mrs. Picariello, in the matter of the Judicature Trial Division of the Supreme Court of Alberta.

Men loitered in the shade of a building, watching the mixer spew forth wheelbarrow after wheelbarrow of a grey mixture. Even Florence strolled to the corner to watch, dainty in a printed yellow frock. Each child in the crowd wanted to leave a hand or foot print with his initials in the wet cement but the trowelers were careful and the surface dried without a mark.

The cement crossing, the first ever in the town, was laid between the hotel and the Club Cafe on September 15, 1921. Picariello and W.A. Beebe took credit for this venture. Wags were quick to remark that the bootlegger's tunnels were in danger of being caved in from traffic and this crossing was merely a roof to hold the dirt ceiling in place. Emilio was amused, the crossing was in one direction only, his tunnels branched out in every direction from the hotel.

On November 21 Maria gave birth to a girl. Even the December 10, 1921 raid on his 2% bar room did not dull the happiness of the Italian.

Picariello's 2% bar room was like many others in hotels and restaurants in Alberta. He paid a fee of $100.00 for a license, took in a stock of 2% brew, put up a sign and was in business.

The license enabled the government to exercise supervision over the bars and if they were caught with anything over 2% the license was taken away and the place closed. A stiff fine and conviction went along with the closure.

The bar room was certainly plain by most standards. The tin embossed ceiling was darkened by the smoke of many cigarettes. A lazy ceiling fan moved stale air. There was a mirror backed bar, a brass foot rail with spittoons at each end, cigarette burned tables and wire tightened chairs. Brown glass ashtrays were on each table. Sticky fly papers hung from several places in the ceiling.

When the provincials chose to raid Emilio's bar they appeared without warning. On seeing them stride purposefully into the place, the crowd grew silent.

A man disappeared from the room in the direction of the hotel and soon Picariello was there, his face expressionless as he leaned his bulk against the bar. The inspectors checked the room, looked through cupboards and underneath the bar. Taking small bottles from their cases, they took samples from his taps and labelled them.

One of the men smelled the liquid. "Picariello, this is more than just 2%!"

With a jerk of his head towards the taps he asked them to prove it. His face was immobile except for one lifted eyebrow. They gave him a ticket for contravention of the liquor act. As they went out Picariello made a fist! He would not be daunted in his work.

As the trial date drew near, Florence knew Carlo would testify for his boss, their conversations at the supper table confirmed her suspicions.

On the stand Carlo swore he had leased the bar room from Picariello on the first of December. He admitted he was the occupant of the bar on the tenth of December when the raid took place and samples taken from the taps.

Carlo said in court he alone was the occupant of the bar and therefore it was he who was in charge when the raid took place. In evidence it was proven Carlo had assisted in selling beer from the taps. He handled it, served it to his customers. This, the lawyer said, showed possession and control. Carlo was fined $200.00 and costs for unlawfully keeping liquor for sale contrary to Section 23 of the Liquor Act.[3] Picariello went free!

The men rejoiced when the decision was handed down. The money for the fine was a mere pittance. A happy Picariello decreed the approaching Christmas season would be the best one ever.

Winter settled in for a stay. Ice, like the niveous beard of an old man, hung from the eaves. The country was bleak in monotonous white. The days of the runs were far behind the girl now but her future was just as uncertain. Not needed by the bootleggers the young girl was free to go her own way.

---

3. Papers of Alberta Provincial Police, Provincial Archives.

Advent season approached. Florence shopped for gifts, strolled through bazaars given by the Ladies Aid in the churches. She looked at the plain and fancy sewing tables, bought cookies from the pantry table for the children. Tea was served from 2 to 4. She ignored the nudges and whispers of the women as they slyly pointed out the girl in the dress of roshanara crepe. They looked at her silk hosiery, wondered about the cost of her coat with its draped fancy sleeves; wanted to touch the bit of fur on the collar. Would you look at her, they said, the bootlegger's woman, as fancy as all get out! They sniffed; pretended not to notice the Irish embroidered handkerchief in her lap, her ribbon bag with its soft puff and mirror Florence looked into at the end of her tea. The women took her money though, happy to sell her Madeira linens, hand crocheted dollies and table centres that she bought as gifts for friends.

In the evenings, she frequented the opera house where Richard Dix was a matinee idol. Most of the time the young girl was alone.

Christmas approached with smells of baking permeating the houses, bits of tinsel appeared to decorate windows. After payday the streets of town were filled with shoppers. Kids sneaked into the beer parlour through spool knobbed doors and did flips for coins before being chased out by the bartender. Then they amused themselves by looking at toys in the drug store window; teddy bears sat fat and contented, drums and blocks were piled with abandon, sewing sets and doll tea sets were priced at 35¢, wind up toys and music boxes filled the corners. Passing by, Florence caught sight of a celluloid kewpie, with pink dimpled cheeks and flirty eyes. She bought it for the new baby. She shopped for gifts for her family; a warm kimono with cord girdle for her mother, senator cut plug, deliciously fragrant for her father. There was a bed jacket of crepe de chine for Maria, eversharp pencils and cigarette cases for the men, fancy arm bands at 35¢ each for the drivers.

In Fernie the mines were working again; there would be money for Christmas. There was relief in the eyes of the women. If there was work for the whole month of December, food would be plentiful on the table and maybe a bit of money left over and a child would have a small toy and candy under the tree. Only then would it seem like Christmas. The women of the miners waited, the children waited; they had done so, many, many times before.

Angela Costanzo walked to the stores in the thin sunlight, pulling a sled with an apple box nailed to the top. In the box a bundled baby bounced along with her parcels. A drug store window caught her eye and she stopped to look at the display of fresh chocolates packaged in gilt edged boxes pictured with a laughing senorita waving a fan. She wished she could buy one for Florence but knew her money would go to the grocery man first. Sadly she turned away.

Inside the store, fountain pens lay in plush boxes under glass topped counters. Pipes, safety razors and fancy china lined the shelves. In the dry goods store there was a rush to buy warm underwear, all wool cashmere hose, sweaters and dresses. The little extra money left in worn purses was used to purchase a blue flowered hair ribbon for a child, a box of initialed handkerchiefs or a splendid patterned tie which came in its own box.

Stores were ablaze with decorations; there was the spirit of Christmas on the sharp December air. Small trees were decorated with tinsel, candles, holly and mistletoe. Children dreamt of dolls and games and begged to lick spoons in kitchens warm with the fruity smells of cooking. In the bakery, the windows were filled with mouth watering pans of fruit layers dribbled with syrupy toppings and dusted with icing sugar.

The stains of a popular new song, 'Three o'clock in the morning', came over the wireless and crowds lingered to listen as they gazed at a selection of powder puff boxes in French ivory, tortoise shell salve boxes, padded hairpin cabinets, pin trays and soap holders all delicately tinted to match. At the opera house, Jackie Coogan starring in "The Kid" made the holiday crowds cry.

The grocer was a busy man after a mine payday. The miners

paid their old grocery bills and charged again for their Christmas groceries. Fresh turkey hung in a butcher shop and sold for 30¢ a pound, chicken cost 25¢ a pound; rabbit was the most expensive, selling for 40¢ a pound. For the miners a better buy was a 2 pound box of dried codfish. The cost was a mere 55¢ and the family would feed on the box for several weeks.

Many of the immigrants were of the Roman Catholic faith. Christmas eve was a day of abstention from meat. The codfish was a traditional meal on that day. The women set the fish to soak in water for several days before it was to be cooked. It swelled to original size and was fried with onions.

Most of the Pass families had a Christmas meal of turkey, chicken, or beef, potatoes, vegetables, cranberries and a favourite dessert. Each ethnic group had a special treat for the holiday meal. Preserved ginger and Madeira cake were popular items. The heady aroma of a scotch shortbread and black bun fragranced the air in some homes.

Soft drinks were available from Lethbridge Breweries Ltd. Coca Cola, Best Ever Iron Brew, Cream Soda, Lemon Sour and Dry Ginger Ale cost 5¢ a bottle. With a lifted eyebrow the grocer asked his friends if they wanted a few bottles out of his new 'stock' and then a few bottles were exchanged in the case.

A waxing moon hung above the small houses in the towns. Smoke plumes rose in a sky that was coldly blue. Children hung stockings and waited in anticipation for morning. Florence took the train home to be with her family.

After the summer runs there was a difference in the girl who returned home to Fernie. Her slight body lost some of its youthfulness, its slim muscularity. Her voice was soft, husky; there was a web of malleability woven around her. Her eyes were lit, torched into a radiant glow by her thoughts; then suddenly the light went out and sadness crept back.

Soon Florence was in her mother's kitchen, encircled with coziness. The coal fire smouldered, caught and flared brightly. The yard outside was lost in grayness, the very air threatened snow. The spruces made a frieze of darkness against the fading sky. Florence was at peace.

She rose lightly to tie on an apron, helping her mother with the traditional piteainhiusa.[4] Together they made the dough of flour, baking powder, olive oil, sugar, beaten egg, water, salt and vanilla. After it rose, Angela Costanzo expertly rolled the dough very thin and covered it with a boiled raisin mixture which had brown sugar, cinnamon, olive oil and paprika added. Florence ground the walnuts and sprinkled them with abandon over the top. They rolled the large circle of dough into a neat roll. On the baking pan the roll was curled into a circle and put in a hot oven to bake.

In the Costanzo home, a traditional Christmas meal included scaili, a dough rolled to fine thinness, cut into fancy shapes and fried in oil, and dribbled with honey.

While the warm smells of the baking floated through the house Florence filled the children's stockings. Her mother had saved wisely; there was a Japanese orange for each toe, a handful of nuts and a few candies. A small tree stood in the corner, decorated with coloured paper and foil circles cut from the tea wrappers by the children. Under the tree the girl put her gifts for the family and brought out her gifts for the children. There were picture boxes of delightful stories of Henny Penny, Wee Peter Pug and Peter Rabbit. Small Ganong's cardboard sleds were loaded with candy. In the stockings she put candy necklets bought for 5¢ a yard.

The cat gave a few whiskered yawns and settled down. Florence stood for a moment at the window, looked out at the coming storm, white against the dark of the valley. The first few flakes, tiny, pristine, brittle, danced in front of the windows rising and falling on the air. The whiteness that obliterated the valley moved down until it encircled the house. Soon the dance of the flakes stopped as they were caught in the driving fury of the storm. Now they moved past the window as if crazed.

Florence blew out the lamp, lay down beside her sister. She

---

4. Piteainhiusa — spellings on this traditional Italian baking varies.

listened to the cadence of soft breaths taken by the warm child. Lulled by the rhythm, she slept.

XI

A NEW BROOM
SWEEPS CLEAN!

AGAIN THE PROVINCIALS leaned on Picariello. On January 11, 1922 Sergeant Nicholson, [1] clutching a search warrant, appeared at the Canadian Pacific Railway yard sheds and seized 71 barrels of bottled beer along with 10 large and 2 small kegs of beer from a refrigerator car. Picariello came to the freight yards to inspect his goods and was astonished to find the police ahead of him.

"This your beer, Picariello?" A finger was pointed to the barrels in the car.

With resignation and a wave at the barrels, Picariello admitted the goods belonged to him.

"Seize it! Do as you damn well please!"

He shook his hand authoritatively. "It's all 2%!" He left the car without waiting to answer their charges.

Elated with their find, the provincials took samples for analysis. On January 27 they were knocking on Picariello's door with a warrant for his arrest. The charge: unlawfully keeping liquor for sale at Blairmore on January 11th.

The case came up before Magistrate Gresham on February 9 and Picariello retained lawyer C.F. Harris to represent him.

Again Carlo testified for his boss. He said Picariello ordered a carload of aerated water from the Fernie Brewery. The car was shipped by a Thomas Smith and it was sent in his name.

1. John Daniel Nicholson was appointed Assistant Superintendent June 21, 1922. He was born Princeton, Mass. September 8, 1865. He was blue eyed, had an anchor tatoo on his left hand, a bullet wound in his right thigh. He spent 25 years in the Royal North West Mounted Police, 6 years as Chief Detective of Alberta.

The bill of lading was sent to Picariello.

Then, Carlo continued, Picariello sent him and his son Steve to unload the car at the freight yards. He was asked what was taken from the car.

"Well sir," said Carlo earnestly, "15 barrels of aerated water were taken to Picariello's cellars and 14 others were taken to Coleman. After we finished with the aerated water we returned to the car and found the balance was all beer!"

Losandro continued with his tale of woe.

"We left it alone. Didn't touch it and went to find Picariello to tell him of the mistake."

"Did you find him? What did he say?"

"Yes, we found him and Picariello, he say notify the Canadian Pacific Railway officials and tell them the car not his. He ordered aerated waters, not beer. He say return the car to Fernie and that's what we was proposing to do, seal the car and return it. Then the police butted in and seized it."

Carlo wisely made no further mention of the 29 barrels already taken from the shipment.

Mr. Harris asked for an adjournment. He wanted to produce a witness from the Fernie Brewery to show what really had been ordered but the judge decided against this. He found the bootlegger guilty and fined him $500.00 and costs. The beer was confiscated.

Picariello chalked this up to expenses but on second thought decided to appeal the case. The appeal was set for May in the city of Calgary.

For the Calgary trial, Emilio retained Mr. McKinley Cameron to represent him. The appeal was made on the grounds there was no evidence the liquor in question was the property of the accused, nor was it in his possession at the time. There was no real evidence Picariello was the keeper of the liquor in the railway car. But the judge thought otherwise and the appeal was dismissed. Emilio promptly forgot about the incident and spent his time devising other ways to get his loads through.

Now rumours of new police postings reached Picariello's ears. A change of police staff in the Pass towns could mean trouble. It was no longer a cat and mouse game; it was a desperate battle of wits. As the police intensified their harassment Picariello outfitted his drivers with guns.

In Fernie a thoughtful man chewed the stub of his pencil and started on a letter to the Superintendent of the Alberta Provincial Police.

February 7th, 1922

Dear Mr. Bryan/

I have no doubt that you will be rather surprised in hearing from me, after turning you down as I did last year, especially after what you did for me, and I want to tell you I have <u>regretted</u> it ever since, for several reasons.

First — I don't like Fernie and never will.

Secondly — Mrs. Lawson has been bothered with Rheumatism of late, and I have come to the conclusion that the climate does not suit her.

I have every reasons to believe that I am giving my superiors satisfactory service, and I have no doubt that they would do their best to hold me, <u>but it would not have any effect on me this time</u>, for I have had all the City Police Work that I require.

Therefore I am going to ask you, should a vacancy occur under your command, will you consider me for same, as I have said before I do not want or look for any favors.

Kindest regards to Mrs. Bryan, and yourself. Trusting to hear from you in the near future.

Yours Very Sincerely,
S.O. Lawson,
Chief of Police.

After the letter of February 7 was typed on heavy paper adorned with the corporate seal of the City of Fernie, Stephen

Lawson put his signature above his title of Chief of Police.

In due course the Superintendent wrote two letters, one to Lawson and the other to the Inspector in charge of D division of the Lethbridge Alberta Provincial Police.

To Lawson he wrote:

13th Feb.

Dear Lawson:

In reply to your letter of February 11th, I beg to advise you that we will overlook the age question in your case; also, that instead of sending you to Strathmore, for the present I am arranging with Inspector Bavin of Lethbridge to see if he can place you at either Bellevue or Coleman, Coleman preferably as there is a very good school there and later on probably move you to some other point. You would be very valuable to Sergt. Scott who is going down from Red Deer to take over from Sergt. Nicholson, and you would get into the system under which we work, and I would be able to put you, probably, in a district of your own. The expense of moving your family from Fernie to Coleman would not amount to very much.

We will arrange for you to get measured by a tailor after you join up. Inspector Bavin will arrange this. I hope this will suit you as I cannot do anything else for the present.

I am wiring you today as you suggested.

Yours very truly,

S.O. Lawson, Esq.,   SUPERINTENDENT
Chief of Police,
Fernie, B.C.

WCB/V

A New Broom Sweeps Clean!

To Inspector Bavin, his letter read

13th Feb.

Sir:

I beg to advise you that Mr. S.O. Lawson, Chief of Police, Fernie, is resigning Fernie and wishes to join this Force. I, at first, thought of sending him to Inspector Brankley, Calgary District, but it has just struck me that Lawson would be the ideal man for either Coleman or Bellevue (and you have married quarters at each place) as he knows pretty nearly every bootlegger and crook running through the Pass. I think it would be a good idea to change Hale from the Pass and he could go to Inspector Brankley's Division for Strathmore to replace Const. Pakenham who has resigned.

I am notifying Lawson today that I will take him on and place him in the Crow's Nest Pass to work under Scott. He will be taken on as a first-class constable.

Kindly let me know how this arrangement will suit you before I take up the matter with Inspector Brankley of Calgary. I may tell you I know Lawson very well; he is a good policeman, conscientious, honest, and energetic, and I think he is the man that we require in the Pass. He would not be able to leave until probably about the 15th March.

I have the honor to be, Sir,
Your obedient servant,

Inspector Bavin,   SUPERINTENDENT.
Alberta Provincial Police,
Lethbridge, Alta.

WCB/V

Lawson, in turn, acknowledged acceptance into the force as he replied to the Superintendent. [2]

February 15th 1992

Dear Mr. Bryan/

Many thanks for yours under date 13th inst, and its contents noted.

I am rather glad that I am going to be placed under an N.C.O. for as you say it will give me the chance of getting on to your system and routine work, for I will be a little green in that line, having been used to City work.

The Mayor has been sick lately and has only just heard of my resignation, which apparently he regrets, for he informed me that he thanked Mr. Bryan for sending me to Fernie, but he DOES not thank him for taking me away, however I understand that he is writing you to recommend him a man for Chief.

From the papers you are very busy, and I won't bother you with any more correspondence, but will stand to and await orders, but would be glad if you would kindly put me in touch with your man at where ever I may be going to, so that I can get size of rooms, and a few particulars. I do not want to crate anything that may be useless to me.

Trusting I will give you satisfaction, it will be my highest ambition.

Yours Very Truly
Chief of Police

WC Bryan Esq
Superintendent
Alberta Prov. Police
Edmonton, Alberta

---

2. Letters from Alberta Provincial Police papers, Provincial Archives.

In the early spring, as the bootleggers were taking their cars down from blocks, Stephen Oldacres Lawson signed his Allegiance and Oath of Office in front of Justice of the Peace and Police Magistrate James William Gresham.

He was a first class constable with a regiment number of 248 and was scheduled to receive a wage of $130.00 a month from which 3% was taken for a pension.

Into the Orders Book of the Alberta Provincial Police the company clerk wrote:

"31/3/22 - First Class Constable in Alberta Provincial Police taken on strength and posted to D. division effective 23/3/22. Reg. No. 248 Constable Stephen Oldacres Lawson."

The 42 year old man taken on strength was born June 8, 1880 in Brixton, England. He was 5 '7 3/4" tall, his lean muscular frame carried a weight of 160 pounds. He had kindly brown eyes and a head of dark brown hair.

Three years of army life in the service of the Fort Garry Horse and 10 years of police work ingrained a smart military appearance in the man. He won the military medal for Meritorious Service overseas in France and after the signing of Armistice, returned to duties of Chief of Police at Macleod from which he moved to Chief of Police at Fernie.

Lawson took his medical in Coleman and Dr. C.O. Scott deemed him to be muscularly well developed, of above average intelligence and of cheerful temperament. He had a small circular bullet wound on his left calf. In completing the medical, the doctor wrote that in 1918 the man had trench fever in France but was physically fit for duty.

In due time, Lawson was issued the uniform of the Alberta Provincial Police which included both blue and khaki breeches, a forage and fur cap, cloth and fur coat, a stetson hat, leggings, and pea jacket. There was both summer dress and winter dress along with miscellaneous items like spurs, chevrons, badges, collar and shoulder sets, leather hat band, belt, holster, handcuffs and key, manual, pouch and ammunition. He was issued with 32 and 28 calibre Smith and Wesson revolvers and a 45.75 Winchester rifle. After the tailor was finished Lawson tried on his tunics, fastened his badges and was ready for work. He was not subjected to the drill and training of new recruits, his conduct and discipline was well known and he went directly to his position.

The other posting that was to put hardship on the bootleggers was the man referred to in the Superintendent's letters — James Ogston Scott.

Scott had risen quickly in his career with the provincials. Taken on as a first class constable February 17, 1917 his regiment number was 7. He was posted to A division where he drew a pay of $3.00 a day. On January 1, 1918 he was transferred to B division as a detective drawing a wage of $3.90 a day.

On February 24, 1922 he transferred to D division, taking over from Nicholson. Scott was made a sergeant on March 11, 1922 and was new blood in the Pass.

Although Lawson knew many of the bootleggers in the Pass area, he needed information on the new and ever increasing inventions in smuggling and Scott was the person to tell him. He knew the problems.

With Lawson installed in Coleman and Scott in Blairmore, the bootleggers knew they had tough opposition. It was the era of the stickiest battles between police and bootleggers.

The southern part of Alberta was a hot bed of liquor transactions. Stiff fines were levied on bootleggers but they paid their fines of $200.00 to $300.00, evaded a jail term and kept on with their trade.

The Blairmore sub district entered 105 cases of which 103 resulted in convictions. Two were dismissed. The fines totalled $12,937.00! In the northern districts of Alberta the convictions and fines were paltry in comparison: Edmonton entered 14 cases of which 13 were convictions. One was dismissed. The fines were a measly $597.00!

Bootleggers, along with enterprising householders, used

every gimmick imaginable in their efforts to smuggle liquor. All over the southern part of Alberta the same scene was re-enacted with many variations.

In a small town a bored provincial constable walked about the streets and finally came to stand in the shade in front of the pool hall. He stalled, not wanting to move from the awning. An August sun blotted the town, searing its streets. Bleached grass poked up through arid soil and was mummified in the droughty land.

The man took off his hat, wiped his forehead and the sweat band of his hat. A car came around the corner and stopped at the garage; dust stirred hung in the heavy air.

The policeman sauntered over, glad to have someone new to talk with.

"Nice car," the constable began. The driver had just come out of the garage. He was dressed in dungarees, high heeled riding boots and plaid shirt with a scarf tied at his neck. In a slow manner he pushed back his hat, coughed and spit phlegm into the dust.

"Yup, I got it new. Just $480.00 and 12 easy payments!" He laughed a coarse laugh. "Just 12 easy payments!" He repeated this reflectively.

The constable looked idly in the car, so obviously new and too clean for a ranch hand. Still, the man had a rag out and was wiping dust from the dashboard.

"Nice saddle. Yours? Bin to a rodeo?"

"Nope, bin to the city. Little vacation, you know," the cowboy winked, "seen a picture show. Rudolph Valentino. Some show!"

"Yeh, I saw him once too. What was playing?"

"Blood and Sand. What a picture! Real Spanish fighting bulls!"

The uniformed man was not interested in the picture, he had seen something of interest and now reached in the car to feel the saddle. It was quite new, no horse hair sweated into the saddle blanket and what's this ... sacks in a new car? The driver shifted nervously, his hands curled and twisted the rag.

"Well now, what do we have here? Oats for your horse, I'll bet."

With a slit of his knife the grain spilled little topaz streams on the dark flooring. Plunging his hands into a sack he drew forth a bottle. There were three sacks in the car, each filled with bottles of whisky headed for Montana.

The cowboy blanched, veins marbled his neck. He knew he was headed for a big fine or 30 days in the pokey!

There were all kinds of excuses used when the offenders came before the judge.

One old man who always found his liquor and found it very often had a likely story.

"Your honour. I swear I never bin this bad before. Why I can't remember what I did and ... he leaned forward to speak confidentially ... I think my medicine ... his voice dropped further ... got mixed up with a little bit of sheep dip!"

"Thirty days or $50.00!"

"But yer honour ..." the drunk expostulated.

"Case dismissed!" was the dry reply.

The judge guessed the old man got hold of home brew. Many people, not having the money to spend at the bootleggers, turned to making home brew. It was noted there was an influx of people out picking chokecherries, much more than needed for a few jars of jam. They made wine in all kinds of pots and with every ingredient. The vilest of these concoctions seized analyzed as high as 110.8 to 115.10%. One man who took three drinks of a home brew was found dead in the alley, still cradling his drink in his arms.[3]

---

3. A report of the Alberta Provincial Police, Provincial Archives stated that "enforcing the liquor act was one of the hardest and most onerous duties we are called upon to perform. The public render very little assistance as they do not want to get mixed up in any way with liquor cases. Complaints have fallen off 60% this year compared with last and I am of the opinion from the reports received at this office from all over the province that as far as actual illegal buying and selling is concerned there is a very large decrease and also in the amount consumed; on the other hand the illicit manufacture of alcoholic beverages has increased. People have acquired the knowledge and habit of making their own beverages, one of the most favoured being what is known as 'bee wine'. It is a simple process ... and the strength of it depends on the people making it. There are scores of beverages made from fruits and vegetables ... known as 'household remedies'.

Police pressure was increasing in intensity and not just in Alberta.

On a hot July morning in 1922 an aging madam struggled to her feet in response to insistent pounding at her door. She hollered coarsely as she tied the cords of her gaudy satin wrapper.

"Get off my property! Bugger off, we ain't open!"

The pounding kept on.

"Damn," she muttered, "whoever it is, they ain't about to go away."

She pushed back hennaed hair that fell in disarray over her sagging face, lit a cigarette and blew smoke into the stale room.

"I'm coming. Hold your damn horses!"

The bolt slid back to reveal four official looking men on the porch.

"What do you want? Hell, can't you let a body sleep?"

"Come on Bell," a trim mustached man spoke holding up an official looking document in his hand. "We have a warrant to search your place."

The sleepy eyes opened, the face paled under last night's rouge. She stood aside to let them enter. The raids had begun.

At the same time 100 warrants were being served to firms and residents across the province of British Columbia. In the days preceding the raid, search warrants were made up and men were armed. Their directions were clear and concise. Stamp out bootleggers! It was an energetic campaign against those engaged in the traffic of illicit liquor.

Alberta was soon to follow with a crackdown of their own. With the flow of liquor stemmed by the British Columbia raids, a new flow to the south started north of Calgary, Alberta. The provincials tried to stop the traffic south of Claresholm by putting road blocks on Willow Creek bridge. If the bootleggers got by this one, there was another roadblock over the Old Man River near Macleod.

By now the general public, tired of discussions and problems caused by the act, ceased to complain and rendered very little assistance in policing the act. There were small groups of people who still put pressure on the government to squash the traffic. Straight-laced individuals were self appointed spies who took a great delight in writing letters to the Honourable J.E. Brownlee regarding suspicious neighbours. [4]

Claresholm, Nov. 17, 1922.

To the Commissioner.

Sir:

I have here the following report on Granum to make.

R__ H_____ Barber Shop and Pool Room handles no soft drinks. Has a poker table in the place, while in there seen a game of High Low Jack and game going on. It was a 4 handed game. Seen no rake off. I tried to buy a drink of hard stuff with the following men, O___ H_____, by J___ M_____ and J__ R___ from here but he had none and said he would not have any before tomorrow.

I learned that O___ H_____ had a still up in the hills, and he supplies Granum and Pincher Creek. He gave me a drink of his moonshine. It was a good brand of that kind of liquor. He sells quart bottles at $5.00. So, as I told you there are stills in the Porcupines for all the liquor in through here is moonshine and it comes from no place but the hills.

Alberta Hotel run by P____ C____ found nothing just soft drinks and 2 per cent. I also tried to get booze from the Blacksmith but he had run out of it too.

On making inquiries found that the town was very quiet and I also found it the same and seen no drunks, on this visit or on the one of Nov. 15.

---

4. Spy letters from the Alberta Provincial Police files, Provincial Archives.

I have received information that there is a still west of Gleichen, Alta., about 20 miles, one of the parties who sells this moonshine runs a tire repair shop. His name is P____ B_____ and if one could get in his confidence he would lead one up to the still. Take this for whatever it is worth, although the person who told me so far has been pretty reliable.

Hoping, Sir, that you find my work satisfactory,

I remain, Sir,
Your obedient servant,

(Sgd) "H 3"

Another letter from spy 'H3" gave more information on his activities and those on whom he watched.

Claresholm, Nov. 17th, 1992.

Sir:

Onthe night of Nov. 15 I visited Granum but found nothing but 2 percent. I am returning there tonight. There has been some beer and moonshine sold during the threshing but now the lid seems to be on, Since Cpl. Hidson got R__ H_____. As for P____ C___ at the Alberta Hotel, I can safely say that if he has handled any beer it must have been very little as I was in Granum a number of times this summer with the ditch gang from Willow Creek and we could never get anything there. Yesterday I took a trip to Barons and I found beer at the Club Pool Room and at the Hotel. I also got moonshine. I tried every place on my list but those were the only two places where I got any. I also took in Carmangay but found nothing there except that I learned from good source that the O.K. Cafe handles beer now and again but that they had been out of beer for about a week. I also visited Champion but could not get a drop, although I learned that the Hotel Prop. does handle some now and again and also the Pool Room, but a stranger in town cannot get a smell unless he is in with the crowd. I visited Stavely once more last night, tried awful hard to get some moonshine of the Pool Room Prop. there but he was out of it, so will try again some other time. I find Claresholm very tight, not a drop can I find and I know this town pretty well. But can't do no good. I made inquiries and I find that the church people here control the town so the lid is on, enough said. The only thing they sell in through here is moonshine and it comes from up in the hills west of Stavely and west of Granum. Trust me, Sir, and give me confidence and a free hand and I will get them. I find the bootlegging element around Macleod, Barons & Stavely are pretty sore at Cpl. Hidson and Const. Jones and the first chances they get they will try to railroad them so as to get them transferred and out of the way, for the men that were here before at these 2 detachments never enforced the law like Cpl. Hidson and Jones, and both of these men have got things under control and work hard, and for doing their duty are Sons of B. as far as the bootleggers are concerned. I will report tonight to Insp. Bavin at Lethbridge after visiting Granum, and give you a report.

I remain, Sir,
Your obedient servant,

(Sgd) "H 3"

Throughout the year of 1922 the hide and seek game continued. Florence looked forward to autumn because winter would soon follow and her part in the ugly scenario would be finished.

156

After a very long dry spell a gentle rain fell in the small town of Blairmore. The rain was followed by a week of blustery winds and deadened skies. Florence knew another large run was in the offing.

She went out in the early morning, walked the streets and felt the ping of rain against her face, let the wind blow her hair. She heard the bird call of gathering flocks soon to be on their way south. She smelled the damp musty smell of summer's rotting leaves.

Metal sounds from the shunt of a train brought her back to reality and she found herself at the edge of town. She turned from the dripping trees, avoided the spongy-needled floor and turning, walked slowly home. The wind was noisy as it slid over the rooftops and swayed the trees, scattering and disjointing their black forms.

Back in her room she changed wet clothing, shivered from the dampness of her skin. Now a voice, echoing from below interrupted her musings and she heard Carlo call, heard the clatter of feet on the stairway.

"Come on, Flo! Don't make the man wait!" The voice was impatient, commanding, slightly peevish.

Before the footsteps could reach the top of the stairs the girl smoothed her hair and slipped her arms into her coat. Her face quickly lost its haunting appeal, the mask brightened to match the stylish figure in the dark green coat. Frivolous light coloured clothes were not in vogue because of the war and the women wore colours of forest green, burnt brown and victory blue.

Donning the phony shell of hardness she used on many of the trips, Florence came lightly down the stairs and got into the waiting car.

Carlo and Tony were in one car, the other stood waiting for Steve and Emilio. Florence would ride with Carlo and Tony. Both cars were loaded, there would be no scout car.

The sky cleared but the wind was bracing. Tumbleweeds moved ahead of the marshalling wind. Thinning trees growing close to houses revealed bird's nests packed tightly into tree forks; they stood out like pock marks on a smooth face.

The cars threaded their way through the bench of blue black mountains, sifted with white, that guarded the western approach. Rugged clouds hung low around their peaks. The twisting road disappeared into outlying hills where the land rolled, treed with wind twisted pines. The mountains parted, the hills gave way and the road slipped between its clefts.

Tony and Carlo were silent and grim. The police had again leaned heavily on bootleggers and nerves were tense, dispositions irritable.

"How do you like them guys?" Carlo was the first one to speak. He was referring to a recent newspaper that asked, 'Don't all speak at once, but who wants 140 cases of booze?' Just last week the whisky had been seized by the police at Macleod. It had been sent from Fernie, billed as household goods, the destination was a household in Kipp, Alberta.

Carlo continued, "some nosey provincial looked at the cases and saw the same name on all of them. He pried off the top and found the stuff in sawdust, was supposed to be china. Was all marked fragile. When they went to see the man whose name was on the cases, all they got was a shrug. Not his stuff. He not order it. Walked away from them, sure made them mad ... serves them right ... interfering, butting their noses in." His voice trailed off.

Police were visiting small towns, making surprise visits and on more than one occasion found barber shops with wet goods and fined them $50.00 and costs. For selling fruit on a Sunday a confectionery store was fined $10.00 and costs. A few weeks later the owner was found with 8 bottles of beer on his premises and fined $100.00 and costs.

The cars were coming to the town of Macleod and Tony slowed down so they stayed well apart from the first car driven by Steve. At a corner store Carlo motioned the driver to stop.

"I'm hungry, Flo. Be a good girl and get a bag of lemon cheese cakes for me."

He handed her 25¢. As she left the car Tony remembered he wanted a bat plug of chewing tobacco and tossed her a coin.

The girl's hand shot out, expertly caught the coin and she turned on her heel to cross the wooden walk. Her face was sullen.

Florence climbed into the back seat again. She declined an offer of a cheese cake and stared moodily out the window.

Outside the town two men in uniform sat silently on a knoll watching the road. Spotting the two McLaughlins discreetly travelling the road several miles apart, they sped back to the Macleod detachment and rang up the police in Cardston. The orders came back, crisp and clear, catch up and search them. The Cardston detachment would try to head them off.

Tony caught up with the Picariello car on the road to Cardston. Florence relaxed in the back seat and escaped into her dreams in a world of make believe. It was always the same; a warm kitchen scene with a polished table on which sat a basket of apples, russet globes with taut skins gathered from a tree behind a small house. There were thoughts of knitting, cosy fires and suppers eaten in a cage of late sunlight, ending with cups of chocolate and long intimate talks. The evening song was of crickets, their song pulsing through the warm air mantle that was evening before the sun lowered, the air turned crisp and clover folded at the touch of dew. It was always the same dream, only the faces were blank; she despaired of having such a life and sat up suddenly in the rocking car.

Fifteen miles north of Cardston just over a small rise the roadblock appeared. Emilio turned around in his seat and gave the thumb up signal to the men in the following car. It meant roadblock or not, they were going through, making a run for it.

Tony tensed, gripped the wheel and with a stubborn look on his face, followed the first car through the wooden barricade the provincials had hurriedly put up. Lumber flew in all directions; 2 provincials ran for their car and the race was on!

For 65 miles the two constables pursued the bootleggers. The police, in their Chevrolet Grand, skidded and turned, following the McLaughlin Sixes through the town of Cardston. They tore down the main street at 50 miles an hour; cars pulled over, horns honked, horses skittered, people ran to doorways to see the commotion.

Carlo turned in his seat, commanding, "Florence, the back window! Attento!"

The girl expertly flipped up the silk roller shade on the back window and positioned herself in the window to watch the following car.

When the police car came within shooting distance they saw the white face of the girl bouncing in the back window.

"Hold your fire!" one provincial yelled to the other, "they got a woman with them!"

Picariello knew the police would not shoot with the girl's face showing in the window. Florence did as she was told, keeping in sight, reporting every move of the following car.

For a short time the police kept within a mile of the fleeing cars. Burning ground beneath them the cars roared through Aetna, Kimball and Taylorville. They raced over all kinds of roads, smooth and rough, ungraded and graded.

They crossed a bridge, bumping over the rough timbers where glass was heard breaking. Through Valleyfield, Richfield and Lenz, Tony's skill as a driver was put to the test as he tried to keep up with the car driven by Steve. Carlo could not help but admire the boy.

When Florence called out, "Attenzione! They're coming up on your side. Careful!" Tony moved the big car over, blocking any attempt by the police to make a run for it and get by thus separating the cars. Steve in the lead car chose the way and Tony followed closely. He hogged the road, slid into the corners, gunned the motor on the straightaway. He threw up dust, gravel where there was any, swayed and drove like the devil was tied to his tail. He had an almost maniacal look on his face, his tongue curled out his open mouth, his eyes were glassy, he was having the time of his life!

Nearing Whisky Gap the bootleggers hit for open country, bumping, bouncing, battering their cars across the prairies. The going was rough and the Chevrolet Grand dropped back, then finally stopped and gave up the chase. A flicker of triumph burned in Picariello's eyes.

Looking back, Tony saw his pursuers stop. He leaned out the window, gave a war whoop, honked his horn and zigzagged over the prairie. Carlo laughed, gave Tony a pat on the shoulder, turned to his wife in the back seat, his eyes flashing with excitement.

"We did it, Flo! Oh, boy, you were great!"

It was unusual for Carlo to give her praise. The girl sank back, took a deep breath and managed a smile. Soon the two McLaughlins were over the border into the United States.

They stopped near marsh land with tree cover to inspect the damage. Florence got shakily out of the car and stumbled to the pond's edge. She was conscious of a pounding, a rushing roar of blood. The young girl sank to the ground where she was part of the earth and it was part of her.

The muddy pond reflected the gray of the overhead sky. The inhabitants of the water logged meadow put on a vocal and aerial display for the intruder sitting quietly at its edge. Prairie chicken moved nervously through the matted grass between the trees. Beige clouds bunched on the horizon and the colours of autumn showed imperceptibly announcing the coming season.

A solace and restoration of spirit came to the girl as she sat quietly and took in the beauty of the pond. Its melody came to her and she took it inside and used it to heal the hurts she felt. As she sat at the water's edge the pond song possessed her and she let its balm wash over her, vibrate within her, felt a quiet joy. The events of the last few months seemed far away now and peace engulfed her troubled mind.

Florence was jolted back to reality by voices beside her. Tony and Steve came to the pond to wash mud from their hands. Tony was vocal in his praise for the job she had done. Steve had only admiration in his eyes. For her, it was enough.

XII

RUN FOR YOUR MONEY!

Emilio stirred in his chair, opened eyes heavy with sleep and looked at his watch. The room was heavy with the warmth of an Indian summer. He ran a hand over bristling jowls and wished for a razor. Maybe his friend, Cervello, in whose home he stayed the night, would allow him to use his.

He yawned, stretched, then walked to the window. Outside, on a patch of sun baked earth, a dandelion did its slow dance of disintegration in the heat. Lethargy enveloped the man, pulling him down. He shook his head; it was not to be, the time had come to make the run.

He looked at his sleeping son. Soon the boy would be eighteen. Picariello shook him by the arm. Steve awoke and sat up, brushing hair back from his eyes. He smiled sleepily.

"Time to go, no?"

Emilio looked at his rumpled clothes. Creases formed in his shirt, in his trousers. The heavy set man was increasingly indifferent to his appearance; he appeared now and then in coveralls, unshaven, with a cap pulled low on his massive head and his huge hands jammed in the bib top. Other times he wore a neat suit and hat; a diamond stickpin glittered on a smart tie. Even with his clothes in disarray he was an imposing figure.

"Vieni, hurry up, get dressed." Emilio prodded his son who had rolled over and gone back to sleep. The older man was anxious to go.

When Emilio descended the stairs he found the table set and the kitchen full of the hot smells of late summer. The woman of the house waved her hand to the table.

"Accomodati!" (take a seat!)

It would not do to leave the house without eating and as she put the noon meal on the table, the woman warned him, as she always did, to watch the road around the lake.

"Is dangerous, Emilio!"

"Yeah, mama," he waved his fork before plunging it into a platter of pork and eggs.

She was not to be put off lightly.

"A car can slip off, into its edges, go down ..."

She broke off, seeing in her mind the mysterious green of the lake's depths. She hunched her shoulders and shuddered.

Emilio nodded to her, his mouth full of egg. He swallowed, gulped coffee, smiled weakly.

"Mama, please, stop the worrying!"

Emilio knew the legend of the Crows Nest Lake, of it having no bottom. He knew of cars resting on its sloping sides in the dark green water.

The woman set a dish of anchovies in brine on the table and continued to admonish the man in a motherly fashion and he, like an unhearing youngster, continued to nod an affable agreement to her cautions.

The mechanic, McAlpine, drove the first car out of the yard. Twenty feet behind him, Steve drove the second car which was fully loaded with liquor. The third car, driven by Emilio, carried no liquor.

As he drove, Emilio wondered about his son, who, so carelessly perfect in his driving, travelled the road in front of him. The handsome boy attracted girls and when two giggling females sauntered in front of the yard as they prepared to leave, he had to bring the boy's attention back to the task at hand. He had been cross with the boy, their angry voices merged and melted together in the quiet heat. He cautioned the boy, if he was cornered, it was better to lose the load than his life! But the son shied from the curbs the father tried to place on him. Even their conversation on this point eased into a sigh by the father as he wondered if he had been forceful enough in driving home his point.

"What you do if you cornered, huh?"

"Cornered? Cornered? By who!" The voice coming back to Emilio was disdainful.

"By the police, that's who!" was the thunder of the reply.

"They won't corner me!" boasted the voice.

"If they do," the elder Picariello said slowly, "Better you lose the load than lose your life! Nothing is worth the breath you take into your body! Nothing!"

The man's dark eyes were unfathomable as they were whenever he thought of his firstborn. He loved the boy dearly, but the youth needed guiding.

The man brought his thoughts back to the present. They had driven through Fernie and were passing through the outskirts, driving slowly on the main road that would take them to the Pass.

The road was relatively clear, their pace unhurried. Shore birds patterned marshy slopes of small lakes hugging the roadsides. Pines swayed in a light breeze which hinted at a rising wind to follow. A stray cloud hung in the blue of a mountain canopy. The cars passed through small towns of Natal and Michel and soon came to the town of Coleman.

The main street was quiet; there were few people about but no one paid any attention to the convoy of cars. Picariello shifted in his seat, looked at his watch and saw it was 5 minutes to 4. As he did so, he was intently uneasy. Something was wrong! He shook his head, relaxed his tensed shoulders. He drove on.

From the shadows of a building two men in uniform stepped away from the shade where they had spent the greater part of the day watching the main street of Coleman. They gave all the cars on the road close scrutiny as they passed and when the McLaughlin cars belonging to Picariello came into sight, they nodded to each other. They knew these drivers!

The men separated; Chief of Police Jonathan Houghton returned to his office, Lawson hurried to the barracks to use the telephone. It was 4 o'clock.

The three cars disappeared far down the road to the east.

In the town of Frank, Alberta, a man in uniform sat at his desk completing a long report. He paused and looked at the date; September 21. He frowned, pursed his lips and chewed on the end of his pencil. With a sigh, he moved to his feet, heavy boots scraping against wood flooring, and removed his jacket.

The day was hot. Flies droned at the dusty window; their muted buzzings mingled with the measured tick of a wall clock.

With renewed determination the man again sat down and continued his report. The shrill ring of the telephone split the stillness.

"Alberta Provincial Police. Sergeant Scott here!"

The man listened intently to the speaker at the other end of the line. As he listened his face brightened and his lips curled.

"Yes ... yes ... how do you know? When did he leave?"

The voice was sharp.

"Yes, I'll watch for him! Okay, okay, got that!"

He rummaged in a desk drawer, found a new pencil and wrote on the paper in front of him. Then he leaned back and contemplated the wall clock.

"So. Pic is making a run, right in the afternoon. Cheeky, thought we wouldn't notice. And from all reports its a wet one! Well, well, a big run, loaded to the locks they are!" Scott muttered to himself.

"Hey Dey, hurry up! Come here!" Scott hollered to a constable in the next room.

The 29 year old Dey answered the call and together they drove towards Blairmore in police car number 7.[1]

The car was buffeted by a strong westerly wind that ground grit into the windshield and sifted dust over the shiny high topped boots of the men inside. Both men were unusually silent during the short drive to Blairmore; each wrapped in

---

1. Dey was an Alberta Provincial policeman stationed in Blairmore.

165

their own thoughts.

Now nearing the hotel belonging to the bootlegger, Dey broke the silence.

"Maybe Pic is making a dry run. He does often you know. Why would he make a big run right in the afternoon?"

Scott, at the wheel, promised the run would be a wet one and outlined what they would do. They had a warrant to go through the hotel, go into its basement, ransack the tunnels they had heard about, peer and pry into every little nook and cranny.

Dey listened intently to the words tumbling from a perpetually sardonic mouth. He watched the streets and spotted Picariello first.

"There he is! See, standing over by his car."

Emilio had parked his car facing north on the side of the street alongside his hotel. The police car came to a stop behind him.

Picariello was uneasy; he had spotted the two police watching the road in the town of Coleman but they had let him come through, had paid no attention to his cars. Intuition led him to believe something was afoot.

The ignition of the police car was turned off. The motor died; the men started towards the bootlegger.

Scott ran around to the back of the hotel thinking he could intercept the other car but it was not there.

He ran back calling sharply, "Picariello, I have a warrant to search all your premises!" He waved a white paper in front of him.[2]

The expression on the big Italian's face did not change as the men came towards him. He turned casually, leaned into his car. His hand found the horn and he sounded it several times in warning. He hoped Steve was paying attention.

The car Steve Picariello was driving was hidden in some bushes. He was impatient; they had come through safely but

---

2. From preliminary evidence files, James Scott testified he and Lawson arranged to have a warrant issued. His words ... "we arranged to try and get him ..."

his father was still fretting, feeling a disturbing dissonance about the afternoon run. Steve was inclined to shrug it off; he wanted a cold drink, wanted to wash the dust from his face and hands. He yawned into the undulating heat pushed along by a marshalling wind. Several short blasts from his father's horn signalled danger. His heart quickened.

Expertly the boy turned the big car around and shot for the corner, went around the block and without a backward glance, turned west along the main street of town.

Emilio, with amazing catlike grace, jumped into his own car and started off around the block. Scott and Dey ran for their car, gunned the engine into life and started to follow Emilio. Scott looked back, saw the younger Picariello go down the street, backed up and took after him.

The chase was on!

Emilio maneuvered his car, tried to get in front of the vehicle driven by Scott. Between the hotel and the telephone office the bootlegger used his powerful car in a race to be first on the road. The sergeant's face was grim as he tried to get every bit of power from his car. Dust billowed from their tires and the road behind was lost from sight.

"I can't get by him, he's all over the road!" Scott hollered.

"Then take the ditch!" Dey urged. "Hurry, get by him!"

"Hold on!"

Scott wheeled his car into the ditch. The car bumped and swerved over the uneven ground, the passenger grabbed for the dashboard, braced his feet. The driver gripped the wheel, his head nearly touched the roof of the car as he bounced over rough ground.

"Damn!" Scott cursed. "We'll never catch young Picariello. He's too far ahead of us." He was fighting to regain control of the car, trying to get it up from the ditch bank onto the road.

"Let me out!" Dey had an idea, "I'll phone from the hotel, call Lawson to stop him!"

Dey jumped from the still moving vehicle, stumbled as he tried to keep his balance. He made a run for the front door of the Green Hill Hotel.

At the Coleman barracks Stephen Lawson stood to straighten his back, to ease cramps in his legs. This subterfuge was loathsome but his orders were to follow the plan. He found himself thinking of what lay ahead. Soon the bootlegger's cars rolling eastward would be turned back to Coleman.

Jonathan Houghton knocked at the door of the barracks and let himself in. He made small attempts to draw the other man into conversation but received only grunts and negligible answers. Into the softness of the afternoon came the neighing of a horse and Lawson turned to run his hand over the smooth luster of his tack. Today more than ever he had an air of insularity about him, possibly from the risky business the telephone call would bring.

Except for the anticipated encounter with the bootlegger the day would be perfect the man thought. Even with the wind rising, the warm sun of the Indian summer wrapped the day hours in tranquility. The cadence of bird calls was slow, muted and there was a feeling of easiness and comfort in the pellucid light that fell on the uncarpeted floor and reflected in the fading pink of the wall paper.

The police chief wondered about the tall man who walked about the room, seemingly unconcerned about the events of the afternoon. Lawson, he knew, would not allow confusion or indecision to come into his work. He went by the book. Even now, his eloquent silence was a statement of his intent, his decision to follow orders, to do what was right.

Houghton left the barracks and went to the train station, waiting for the local to come in.

In the barracks the shrill jangle of the telephone broke the quiet. Lawson turned on his heel and with one stride reached the receiver. He listened intently.

Lawson stepped into the simmering heat of the pitiless September sun. He sniffed the faint fragrance of wood smoke, noted the new glint of snow in the high country. Lawson did not appear to hurry but in his bearing, in his decisive singular movement to the train station his intent was clear. Picariello would be stopped.

At the depot, Lawson called to Houghton; "Jack, get the biggest car you can find. We will need it. Picariello is doubling back with his load!"

Lawson and Houghton hurried back to main street on foot. Houghton ran across to the Grand Union Hotel, owned by a Mr. Bell, and asked him to start up his car. As Houghton entered the hotel a car came from the east and proceeded down the main street travelling between 50 to 60 miles an hour.

In the large McLaughlin Steve felt mounting power as he left the dust of Blairmore behind him. He barely glanced back to see his pursuers until he put a deepening distance between them. With practiced ease, he put the gas pedal to the floorboards until the other car was a speck on the road which fell away from him in a clear unwinding image.

Steve knew the police would follow, try to catch up as they always did, try to force him off the road or follow so close he would lose control when trying to watch behind.

When no car was seen in the distance Steve was tempted to stop. He resisted an even stranger temptation to turn around; he could easily make it over the provincial border and his father would find some other way to bring the load down. He was approaching Coleman now and the town's outskirts flashed by him then he saw the shacks of the miners, the feed corrals and wooden fronts of mercantile stores. On the long street that ran through the town he scarcely slowed his speed. People were startled to see the car speeding through the town.

After Houghton left Lawson at the corner of Pat Burns Butcher Shop, Lawson crossed over to the Coleman Hotel. He, too saw the speeding car come down the road, a cloud of dust billowing behind it. Lawson stepped purposefully into the middle of the street.

He raised his hand in an authoritative gesture meant to stop the car, but the McLaughlin, still at top speed, bore straight on. Lawson hollered at the driver. The townspeople cringed in fear as the car made no deviation in its direction or speed.

It was the sort of drama the town had never seen before.

Wide eyed, the onlookers stood transfixed as Lawson pitted his will against the force of the moving car. He was in a precarious position, a reckless stance and the people watching shrank back as the distance lessened by the second.

Lawson, too, seemed frozen. Then, at the last minute, he jumped aside. The driver had been shocked into a reciprocatory move, the car swerved to the other side of the officer and continued on down the street.

As the dust swirled around Lawson, choking him and blurring his eyes, his arm moved instantaneously. His revolver was whipped from its holster, two warning shots were fired. At the sounds of the shots the watching crowd fled the streets to take up seemingly safer positions in doorways and windows. The McLaughlin was not going to stop.

Lawson raced to the car found by Houghton and gave the startled driver, William Bell, orders to follow the speeding car.

Jockeying for position, the cars tore down the road at top speeds. The bootlegger's McLaughlin out powered the car owned by Bell and Lawson gained only briefly as the cars rounded Crows Nest Lake. At one time the pursuing car gained on the young driver, coming to within one hundred feet of the other car, but Steve stepped on the gas and the big car's powerful motor gave him the speed he sought. It roared with life and he easily pulled away from his pursuers.

By ordinary reckoning, the winding road was a nightmare. Leaning out the car window Steve saw far below him the wind whipped lake where the water surged into white foam that hit the rocks lining the edge. He tightened his hands on the wheel, controlled the swaying car on the turns.

Moving fast, Lawson leaned out the window, took an unsteady aim and fired another shot at the fleeing car. As far as he could tell the shot went wide. Lawson did not see the blood that ran down the door of the other car.

Lawson became aware of one other bitter reality. Bell was slowing the car, applying the brakes.

"Why are we stopping? Come on man, we were getting so close! One more shot at the tires was all I needed."

"Flat!" The car rocked precariously to the side of the road. Driver and constable got out. Flat it was.

Lawson shook his head in disgust. Few men had ever seen him give way to any show of anger. Squinting into the sun, Lawson's eyes searched for the dust of the escaping vehicle.

William Bell got his tire irons out. He was looking for a flat rock to put the jack on so the weight of the car would not sink the jack into the soft soil.

Lawson turned to help, the chase was over, for now. There would be other times, he was sure. He kicked at a puff ball growing on the side of the road.

As they looked at the tire, another car came from the east and stopped about 20 feet away. It was the car belonging to Emilio Picariello.

Houghton and Bell watched warily as Lawson approached the Picariello vehicle. Picariello spoke to Lawson from inside his car but the wind took the words away and the watching men could not hear them. They did, however, hear Lawson's reply.

"You had better bring your son back, because if you don't get him, I'll go and get him!"

The face of the elder Picariello was grim with rage.

The driver of the other car had hurriedly finished the tire change. He heard the sharp command of the lawman to the notoriously strong minded Picariello. Bell indicated his car was ready to roll again.

"Let's go, Bell!" Lawson's voice was crisp, sure again. He was silent on the road returning to Coleman.

At Sentinel, the travelling car met a vehicle driven by Sergeant Scott. The Dodge car pulled to the side of the road, turned around to follow Bell's car. Both cars stopped and Lawson got into Scott's vehicle for the return ride home.

"What happened in Coleman anyway?" Scott was curious to know the details. The look on the Englishman's face told him it was a subject to be left until later, maybe in the barracks after supper. Scott left the constable in Coleman and continued to his home in Blairmore.

Just a short distance from Coleman Scott came upon Emilio Picariello's car. The door on the left hand side of the car was open and Picariello put his hand out as a signal to stop.

To Scott, Picariello said, "You did not get the load."

Scott replied, "No. But we are not through with you yet, I am going to lay charges against you under the Motor Vehicles Act for speeding and also blocking the road and furthermore, the Constable is going to make charges against you and Steve for speeding through Coleman and failing to stop when signalled."

Emilio shook his head.

"That don't worry me. I don't care how many times I put you in the ditch. I saved my load and that is all I care about. All I care about is saving my load and it is lucky for Lawson he did not shoot my boy. If he did, I would kill him."

It was a statement simple in its utterance. It was a statement as old as his people, an eye for an eye.

"Pic, you are crazy! I have heard these things before."

Emilio stepped on his gas pedal and drove in the direction of Blairmore.

It took Scott another ten minutes to come to the town of Blairmore. On the way he passed a car heading west with two of Picariello's men in it. In Blairmore, Scott saw Emilio again, standing on the corner near the Alberta Hotel. He was talking to three men, Mr. Christopher, M.P., Mr. Risk of the Pass Clothing Store and George Allen. It was 15 minutes after 6 p.m. It was the supper hour, soon the murk of the mountain night would fall about them.

By Picariello's own account of the day, he returned to the hotel and went to the lobby to think. He needed to get Steve back home. The loaded car could be left over the provincial border. Steve would know where to hide the car and with someone else driving, Steve could come back into Alberta and no one would be the wiser.

Picariello went to the garage and sent McAlpine on his way to find Steve. Emilio lingered, stony faced, worrying about his son, wondering if he had safely navigated the winding dangerous road around the lake.

The shrill jangling of the telephone made him start. He moved quickly to answer it.

"Emilio?" The voice was Italian, that is all anyone ever learned of the caller.

"Emilio? Patrone?"

"What is it?"

Picariello's face went white, then dark, as he listened to the voice on the other end.

"Shot at him? Why?"

The voice went on, cautious but insistent in Emilio's ear.

"The dirty bastards!" Hatred spewed from Picariello. "How bad they hurt my Stefano? He not dead?"

There was no reassurance from the telephone.

"I do not know, patrone ..."

The Italian's face was gray as he hung the receiver back on its hook. He turned blindly and stumbled out the door.[3]

---

3. Many details throughout chapter from inquest and trial papers including verbatim statements made by people involved. McKinley - Cameron Papers, Glenbow Alberta Institute.

XIII

THE
VENDETTA

IT WAS EVENING when Stephen Lawson made his way to the barracks and home. The wind died to a quiet whisper; gently rippled the tangled grass studded with the summer's last colour. The setting sun gave hint of a poppy sky to follow but the man did not notice; he had failed and his neck was corded with anger.

Stephen Oldacres Lawson was tired; the weariness showed in his face, in the slump of his usually ramrod shoulders. His dejection was heightened by a dusty sweat-stained uniform and, although to most he appeared singularly unconcerned, he was deeply dejected by the failure of the afternoon.

His wife met him at the door. She reached up to smooth the frown that started on his face and he relaxed. Their eyes met; the look between them recalling moments their hearts touched and laughter they shared.

She leaned against the door frame and wiped her hands on her apron. Supper was almost ready. Maggie Lawson's face was flushed from the heat of the kitchen stove and behind her a spicy aroma permeated the house. She pushed back small tendrils of hair that curled and clung to her damp forehead.

"Hot today," she smiled up at him, "looks like a storm brewing." She had a smudge of flour on her cheek.

He didn't answer. She knew the events of the afternoon, could tell by the set of his shoulders that he was troubled.

She knew instinctively what was bothering him and she

avoided the subject; whispered pieties would be scorned by him.

Lawson was a conscientious officer with a very high regard for the work he was to do. When he resigned his post in Fernie, the police commission prevailed upon him to stay; they knew they were losing a good man. But the 35 year old man had made up his mind.

The man caught his horse, took a brush to his back, watered him at the mossy trough and swatted him gently on the rump, turning the gelding out to graze. A dog jumped around him, held its head to one side and gave the man a quizzical look while playful growls and barks came from deep in his throat. The screen door slammed. A child came from the house to pour a little milk in a cat-licked dish. A purring ball of fur was quickly at the dish, forepaws together, haunches low.

" 'lo Daddy."

The child, receiving his tight smile, was satisfied and moved off to the footbridge where she filled her hands with the last of the wild pea flowers.

At the house Lawson removed his belt and holster and hung his tunic on a peg. His undershirt was darkened by sweat. He broke open his gun, emptied it of shells, put the shells and gun on top of a chest of drawers. Feeling eyes upon him, he turned to see his daughter watching him.

"I'm going to the show, Daddy! Mama said I could. The one at the Grand." He nodded to her statement and looked at his watch. It was almost 7 o'clock. He ran a hand over the wiry stubble on his chin and walked into the kitchen.

Lawson heard the sloshing sounds of batter being beaten. The laughter of children playing in a vacant lot mingled with the sound of crickets under the wood flooring. Soon the evening light would be claimed by the high peaks overshadowing the valley floor. He picked up the axe from behind the stove, remembered it needed a new handle and absentmindedly went to the office, swinging the handle from a strong wrist. His thirteen year old daughter followed him, hopping from one foot to the other. She tried to draw her father into a conversation.

"It's called, 'For Big Stakes' Daddy, and Tom Mix is in it. All about a mysterious rider on a big black horse. That's what the picture poster says."

Lawson turned to nod at the girl, a faint tired smile on his lips. He watched her as she left, moving at a dog trot across the yard to the footbridge. The girl turned and waved to him as she skipped happily down the road.

In the kitchen of the bootlegger the air was not as tranquil.

Maria met her husband at the door and not knowing of the events of the afternoon she greeted him almost gaily, asking if he was ready to eat. In her hand she carried a bowl of black olives swimming in oil, sprinkled with garlic and pure oregano from Greece. Behind her on the table among many plates set for the evening meal, la sogliola and a plate of le patate fritte[1] graced the table. A whole ball of provolone cheese sat on the sideboard. To her bewilderment the man turned on her, his fist clenched.

"How can I eat, woman? How can you think of putting food in your mouth, when your son, your Stefano, may be dead? Dead! I said, Dead! "

The woman sank into a chair, colour rose high in her face, then quickly faded. Her face contorted and tears sprang to her eyes. She covered her mouth with her hands.

"What? Where?" She bit her underlip and a drop of deep red stained the fullness of her lips.

"It doesn't matter," he raged, not wanting to go over the painful events of the telephone call.

"They have shot him, they have hurt him. My son!"

His face was drained of colour but his voice was firm.

The big man's face was stony; he seemed larger in his anger as he strode through the rooms, his passion barely concealed.

In a burst of anger and frustration he swept a table of pictures and ornaments to the floor. An old vase, its sides

---

1. La sogliola — dish of fish (sole); le patate fritte — fried potatoes.

painted with pink roses lay shattered, its white chips a sharp contrast to the dark flooring. Motes of dust spun dizzily in the last glittering rays of sun that entered the room. There were tears of sorrow on Emilio's cheeks; he stamped his feet, shouted and roared, lapsing into his native dialect as the pain from his heart seeped through his body.

Carefully the people of the house crept to the kitchen; supper was forgotten and the cheese curled and darkened in the hot air.

Emilio, his massive head sunk down on his chest, told the events of the afternoon chase. With glowing rage he spoke of the shooting to the stilled, silent people gathered around him, who, sick at heart, did not want to believe the story they were hearing.

His tale ended, complete and final; now all that remained to be done was to get his son back, dead or alive! His face was flushed now and he turned to walk to the window. Quietly in the silent kitchen came the voice.

"If they will use guns, then so do we!"

Now Emilio calmed a little as his family gathered around him. Seeking consolation for the injustice he felt was done to him, he sought their advice and help. They were his allies; his accomplices that would soothe and aid him in his time of trouble. He looked to his family for refuge, for support, as a balm; the load had been saved but the price paid was too high.

He had been opposed; the Provincials were trying to intimidate him and they seemed determined now that his loads should not go through. It was odd he thought, most times the loads went through with no trouble but recently, they seemed to know of his every move. His thoughts were interrupted by voices in the room as the shocked people at once seemed to find their tongues. They questioned him and one another about the shooting.

The bootlegger needed to feel his family's loyalty and as he sought to gather them together during this crisis, he thought of his family's honour, and the reasons it had been tarnished by events of the afternoon.

This episode would be avenged, to be sure. It was an affront, the happenings of today, an affront that the authorities should now be hostile to him, as all along they had treated him with friendly camaraderie.

They knew what he was doing and when he was caught he paid his just dues. They had never before become ugly or aggressive in this manner, had never been so determined to stop him and thinking about the turn of events he knew he had to see Lawson, had to square up with him to get his son back. He didn't care about the money, the fines or the bother of the court; he only wanted his son back. He would see Lawson.

The people in the kitchen were all talking at once, working themselves into a passionate babble of voices as they pelted each other with questions. The only person not excited was the giant Tony, who, not of a fiery and passionate nature, was nevertheless concerned and troubled as he sat, dumbfounded by the heated conversations swirling around him. He sat tilted in his chair, gazing dolefully at the people in the room.

Tony's eye caught a movement near the door as Florence crept into the room. Her face was ghostly, her eyes enormous and he knew from the look on her pinched face that she heard everything from just outside the door. He felt sorry for the girl, knew she was put upon to take risks on the runs.

Supple as a wand she crouched on a stool near the stove. Nobody paid heed or noticed she was there.

All at once a heated argument developed. Picariello was determined to confront Lawson; Maria was equally determined that he not go. Her intuition told her it would be fateful for the two to meet while the Italian was in so explosive a mood.

"Please, Emilio, please... he may not be dead, wait and see, oh please my husband, I understand...." her lips trembled, tears coursed down her cheeks.

"Siete Ignoranti Tutti!" (you understand nothing)

The man was brutal in his disillusionment.

"Be quiet, be quiet, I say! I will decide here." His broad features were distorted by surprise at his wife's interference.

But she continued on, not paying any attention to her husband.

"If he were dead," she sobbed, "somebody would come tell us." She moaned and crooned, almost to herself, her voice dropping so low the people in the room strained to hear her. "Somebody would come and tell us.... of Stefano... of my bambino."

There was silence in the room. Guido lifted the lid from the burner and spat into the fire; he spoke nervously, haltingly.

"Where's McAlpine'?" He looked around the room, seeking the man who should be there.

Picariello straightened his shoulders, turned and said quietly, "I sent him to Michel, to find out what he can, maybe bring the boy home."

"Let us wait then, patrone."

Guido pleaded with his boss. He was anxious for the wild eyed man who seemed to oscillate between his own impulses and the pleas of his wife.

The kitchen was airless, stifling in the late autumn sun. Picariello sat with his head in his hands, not hearing the arguments swirling so about him. The angry outbursts rose and fell like waves in a brutal sea.

Finally he ran his fingers through his cropped hair. Quietly, almost deadly, he spoke.

"I'm going to see him, he hurt my son. He can go with me, get my son back. We see about the load later."

Restlessly he searched the room with dull eyes as he debated who was to be his companion on the trip to Coleman. Guido sat perfectly still. Tony licked dry lips, he wanted no part of this trip.

The girl Florence rose hesitantly from her seat. Her voice was mellifluous as she started to suggest a plan to get Steve back.

The Italian boss was immediately irritated by her nerve. He started to rave at her, then stopped suddenly, a dawning light etched in his eyes as he gave her a long, searching look.

He chose her. "Get your coat," he commanded.

The girl disappeared from the room. Maria started to speak, found nothing coming from her mouth and her hands traced hopeless patterns into the stillness of the air.

It was two quiet people who travelled the dusty road back to Coleman. The Emperor was sullen and morose. He hunched his broad shoulders, his fingers tightened around the steering wheel. He furrowed his brows against the sinking sun and his full fleshy face was ruddy in its dying light. Beside him on the seat the girl was a shrivelled figure as she appeared smaller, her face impassive as she watched the roadside, seeing only a dusting of minute violet flowers in the grass.

In the mountains there were blotches of glowing orange amid the dark green of the pines. The hot wind, torched by the sun's furnace, rouged the leaves of the aspen, turned them to flaming gold. Now the wind quieted, the leaves drooped and were still.

They drove in silence, broken only by the rumble of the car on the uneven road and the tuneless whistling of the man beside her. The whistling got on Florence's nerves. It was an irritable sound of breath forced through tight lips with no attempt at a tune or the avoidance of dissonant sounds.

Looking up, Florence saw familiar landmarks of the town where Lawson lived. She turned, broke the stillness, her voice husky with nervousness.

"Whose car is this?" She looked around the car as for the first time, noting it was not one of Picariello's fleet, although it was a McLaughlin Special Super Six.

"It's Petrie's, from Hillcrest." Picariello replied caustically. "McAlphine got it this morning to work on." He blinked and gripped the wheel tighter. It was the only car left in the garage; McAlpine had been sent to Michel with his car, Steve had fled with another and Carlo was away with the third.

Again the pair fell silent. At the outskirts of the small town, Emilio pulled to the side of the road, pulled a gun from under his coat, loaded it and put it on his lap.[2]

---

2. Picariello had two permits to carry guns; one for the 38 revolver, the other for a 32 calibre Colt Automatic, both issued for business protection on April 23, 1922.

Near the post office he stopped the car again and drew another gun from under the seat and thrust it into her lap. It lay on her lap glinting darkly against the paddy green of her coat.

"For protection!" He offered the explanation tersely. He showed his teeth, "...they used guns this afternoon," he paused reflecting, "...we meet them on their own terms."

Pellets of sweat formed on his brow. For all his earlier agitation he now appeared steady, unruffled, though bitterness seeped into and through his words. The girl wanted to refuse the gun but it was difficult to gauge the mood of the man, and she thought better of it.

She looked at the gun, her coal black hair, bobbed to the shoulders, fell across her cheek as she bent her head. The gun was impersonal, cold, an awesome thing. She curled her small hand around its bulk and it slid into her fingers to nestle coldly against her flesh. She hated the feel of the gun, its smallness and the power it had to destroy. She hated too the sharp sounds, the gunpowder smell, the feeling of death surrounding it.

A small grimace crossed her face as she nodded her head to the man, said, "thanks," and slipped it into her pocket. She felt its heaviness against her thigh. Neither of them saw a young girl watching them from the sidewalk as she waited for the show.

Police Chief John Houghton of the Coleman Municipal Police left his town office shortly before seven o'clock. He decided to walk the short distance for his mail. Meeting the Reverend D.K. Allen, they walked slowly until reaching the post office. After a few minutes Houghton left Allen at the post office and walked towards the Price residence. On the way he stopped to talk with Sam Moore and Tom Jackson, two residents of the town. While they stood on the wooden walk a car approached and the men turned to look.

"It's Picariello, back in town." said Sam.

"Yeah," Tom spit into the dusty road, "you think he had enough this afternoon." He laughed and licked his lips.

Houghton heard their comments, watched the car as it went by at a moderate speed, noted the Losandro woman was again with the Italian. The car was going in the direction of the barracks and Houghton frowned, feeling uneasy. He left the men and started to walk again, moving leisurely in the direction of the Grand Theatre, intending to stop by the barracks to see Lawson and talk over the events of the afternoon. At the Grand Theatre he saw Lawson's oldest daughter waiting with other children for the evening show.

Back at the barracks home of Lawson daylight was giving way to dusk.

"Can we go to the picture show too?"

To this question Maggie Lawson replied, "If you get the war tax tickets, we'll go." She put her arm around her young daughter giving her a gentle hug.

Mrs. Lawson took out the washbowl, picked up a towel to wipe her hands and face. The sounds of a motor car cut through the autumn stillness. She went to the half open door of the barracks.

First she said, "It's the sergeant," then she corrected herself, "Stephen.... there's a man here... man and a woman with a red tammie on."

She walked back to the sitting room to look for the war tax in the library table drawer. He passed her and she smiled gently.

"Don't be long, supper's about ready. Then I promised we'd go to the show."

The car came to a stop in front of the barracks, the motor died. Lawson came to the door; his greeting was terse, his eyes narrowed.

"Yes, Sir?" Lawson was always correct, whether in or out of uniform.

Lawson's nine year old daughter left the kitchen and came around the corner of the house to see her father rest his foot on the running board of the car. His hands were hooked in the pockets of his breeches. She watched curiously as the sounds of an argument reached her.

Emilio leaned out the window.

"Where's my boy?" he asked, his voice was low, modulated.

"I don't know," Lawson replied. He leaned his arm on the car.

"Well," Emilio replied, "you shot him, you are going with me to get him, find him!" His voice started to rise. Lawson raised an eyebrow, quizzically.

Picariello was now excited, his suppressed rage rising within, about to burst into flame. He spoke hoarsely, "Do you know you shot my son!"

Lawson cooly replied, "I didn't shoot your son, I shot at the car, at the tires which I was allowed to do. [3]

Lawson changed his position, he stood on the running board and stooped to lean on the window frame of the car. Picariello's face was now livid with anger.

With deadly earnestness Lawson continued, "Picariello, this bootlegging has to be cut out and these are my orders. I am going to do it."

Picariello's eyes were glassy, his breath came in short gasps and he said, through barely parted lips, as he pointed to the gun in his lap, "if you don't cut out this shooting, I can shoot too!"

Lawson, seeing the gun, leaped forward to grab it. He put his arms around the bull neck of the man, forcing the arm that had the gun downwards, away from him.

With growing horror Florence had listened to the conversation as it grew to monstrous proportions and she pleaded with the Italian to leave. Picariello silenced her with a look. When the scuffle broke out she watched wide-eyed, twisting away from the man in the seat.

There was a deafening roar in the car. A bullet whizzed past close to her feet.

Standing at the washbowl Maggie heard the first shot and thinking the child had knocked something off the library

---

3. Many details throughout chapter from interview files with the late Charles Costanzo, uncle of Florence.

table, called out, "What have you knocked over?"

"Nothing, Mama."

More shots went wild, one hitting the speedometer, the other smashing through the windshield. Glass rained over Florence and she smelled gun powder.

Maggie looked up and walked to the sitting room door. She paused, a frown creased her face. Talking to her younger daughter she said, "Daddy probably wants to arrest that woman and put her in jail and she doesn't want to go."

Lawson heard the roar of the gun in his ears. He loosened his hold on Picariello, turned and ran towards shelter at the side of the barracks.

One shot, its flash cutting through the gloom of the evening, struck the running man and he fell to the ground. The child around the corner of the house screamed and ran to her mother. Her mother threw down the towel and ran to the front door.

She found her husband lying in a heap at the corner of the house and screamed as she ran to him, kneeling at his side. She saw the blood splotched hole under his shoulder, saw the red blood oozing from the wound.

Anguished cries came from her trembling lips. Maggie lifted his head, cradled him to her crying, "No, no...oh God, not Stephen...please, not Stephen..."

Emilio was dazed, at his side the girl sobbed. The big car roared to life, he gunned the motor and drove across the vacant lot, scattering glass behind him.

Just then a man ran across the lot and Picariello leaned out of the car, swore and yelled at him to get out of the way. He wanted to flee, and headed the car east, down the main street past incredulous onlookers and people running in the direction of the barracks. A crowd gathered around the fallen man.

Police Chief Houghton heard the shots as he walked to the barracks. Lawson's daughter was standing in front of the theatre.

"That's your daddy!" He grabbed her arm and she turned to him in fright. Together they ran in the direction of the shots. At the barracks Maggie struggled to her feet, turned towards the house, crying incoherently for help. Fred Cole, visiting his mother in the hospital across the way, ran with nurse Thorpe to the man on the ground. People were running, across fields, down streets, as the word spread. Houghton took one look at the fallen man and ran to the telephone. Inside, Maggie stood, holding onto a chair for support, the telephone receiver swung gently from its cord at her side.

Her lips barely moved, her words frozen to her mouth.

"I've called."

" Who?"

"Sergeant Scott."

She turned from the telephone; Houghton eased her down into a chair. Houghton then rang up the Inspector at the Alberta Provincial Police detachment in Lethbridge.

Dr. Charles Vincent Scott left the Coleman Hospital about seven o'clock, going to his office across the street. He glanced about as he walked wearily down the steps. The road was clear; a few children played about the police detachment. It was quiet and the dusky evening air was soft.

Scott sat in his old swivel chair and started to fill out orders for his patients. The screen door banged and two lads rushed in.

"Quick, Doc, somebody's bin shot!"

The doctor grabbed his black bag from his desk and running with the boys to the detachment found Lawson lying on the ground, his head cradled in a man's lap.

Dropping to his knees, Scott searched for a pulse. The man was barely alive. The doctor felt for his heart; it was still beating.

"Lift him, careful now! To the hospital, and quickly!"

Husky men lifted the still living constable and carried him to the hospital nearby. Administering stimulants, the doctor tried to keep the man alive. The heart, however, continued to flutter, then stopped.

Houghton ran in. He started to speak but his words trailed off as Scott looked up and he read what was in his face.

"He's gone... what bastard did this to him?"

The doctor started to undress the slain man. Houghton, his face ashen, helped. The doctor found the wound on the right scapula (right shoulder blade) near the fourth rib. There was a patch of bruising on the left breast. His probing fingers found and extracted the bullet.

He held it to the light, spoke slowly.

"Looks like its notched!" He handed it to Houghton to examine.

"Yeah, it is," Houghton wrapped the bullet in a piece of cotton wool, "it's from a 38!"

Slowly, his face grim, the doctor pulled the sheet over the man's face. He looked up, the same sadness came to his eyes as it had so very many times during his long career as a doctor. He spoke to Houghton.

"His wife is waiting, she's taking it bad. You'll have to tell her."[4]

---

4. Many details throughout chapter from trial papers including verbatim statements made by people involved. McKinley-Cameron Papers, Glenbow Alberta Institute.

XIV

TWO FOR THE SHOW

THE BIG CAR sped back towards the town of Blairmore. The girl's sobs combined with sounds from the car as it hit the bumps in the road. More than once Florence grabbed at the wheel to steady the car in its erratic movements. Picariello then started to talk.

"He tried to get the gun!" Picariello was adamant. He half-turned to the girl and told her to load his gun. Florence didn't know how and her hands shook. Picariello commanded her to steer the car while he quickly loaded. They were nearing home but the man drove past the hotel, stopping at the far side of town near the tracks where the scrub brush was high.

"Wait here!" he turned to push the girl from the car but she braced herself, wouldn't open the door. Florence was horrified; she fought against going into the darkening thicket beside the road. Awkwardly she fastened the buttons of her coat.

His big hand shot out to grab the front of the coat, drawing the material into a bunch. His wrist twisted the material, straining the buttons. His heavy jowled face seemed bloated as he came menacingly close to hers.

"You have to wait here. I come back but first, I have to find out how the boy is!" Now he pushed the girl away, loosening his fingers from the material and a button, a bit of material hanging to its threads, fell unnoticed to the floor boards. He sought to reassure the eyes that never left his face.

"I come back. You wait, close to the road. Hide. Nobody will see you. Here is my gun. Take it for protection."

He had forgotten about the gun in the girl's pocket. He seemed anxious to rid himself of his gun.

As always, Picariello had his way. Florence took him at his word and with a short, abrupt motion she was out of the car and into the brush.

The man turned the car, skidding in the loose dirt of the road. Again he headed west, to where he hoped to find McAlpine and his son.

As Picariello travelled the Pass roads he passed friends from the town of Fernie. They waved but he was intent on his driving, lost in thought, anxious about his son and he did not return the greeting. He could not find either of the two he sought and he drove aimlessly now, distracted by worry. He hunched his massive shoulders, feeling fear and the need to hide, the need to get off the road. He wanted some place where he could think clearly, sort out the crowding events of the day and decide what he should do.

He turned his car back to Blairmore and left it at the back of the Cosmopolitan Hotel. Cautiously he paused beside a spoke-rimmed dray while he surveyed the street. Panting, he could feel his heart thudding deep in his chest. The street was deserted. There was the dampish smell of coal fires, the night smells of approaching winter. He headed into the brush where he left the girl.

After Emilio left, Florence hid in the scrub brush, alone and afraid. The silence of the night was broken only by the sounds of a rising wind running through the brush above her head. She sank down on a rotted log, closed her eyes and tried to stop the churning feelings she felt through her body. She started as a sound was heard. Someone was coming! In the gloom Picariello's bulk loomed before her.

He spoke brusquely, "I find nothing!" He spread his hands flat with aggravation. "We hide, decide what to do..." She questioned him hesitantly. "Steve? And the policeman? How are ...?" He cut her off. Some of his old confidence was coming back as he reasoned to himself. He was the person dishonoured. He avenged his dishonour. The vendetta was done, an eye for an eye.

"I don't know," he grunted, "we hide, wait and see."

They moved furtively down the tracks in the windy dark. Again the man spoke, his words punctuating the darkness.

"We hide in the old shack for the night." He moved to a decrepit old building and pushed in the decaying door.

A soft rain fell, coursing down the soot-covered panes of the shack window like tears on the dirty cheeks of a child. Outside, pines dropped their wooden carvings onto a mossy roof.

Florence sank down on an old bench near the wall and slid her cold hands into her pockets. She felt the guns and recoiled at the touch. She moved restlessly and felt their heaviness as she moved to the window to stand beside him. Picariello was wiping a hole in the dirt encrusted pane.

Florence tried to hand him the guns but he took only one and left the shack saying, "Tell them, only one gun in the car." She knew he was disposing of one gun, leaving the other one with her.

A hotness went over her body as she realized the implications of what he was saying. He came back into the shack and continued slowly, "Tell them it was an accident, tell them ... only one gun was in car. You say you shot ...," he was drawing her into his private warfare, making her the scapegoat of his revenge. She wanted to shriek at him, deny him the right to do this, but he continued on, ignoring her hand that clutched his sleeve. "You shot, ... just you, in self defense."

His voice was commanding as he moved slowly about the shack, stumbling in the silence of the night. Each sound of his footsteps shattered the quietness and she was sure the sounds could be heard from the shack. She wanted him to be quiet, sure that search parties were out. Somehow they had to escape detection.

As the man outlined her place in the drama Florence became feverish, throwing her coat on the dirty bench. She heard a sound and went to stand by the door, peering anxiously outside into the dark. She rocked herself back and forth, her hands, folded across her chest, dirtied the fine white cotton of her flounced sleeves. Her blue skirt was wrinkled, her black stockings were snagged and torn from the brush.

"You shot ... yes, by accident ... tell them you shot ... when you saw his gun ... someone shot at you and you shot back in self defence!" The man was searching for a clever stratagem as he rubbed his large hand over grizzled jowls. "Look here, you shot by accident. A woman can, you know. To protect herself ... a woman can. They no touch a woman." He was coolly appraising the situation, indifferent to her feelings or thoughts.

Florence was gullible and she wanted him to reassure her, to tell her it was all right, that she would be safe in his explanation of the shooting. Besides, she thought, the man may not be badly hurt. She started to speak.

He again cut her off quickly. He was losing patience in his struggle with himself. "No mind. Listen! You say you did it. I go free and with money I get the best lawyers. Then you go free too."

His voice was anxious, he pleaded with her. Carlo had always testified the way Picariello wanted him to, now he wanted, no commanded, her to do the same.

"You and Carlo have money then, maybe $10,000 heh? You start a new life somewhere."[1]

His pleading voice crept inside and hammered at her brain. He seemed to know her innermost dreams. She turned her head, rubbing her temples as she tried to think. In his soft pleading way, he had some of Steve's careless charm and she was engulfed in a wave of unbearable pain as she thought of the predicament they were in.

The wretched girl struggled into her coat. She sighed deeply as she sank to the bench, a stricken look in her eyes. The two fugitives finally dozed fitfully in the cold shack, unaware of the storm of activity gathering about them in the Pass.

Telephone wires crackled up and down the Pass. News of the shooting stirred the small towns from end to end. In each

---

1. Taped interview files with the late Charles Costanzo, brother of Vincenzo and uncle of Florence.

division, every man in the police forces in Alberta and British Columbia steeled himself for the manhunt that would follow.

In Lethbridge, Inspector Bavin had, on receiving the news, placed a call to Royal Canadian Mounted Police Superintendent Junget and Inspector Dunworthy of the British Columbia Provincial police. In Fernie it was 8 o'clock when Sergeant Hanna informed Royal Canadian Mounted Police Inspector Bruce of the East Kootenai sub-district of the shooting. Bruce gave concise orders:

"Send the following party under Sergeant J.A. Wright: Corporals Gallagher, Wilson, and Smith. Constables Ellison, Reed, Doree and Anderson. Send them by car to the Crow's Nest. Make sure all are fully armed! Have them search all vehicles coming through the Pass!"

The men started their journey about 8:30 p.m. Bruce telephoned Inspector Dunwoody who quickly decided to accompany the police to the Pass. Dunwoody provided the private automobiles for the trip. Turning again to the telephone Bruce instructed the Royal Canadian Mounted Police officers at Michel and Blairmore to assist in the search.

In the Pass, police patrolled the roads and searched all trails leading to logging and mining camps. During the long night quiet conferences were held. There were hushed calls and tense movements as carloads of police converged on the scene. Police in all towns and cities in both Alberta and British Columbia were alerted to watch for the pair. All outlets from the Pass were blocked at each end. The Inspector from Lethbridge arrived in the Pass at midnight to take charge of the search. With him came two carloads of police.

Commissioner Bryan of the Alberta Provincial Police sent five men from Edmonton on the night train and in his terse statement to the press stated:

"This is the third policeman to be killed in three years while engaged in the work of stamping out bootlegging!"

After a call from Coleman, two more policemen arrived on the Friday morning train from Edmonton along with Alberta Provincial Police Assistant Superintendent, John Nicholson and Detective Pass.

On the morning of the 22nd, Bruce received a telephone call from the Royal Canadian Mounted Police Commanding Officer at Lethbridge. Ten members of his force were being sent to assist. Bruce consulted with Inspector Bavin, then proceeded to station his men at strategic points throughout the Pass. He stationed 5 men to work under Sergeant Wright at the Crow's Nest, increased the Michel detachment by one man, sent a mounted patrol to Coleman, and detailed Constables Tutin and Clark to assist in the Blairmore search. He kept the remainder of his detail in reserve for the night duty. Throughout the long night calls were made to all detachments and barracks in southern Alberta. The barracks in Bow Island, Alberta received such a call.

In the Bow Island kitchen of the police detachment a 35 year old man cleaned and checked his revolver. To his wife's quizzical look he said, "I've been called in. One of our men has been shot. Lawson by name." He turned to look in the small mirror, brushed his short brown hair.

"Where do you go?" she sounded nervous. Their four children spooned porridge into hungry mouths at the small table. It often crossed her mind; what would happen to her and the children if he should happen to have an accident. She thought of the slain policeman's wife and shuddered.

Bradner [2] walked across the room to take the shirt she had just finished ironing. "Blairmore," he answered absentmindedly. She watched him as he put on the fresh shirt, covering a tattoo on his right forearm. 'Might not be back for several days. Those Italians are crafty, might be hard to find."

Before he shrugged into his coat, he mashed his cigarette into the tin can that served as an ashtray. While in uniform members of the police force were obliged to refrain from

---

2. Irish born Bradner, a man of 6'1", joined the Alberta Provincial Police November 16, 1918 coming from 7 years of duty with the Royal North West Mounted Police. He was a first class constable with the A.P.P. with the regiment number of 100. His military decorations included the 1916 Silver Badge for Honourable Service. His posting was to the barracks in Bow Island, Alberta.

smoking on the streets or in public places. It would be some time before he could have another cigarette. He turned to give his wife a nod and was gone.

In Blairmore, Bradner received his orders from Inspector Bavin. He was to search all houses on the south side of the tracks. Also assigned to this duty were Constables Tutin and Clark of the Royal Canadian Mounted Police.

Bavin cautioned the men. "There is a very large Italian population in this area and these people have been influenced by this man as he has risen above them. For the most part the Italians are bound by custom and language; they instinctively aid and support each other and keep to a tight impenetrable circle. They will be wary of you and of anyone in an official capacity. They are quick to defend their honour and that of their friends and families. They will aid Picariello in his bid for freedom. You cannot expect any help from them."[3]

A concentrated hunt was to start in the ragged light of a madder dawn. Clouds like mare's tails hung low in the sky. All available men were called to headquarters for a briefing.

Pacing up and down, the Inspector again spoke tersely.

"We believe the fugitives are still in the Pass. The man is Italian, a big man, name of Picariello. He is stockily built, five foot, seven inches. Weighs 200 lbs. Has black hair streaked with gray, moustached. Last seen wearing a gray suit and cap. He has a woman with him. Losandro, wife of one of his drivers, is a small person with dark hair. Picariello knows this mountainous country minutely and has many friends. He is very wealthy and could buy his escape. Be careful! They are both armed!"

The booted and spurred men dispersed to their assigned duties while another group manning the stations came in for their briefing.

Having received their orders, Sergeant Scott, Corporal Stevens of the Royal Canadian Mounted Police stationed at

---

3. Chapter contains details from police records including verbatim speech; direct quotes and factual information from inquest papers, newspapers and preliminary trial papers.

Blairmore and Detective Lawrence from Lethbridge along with Constable Moriarity went to the door of the Picariello home.

To Scott's knock there came a call. "Chi e?" (Who is it?) A white-faced but fully composed Maria opened the door. She was still fully dressed. "He is not here," she shook her head defensively, "not know where he go." She gave them a dissembling look, aware that they had not spoken to her.

Without a word they brushed past her into the kitchen. Several of the drivers were there but no greeting was given. The Italian community was closing tightly around their own.

Scott and Moriarity went upstairs to search the bedrooms. Stevens and Lawrence were to search the downstairs and the garage. Scott remembered he didn't have a search warrant but the woman at the door hadn't asked for one. She followed them from room to room.

"Where is her room?" Scott asked brusquely.

"Philomena?" Maria reverted to the girl's Italian name.

"Yeah, Florence!" he nodded his head affirmatively.

"Philomena, she sleep here, with the bambino," She pointed. "Carlo, he sleep upstairs, in hotel." She inclined her head towards the stairway.

Scott stepped into the bedroom, flooded it with light; a sleepy child stirred.

There were women's clothes in the room. Scott thought he recognized some of them as belonging to the girl. Still, he could not be sure. He walked over to the dresser, rifled through some letters on top. They were addressed to Mrs. C. Losandro. The photographs on the dresser, in gilt frames, were of an older couple and children. Scott did not recognize any of them. He opened the drawers, pushed clothes to one side, his fingers caught on the satin of the garments. There was nothing of interest in the dresser. Moriarity whistled softly and looked up from the trunk he was ransacking. Scott looked over his shoulder; the smell of moldy leather floated up to him. Moriarity straightened and turned, in his outstretched hand were 2 Dominion cartridge boxes with 31 shells in one and 17 shells in the other. They were 32 calibre automatic shells!

The two men went across the hall to another bedroom. They rummaged through documents and clothing as Maria stood ashen faced near the door. Scott combed the drawers of a tall chiffonier, tossing papers and clothes aside in abandon. In the bottom drawer he found what they were looking for; 36 shells of two different makes for a 38 calibre which would fit the gun used by the bootleggers. There were also some 30-30 shells of Dominion cartridge.

On the lower floor Detective Lawrence searched the parlour and walked around to the hotel. Corporal Stevens did a quick search of the kitchen. As he was doing this he heard a motor car drive up in the back. Stevens went to the window and looked out. He then ran to the back of the house to see a man getting out of a McLaughlin car.

"What's your name?" he asked warily, instantly on the alert in case of trouble.

"I, Steve Dorenzo."

"This your car?"

"No! I jist bringing it back." The car was damaged. There was a jagged hole in the windshield. Opalescent light glinted on the silvered edges.

"Where'd you get it?"

"Behind the hotel," the man waved his arm wildly in the direction, "Cos..mo..politan." He had trouble with the pronunciation of the name. The other men hurried from the house at the sounds of voices outside. As they ran around the corner Stevens was starting to inspect the car.

"You! Dorenzo!" Scott called out. He recognized the man.

"Yah, I Dorenzo!" the man was frightened at the sight of the uniformed men.

"You know the headquarters in the town of Frank?"

The man nodded his head affirmatively.

"Take this car there. Don't touch anything in the car or let anyone take anything out! You understand?"

"Yes sir! Yes sir!" The man climbed quickly into the damaged car, anxious to get away from the officers. He wanted no trouble. He didn't care how he was to get back to Blairmore, he would walk if necessary. He started the car and drove away.

"Good work Stevens. We'll search the car in the morning when the light is good."

"Yes sir! Thank you sir!" came the crisp reply.

It was mid-morning before the suspected murder car was searched. A group of officers stood by as a constable on his hands and knees ran his fingers carefully over the floor boards trying to avoid the broken glass. He whistled, stood up from his crouching position and held out what he found.

"They used two guns!" He had an unexploded 32 calibre shell and an empty one in his hand. He picked up bits of glass and a button and handed them over to Sergeant Scott. He looked over the floorboards carefully again. "Nothing more here, sir." Scott was thoughtful, "The car should go into police custody in Lethbridge. Get the mechanic McAlpine to drive it down."

"But he works for Picariello! And, isn't he in custody? I thought they were holding him in Michel?"

Scott stopped and turned. "Yeah, they were. McAlpine, Losandro and young Picariello were in the pokey at Michel but they released McAlpine and another man they were holding. They're still holding Carlo Losandro as a material witness. They got young Picariello's car too."

"Steve Picariello make a statement yet?" The constable was curious for details.

The sergeant was thoughtful, "… no, of course, he refused. All they got him for was a $100.00 fine for carrying a gun. The boy's as tight-lipped as the rest." He smiled a wry smile, he too was given to laconism.

In Coleman, Coroner Alex M. Morrison completed an affidavit, swearing before a Commissioner of Oaths that Lawson did not come to his death from natural causes or by mere accident or mischance but that he came to his death by violence. He then summoned a jury.

At 2:30 in the quiet afternoon on Friday, September 22, a hushed group of jurymen and witnesses gathered for the inquest into the death of Stephen Oldacres Lawson.

Maggie Lawson arrived holding tightly to the hands of her two young daughters. The coroner cleared this throat and somberly took charge of the proceedings. He looked over to reporter Herbert W.T. Sydenham-Maisey of Macleod to see if he was ready. Maisey was sworn as reporter and the coroner opened the inquest.

J.W. McDonald, K.C. represented the Crown while D.G. MacKenzie of the firm of Gillis and MacKenzie represented Picariello. The jury were in their places — Harold Houghton, Ernest Houghton, William Burrows, Charles Scott, Jerry Lonsberry and D.K. Allan. Reverend Allan was to be the foreman.

Maggie Lawson was the first witness called. McDonald rose to question her.

"What is your occupation or who were you the wife of?"

"The wife of Stephen Lawson."

"What position did he hold?"

Quietly came the firm reply. "Constable in the Alberta Provincial Police."

"You remember the afternoon of the 21? Something happened very unusual in the evening of that day?"

"Yes." The voice was soft, tender, composed. "Mr. Lawson and I were sitting in the house ..."

"About what time?"

"About 7 o'clock. Mr. Lawson was putting a handle on the axe for me, and we were sitting and talking together. My little girl asked to go to the picture show."

"Which girl was that?"

"Tibbie. I said if she would get the war tax we could go. The door was half open and I thought the Sergeant had come. I looked out and said, 'No. It's a man and woman with a red tammie on'."

"Did you notice anything else about her clothing?"

"She had a dark coat." The people in the room looked intently at the woman as she recalled the events of the evening. When she recalled finding her husband her voice broke and she paused. Deliberately, carefully, holding down the tremors in her voice she swallowed, then continued. "... I turned him over and I saw he had been ... had been shot ... in the back ... somewhere ..." Again her voice trailed off. She took another breath, lifted her head and continued.

"The nurse and a young fellow from the hospital came and I said, 'you take care of him for a minute while I phone for Sergeant Scott'." The next sentences came out mechanically, "I went and phoned him, then Mr. Houghton came in and when I came back Dr. Scott and someone was carrying Stephen to the hospital."

"Was he dead then? Did he speak to you?"

Dully came the answer, "No, he didn't speak."

"Did you see him when he was dead ... about 5 minutes after?"

Tears welled into her eyes and spilled over, coursing down pale cheeks. "I saw him after ... when he was dead."

"Did you see the car that was there?"

"Yes, I saw the car and I saw it drive away just as I ran to him, the car hit close to the garage right like that and made for the Blairmore road. I mentioned that when I phoned for Sergeant Scott."

"Did you see the people in the car?"

"I didn't pay any attention. I just know there was a man and woman in the car, a woman with a red tammie on."

"Did you know the man?"

"No."

"Or what kind of man he is?" The question was loaded with prejudice.

"No."

McDonald turned away; he had finished his questions. MacKenzie declined to question the witness and she was allowed to leave the box.

One of Lawson's daughters was the next to be called. She was too young to be sworn but McDonald rose to question her, asking what happened on that night.

The child shook her head and started in. "Daddy was

standing at the car. He put his arm around the man's neck and then they shot him, the lady shot and then the man shot, and then they shot again, the lady let off the last shot and Daddy fell down. A nurse came out and then a man came out and they took him to the hospital." The words fairly tumbled out of the child. She took a deep breath. Her testimony charged that the first, second and third shots went wild. The fourth shot was the fatal shot.

"Did you see your Daddy fall?"

"Yes."

"Did you see anyone in the car?"

"No. I just saw the man." Here, the child contradicted herself, forgetting about the lady in the car. "I don't know if I could pick his face out now."

"What sort of man was he?"

"He had a moustache."

"Was he a fat man or a thin man?"

"He looked to be thin to me. I don't know if he was or not." The child looked confused.

"You saw your Daddy fall, did you?"

"Yes."

"Did you see what the car did then?"

"Yes, it went away around to Blairmore."

"You were out before your mother?"

"Yes. I was standing in front and I saw them. I ran and called Mama. I went up to the front door and saw her out there."

"Did your Daddy get up again after he fell?"

"No, he never got up." The child shook her head sadly. "They took him to the hospital."

"Now, whereabouts were you standing, girlie?" The man started off on a different line of questioning.

"I was standing around the corner of the house."

"Whereabouts did your Daddy fall?"

"Daddy fell down right by the hospital."

"You weren't very far off when the shouting was going on?"

"Yes, but when I saw him shoot, I went around the back."

Here was evidence that the man had shot too! There were no

further questions and the child left the stand. She ran to her mother's arms and buried her head in her lap. Maggie smoothed the child's hair, drew her into her arms. The other daughter was called next. She, too, was examined by Mr. McDonald.

"Do you know what it means to take an oath and kiss the bible?"

"Yes Sir."

"Do you know what will happen if you don't tell the truth?"

"I'll go to the bad place and the bad man will get me."

"How old are you?"

"Thirteen." She took the oath solemnly, her right hand holding the bible.

McDonald took the child through all the questions of who her father and mother were, how her father made his living, where they lived and then asked, "Do you remember the night of the 21st? Was there something unusual happened that night? What happened? Tell us all you know." The voice was probing, coaxing.

"I went down to the show. I left the house about 7 o'clock, around there, and by the show Pic came through with a girl in his car."

"Who is Pic?" The man seemed surprised at the use of the name.

"A kind of man with a moustache on. There was a bunch of boys standing by the show and they told me. I didn't believe them and I looked, then I saw Pic and this girl."

"Do you know what sort of clothes the girl wore?"

"She had a red tam and a new coat. We followed them up, and I said to my friend Effie, I said we would follow them up, just out of spite. They were between Graham's and the Post Office, and he took something out of his pocket and put it in the girl's lap and she said, 'Thank you' and he said something else, I wouldn't say for sure what, but something like Crow's Nest. I thought he was going to the Crow's Nest. They went up and we followed them until they turned down our street. I said to Effie, 'Let's go up and see where he lands' and he went up and we went to our door. We heard shots and then Daddy dropped. He started up the car and drove away. He was swearing at a bunch of men to get out of the way. He had another car to follow him. He waved his hand and this car stopped at the garage and put out his light and stopped his engine. He waited in the car and when he saw Pic he beckoned to him and went towards the Blairmore road. I saw Mr. Houghton and he said it was Daddy and we went home. That's all I know about it." The girl finished in a rush, her face was flushed and she was close to tears.

McDonald paused, looked off in the distance. He ignored the reference to the other car. Again he questioned the girl.

"Where were you when the shooting was going on?"

"Down at the Grant corner."

"Is that very far from the house?"

"No, not quite a block."

"Do you know who was shooting?"

"I think it was Pic and the girl, because he put something in the girl's lap."

"Was the shooting near the car, could you tell that?"

"No, I don't think I could. I seen just around the door."

"You saw it was Pic's car?"

"Yes."

"Was it from near that direction that the shooting came?"

"It was near our place I know. I saw Daddy in between our house and the hospital. Pic shot his last shot and got his car in full speed. He ran over all the tin cans between the house and the pole, then lit out for Blairmore. That's all I saw. I went and stayed home."

At that point Picariello's counsel, Mr. MacKenzie rose to question the girl.

"When Picariello, or whoever was in the car, put something in the girl's lap was the car stopped?"

"Yes."

"At the side of the street?"

"Yes, he said something to the girl and she said, 'Thank you', when she saw this in her lap, and he started to go."

"Where was he stopped?"

"Between Graham's and the Post Office."

"Close to the sidewalk?"

"Yes, I stood right by the car and pretended I wanted someone." The girl tilted her head, a bit of mettle in her voice.

There were no further questions from MacKenzie and she too stepped down to hurry to her mother's side.

At this point the men representing the Crown and Picariello conferred with the Coroner. Mr. Morrison turned to those assembled, "This inquest is adjourned until Saturday morning, September 23, at 10 o'clock. You may all go now, except the jury who will view the body."

His tone was matter-of-fact, the tone of a man used to events that were shattering to those involved but ordinary to him in his day to day work.

Maggie took the girls back to the barrack's home. There were people about, coming and going, carrying food, asking what they could do to ease her burden. Her mother, Mrs. Mckenzie, arrived from Macleod to find her wan-faced daughter steady and composed.

"Have they been found ...?" the older woman's voice trailed off. What if they should come back here, she wondered to herself.

"No," her daughter answered, "but they will be!" She added this firmly; from long experience she was used to the time it took.

At the time the inquest was starting, Bradner and the two men assigned to him, Clark and Tutin, started their methodical search of the predominantly Italian homes on the south side of the railway tracks in Blairmore. It was 2:15 in the afternoon.

The Italian community was silent; inscrutable faces watched as the officers went from home to home, prying into sheds and coal bins, peering into closets and under beds in a systematic search for the fugitives. Their questions met with no response.

The men stopped at the last house on the street. An old woman stood in the doorway, leaning on a cane. Clark and

Tutin searched the house; the woman, her eyes kindled with hatred, ogled Bradner as he searched a motley group of sheds in the weed filled yard. Bradner turned to appraise the view around him. He spotted an old shack near the cement mill at the base of a steep slope.

"Whose shack is that?" He spoke to the old woman who followed his every move across the yard.

"No speak, no speak Engleesh!" was the snarled reply. She brandished her cane at the man.

Tutin and Clark emerged from the house. Bradner looked at his watch. It had been a long day and they were tired. He started to speak. "It's 3:30 now and we've finished ...," he broke off, "look there, there's a man running ..."

A man had slipped from the shack. He crouched as he ran, trying to conceal himself as he moved clumsily up the side of the slope towards the east.

"Where?"

"There! Up the side of the mountain ... there he goes!"

The three officers ran after the man and started up the slope. There was a flash of blue in the doorway of the shack but the men did not notice. The man climbed the incline and looked back for a brief moment. Only then did the officers get a look at his face.

"It's Picariello! It's him!" Tutin cried. In a split second the man was gone from the top.

Bradner wished he had his rifle to shoot ahead of the man. He pulled his gun into his hand as he scrambled up the side, his feet slipping and sliding in the soft shale of the incline. Rocks, dislodged by his feet, clattered to the base below. Bradner shouted to the other two.

"Make a circuit! Cut him off!"

"Hurry! Get him!"

The officers shouted to each other as they panted and scrambled up the slope, pulling at their sidearms as they climbed. Dust, blown up by strong winds, smarted their eyes.

At the top, they took cover. Clark spotted the man in the brush not far from the rocky ledge. Picariello was bent over, rubbing his leg.

"Look out, he carries a gun strapped to his leg!" With drawn guns they cautiously approached the man.

"Emilio Picariello, you are under arrest!"

"Don't be afraid," came the calm reply, "I no shoot you signori!" There was defeat in his voice.

Bradner, in his soft Irish brogue, gave the man the warning as he put him under arrest.

"You need not say anything. You have nothing to hope from any promises or favour and nothing to fear from any threat whether or not you say anything. Anything you do say may be used in evidence."

Clark and Tutin searched the man; to their surprise they found nothing but two pockets of twelve gauge shotgun shells.

Bradner took Picariello's arm and started back down the hill. The bootlegger stopped, rubbed his leg and complained of cramps. Tutin, his gun still held on the man, asked Clark to get a car. Then the bootlegger, resting on the side of the hill, started to talk. Picariello needed to know; his eyes were anxious in his sad face.

"How is my boy? Is dead?" The words came hesitant, soft.

"No." They answered, "he was just shot in the hand."

Softly, almost to himself, the bootlegger said, "... damn, damn them, that bastard in Michel told me he was shot."

Bradner queried, "And you thought he was dead?" To this, Picariello nodded yes.

After a pause, Picariello asked, "How is Lawson?"

Bradner replied tersely, "He's dead!"

Picarello flinched, his face blanched, he seemed to shrink into the rocky face of the hill. Bradner commented, almost to himself, "Lawson never had a chance to defend himself." Picariello moved his lips, his words were disjointed, confused as he mumbled about Lawson and a gun. Then he was silent, stony-faced.

They walked him to the roadway where the car had come up. Bradner questioned him as to the whereabouts of Florence.

The man was uncooperative, morose, first saying he did not know, then almost as an afterthought, "you know where the car was found, well, I leave her there." They asked him where his gun was and his reply was, "I got no gun."

Picariello was taken to the headquarters at Frank and handed over to Inspector Bavin. Bradner and the two constables returned to the area where Picariello was found, searched the area minutely for weapons and finding nothing, returned to the barracks.

News of the capture of Picariello spread quickly throughout the town. It was shouted with glee in some sections; whispered with quiet remorse in the Italian community. When told of the capture, Maggie Lawson collapsed from strain.

About 4 o'clock Scott and Moriarity returned to the barracks in Blairmore. The telephone rang and an unidentified voice on the other end told them where to find the Losandro woman.

Scott drove the car. As soon as the Gibeau house was sighted and before the car could come to a complete stop, Moriarity was out of the car and running towards the house. Scott came puffing up behind as the door opened; a small woman stood in the hall. Confused at her sudden appearance Moriarity said, "Don't be afraid."

To this remark, Florence replied, "I have nothing to fear. He's dead and I'm alive and that's all there is to it!" Her face in the shadows was resigned. She turned on her heel and went back into a room. The officers were taken back by this show of unconcern.

The girl put on her tam and coat. Moriarity gave her the warning and told her he would have to search her. She raised her arms slightly while he made his search. In her pockets he found several cartridges.

With her quiet capture Florence had disarmed the men. They expected more, some violence such as scratching, kicking, some verbal abuse. It was obvious the girl had no idea of the extent of the predicament she was in. Right now her only thought was of her hunger and she complained bitterly of her starvation.

Back at the police barracks Scott led her into the kitchen. Florence sat at the table while he made coffee, fried several eggs and cut slices of bread. The girl removed her tam and coat, then devoured the food. Over her coffee Florence was inclined to talk.

Moriarity came into the kitchen and leaned his tall frame against the drainboard.

"Has the car been found?" She addressed neither of the two men in particular.

"Yes, the Provincials have it down in Lethbridge"

The girl was silent for a minute. Finally, "... and Steve, how is he?" She appeared to be nonchalant but there was a small catch in her voice.

"He's okay, just a scratch."

She seemed relieved. She finished her coffee and asked for more. After a pause she continued, "Have you seen the gun?"

"No, where is it? The men have been out looking ..."

She interrupted him, stating matter of factly, "It's down at Gibeau's place!" indicating the house they had just come from.

Scott left the girl in the kitchen under watch by Moriarity and another constable while he went to get the gun. When he came back Florence turned to him and said, "There could have been some shooting but two shots were fired at us in the car!" She paused and bit her lip. "I did not shoot till I saw a gun pointed at me!"

"Yes!" The man leaned forward in his chair. It was a question, he was urging her on. His face showed greed for the information she was about to impart.

"One grazed my leg, the other broke the windshield."

"Did you fire?"

"When Lawson put his arms around Mr. Picariello's neck, I fired." She paused, considering what she was supposed to be telling. "Mr. Picariello didn't fire at all. Lawson had hold of him around the neck." It was a flat statement given without emotion. A regurgitation of events from a mind completely obliterated by a power greater than hers. Again as in all her life, Florence did as she was told. She turned to Scott, her eyes like quiescent pools, and stated firmly, "I killed Lawson by accident. There was only one gun in the car!"

Scott's eyebrows raised. He let out his suspended breath. There was evidence of two guns from the spent shells on the floor-boards of the car.

Scott locked the girl in a cell and went back to the kitchen. He was acutely conscious of not having made notes of the conversation nor did he have the girl sign a statement. Just at the time he was pondering this, his thoughts turned to the gun found at the Gibeau house. The gun had been found under a cushion and still had five shells in the chambers. It was a.38 calibre revolver.

Moriarity came back into the room and Scott showed him the gun. Florence had told him the gun was hers but the shells found in her room were for a 32 calibre and wouldn't fit this gun. Scott put the gun in a paper sack, then tagged the sack. Saying nothing, he left the room.

It was difficult to gauge the mood of the Italian population. In the early evening a consultation at the Frank headquarters raised doubts about the security of the prisoners. It was decided to move Picariello to the Alberta Provincial Police cells in Lethbridge. A special court sitting to charge him with murder was scheduled for Saturday morning, he had to be taken down to Lethbridge anyway, and a move now would get him out of the turbulent Pass area.

At the cell door Corporal Hidson motioned Picariello to his feet. He held handcuffs by his side and seeing them, Picariello asked that he not be bound.

"Sorry!" Hidson said, "orders!" He led the man through the rooms of the headquarters and was joined by Detective Pass and Corporal Drummond. The Italian had not yet made a statement.

Picariello settled himself in the back seat of the car. He was flanked by Pass and Drummond. Hidson would drive. Through the window Emilio caught sight of Scott in the midst of police officers watching the scene. He leaned forward to call to the man and Scott sauntered over to look in the window.

"Can anything be done to get my boy home from Michel?" Scott hesitated. It seemed strange to hear a plea in Picariello's voice. Without waiting for an answer from Scott, Emilio continued, "They told me Steve, my son, was shot. I don't remember anything after that." The man was obviously distraught. He was denying any knowledge of the shooting. The Italian looked down at his manacled hands, Hidson started the car and Scott moved back as the car moved away.

There was a chill in the air on Saturday morning when the inquest again opened at 10 o'clock. A late rising sun warmed the frost rimmed streets as birds, late in their migrating patterns, clustered into balding trees, vocal in excitement of the long flight before them.

Again the jury took their places, the witnesses filed into the room and the reporter was sworn in. The coroner shuffled through his papers and to the hushed room, said loudly, "The next witness please, Dr. C.V. Scott."

Scott came to the stand, put his hand on the bible and took his oath. He was asked if anything unusual happened on the evening of the 21st of September.

"Yes, a remarkable occurrence. I left the hospital building at the hour of 7 o'clock on the night of the 21st and passed to my office across the street. As I walked down the steps the road was clear. There was nobody about the police detachment except some little children. When I was in my office for a few minutes some lads came and told me a man had been shot. I rushed out and ran over to the detachment of the police, right next to the hospital, and found Lawson lying on the ground with a small crowd of people around. No car was in sight at that time. Lawson was practically gone at the time."

At his words, Maggie Lawson's lips tightened and she drew her daughters close to her. The Doctor continued.

"I felt his heart and it was still beating. I had him removed immediately to the hospital in the hope that I could do something for him and the heart continued to flutter for a few minutes after I brought him in."

Scott was silent, reflective for a moment. "I did all I could.

After examining him, I pronounced him dead."

McDonald then asked, "What, in your opinion, did cause the death of Stephen Lawson?"

"Hemorrhage from the aorta caused by a bullet wound passing through the right shoulder to the left breast."

McDonald asked the doctor about the bullet he removed. Scott was confused about the size of the bullet but noted it had been notched by some sharp object.

"Would that be caused by coming into contact with any hard substance during the course of it through the body?"

"The bullet only passed through the scapula and one rib. I don't think it would be possible for these bones to cause any mark on the bullet."

"Your observation on the bullet leads you to what belief in reference to the direction that the bullet took before entering him. That is the direction with reference to himself, did it hit him in the front ... or ...?"

The room was deadly silent as the Doctor slowly answered the question.

"The bullet hit him ... in the back!"

"In the back?" The question got the anticipated response from the jury it was designed to.

"Yes."

"No further questions."

The Crown counsel inclined his head towards Mr. MacKenzie and said crisply, "Your witness."

MacKenzie had only one question of the Doctor. "What is the right scapula?"

The answer, "The right shoulder blade."

At this point the foreman of the jury requested that the bullet be produced and it was sent for. Dr. Scott was allowed to leave the stand.

One by one, the witnesses rose to tell their version of the events and of the part they played in the aftermath. A question rose over the suspected murder car. The witness was a hoistman for the International Mines.

"I was coming up by the corner of the Coleman Hotel and

met a fellow by the name of Jackson. Houghton came along and we talked about the chase. While we stood there a car turned the corner and I said, 'Here's Pic's car!'. With that I walked off." The man nodded his head for emphasis.

"You said that to Houghton, did you?"

"Yes, sir! I said 'Here's Pic's car!' just like that." He repeated himself, satisfied with his account. "I went away and Jackson went across the street to Bell's. I walked for a while and waited for him to come out. As I came to the corner of the bank, Mrs. Emerson came along and said, 'Help, help! That fellow in that car has shot Lawson!' We went along to the barracks but by the time we got there, Lawson was inside the hospital."

"Did you see where the car went?"

"No, I didn't see where it went. In fact I couldn't say I saw his car. I said the car was Pic's car but I couldn't swear who the occupants of the car were. In fact, I couldn't swear it was Pic's car. It was one very like his." The man was back tracking.

MacKenzie rose to question him.

"What made you say this was Pic's car if you didn't see who was in it?" His tone was accusing.

"It was a McLaughlin Special and there are not many of them around."

MacKenzie raised his eyebrows, "I thought there was quite a lot of them around here?"

"Not with those handles on the door!" The witness was smug.

"Did you see the handles?"

"Yes, the light shone on them."

"It was just because you saw a McLaughlin Special you thought it was Pic's car?" He prodded the witness, getting his point across to the jury members.

"Yes, with those handles on the door. There's lots of specials in the country but not with handles on the outside of the doors."

Now the jury took a greater interest in the witness.

"Did you see which way the car turned when you said, 'Here comes Pic's car'."

"Yes, it turned around by the bank there."

"No further questions, you may step down."

Dr. Scott was recalled to the stand. He was asked to look at and identify the bullet. "That is the bullet I removed from the body of Lawson. I identify it."

The bullet was sealed in an envelope and marked Exhibit one.

The jury members questioned the doctor again about the markings on the bullet, asking if it were possible for a bone to mark the bullet as it was marked.

Scott replied, "It would be possible for bone to do that. In this case it is not possible that the bones through which it passed, the shoulder blade and one rib, could have done that. It would be impossible for these bones to mark a bullet with sharp edges on it."

With that, the parade of witnesses and exhibits had come to an end. The jury had one final question of the court.

"Have there been any guns found on Picariello or the person of that woman?"

The response was negative. McDonald turned to address the jury.

"All evidence in this case has not been submitted. We have only heard evidence as to whom, where and by what means Constable Lawson came to his death. You, as members of the Coroner's jury, do not have to find out who killed Stephen Lawson."[4]

The jury was ushered into a private room for the deliberations. The witnesses arose to escape the stuffiness of the courtroom. They emerged into bright sunlight and stood blinking on the steps as the light hit their eyes. There was an uneasy silence as they exchanged small stilted remarks about the weather. They did not have long to wait; the jury was out for only 30 minutes.

The foreman of the jury read the verdict:

---

4. Direct quotes and details from the Lethbridge Daily Harald, 1922, along with verbatim statements from inquest, McKinley Cameron Papers, Glenbow Alberta Institute.

"That Stephen O. Lawson, Alberta Provincial Police Officer, stationed at Coleman, Alberta came to his death on September 21st, 1922 at or about 7:00 p.m. in front of the Alberta Provincial Police detachment, Coleman, Alberta by a bullet fired from a revolver in the possession of the occupant of a car which stood in front of the Alberta Provincial Police Barracks, Coleman, Alberta."

The jury did not mention the names of the occupants of the car. The inquisition form was signed by each juryman.

After the inquest Coroner Morrison submitted a billing of $71.00 to the Attorney General's department for the witnesses and jurors. The coroner received $20.00, 6 jurymen received $2.00 each, E. Houghton, the guard received $5.00 and all the witnesses received $1.00. The doctor received $25.00 for his time. Herbert-Maisey completed his transcripts. He made three copies, one for the agent of the Attorney General, one for Inspector Bavin, the Officer Commanding at Lethbridge and one for Sergeant Scott. His bill came to $44.65. The cost of his transcript was $35.95; his hotel bill and meals came to $4.00. The remainder of $4.70 was for his return train fare from Macleod to Coleman.

While the complexities of justice were moving forward, another scene was taking place in the holding cells of the Frank gaol.

Shortly after the news of the verdict was heard in Frank, a car was brought around to the front of the detachment where Florence was being held. The surprised girl was hurried from her cell into the waiting car. A frown creased her forehead as a matron and several policemen got into the car beside her.

"Where are you taking me?" she demanded to know.

The reply was off hand, she was no longer a person but the property of the law. "To court ... in Lethbridge ..."

She sat back in the cushions of the seat, wondering.

In Lethbridge, Provincial Magistrate E.N. Barker was preparing to preside over a special sitting of the Alberta Provincial Police Court. A formal charge of murder was to be laid against the man now lodged in the cells below, and his woman companion. As soon as Florence arrived at the court house, the sitting would start.

Picariello's counsel for these proceedings, Mr. C.F. Harris, arrived at the court house early in the day. A worried looking Emilio was brought from his cell to meet with his counsel in the detective's room. After a short time, Picariello came from the room. He was smoking a cigar and was visibly less tense.

At 4 o'clock, Emilio was taken from his basement cell. Manacled and heavily guarded, he was brought into the court room to face the magistrate.

Emilio looked around the room. For once he was conscious of his appearance. He ran his hand over his unshaven chin, pulled at the front of his blue serge suit jacket. The pants were rumpled and creased from the long hours sitting in a cell. He wore the same shirt with no collar or waistcoat and his cuffs were dirty, the shirt front stained. He rose only once during his court appearance and that was to hear the charge of murder read against him.

"That one Emilio Picariello did, on the evening of September 21st at Coleman, Alberta murder Stephen Lawson, Alberta Provincial Police Constable."

After hearing the charge he sat down heavily and watched with keen eyes as his counsel asked for a one week remand instead of having the preliminary hearing start the next Thursday.

Approaching the bench Mr. Harris told the magistrate that if for any special reason the Crown Prosecutor at Macleod desired to have the preliminary hearing on Thursday next, he would certainly endeavour to get ready but it would suit his client's interests and the court if it could be postponed.

The judge shifted in his seat, shuffled some papers and said, "The court will consider your request. We will have the next prisoner please."

At his words there was instant activity, almost feverish in haste. Again tightly guarded, Picariello was taken from the room as Florence was brought in another door. She did not see

Emilio as he left.

There was someone with some compassion as she was not manacled but the guard assigned to her was heavy. It was ironical they should fear her she thought, looking at the heavy flank of guards around her. Florence stood straight as the charge of murder was read; she appeared nonchalant to the rest of the people in the room. The charge did not seem to visibly move her and they thought her hard. Then the magistrate deemed the preliminary hearing would take place Monday, October 2 at 10 o'clock in the morning in the town of Coleman. Court was dismissed.[5]

To the newspaper reporters clustered outside the court house, Harris stated only he and J.E. Gillis of Blairmore had been retained for the defence.

"No," he said, "Picariello has given no thought to any outside counsel until after the preliminary. "In fact," he added with a raised eyebrow, "We are taking this action as we believe there are facts in the case that have not as yet been disclosed to the public and at the preliminary hearing charges against both the accused will be dismissed."

There was an instant clamour at this remark and he was besieged and pushed at for clarification of his statement. But the counsel stated firmly, "no more now, terrible sorry, I'm very busy, sorry ..." and walked away.

Florence was returned to her basement cell and as the heavy door was closing upon her, she was acutely aware of a feeling of dread growing within. It was a nameless horror of doubts that whirled around in her mind until her head began to spin. Mr. Pic had promised; it was just a matter of time before she would be free, but hour by hour her life was slipping into a parlous state. Her emotions wavered, slipping between wonder at the attention she was receiving, to fear and rage at the nonentity she had become in the hands of the police. To them she was more than a number, she was a criminal, a killer of one

---

5. Ibid.

of their kind. Florence wanted to run away, to escape, to seek safety at her mother's side.

Again, thinking of her family, she sat down hard on the thinly covered bunk and looked wildly around her. At the end of the night she would come to know every inch of the cement poured ceiling, tracing and retracing with her eyes the imprint of wood in the cement. Outside the heavy barred door, the white painted brick was crumbly looking and scarred. A naked bulb, covered with only a green shade, hung from the ceiling. Pipes went thither and yon down the cold corridor. Small shreds of evening light sank into the cell through cross barred windows. There was a nose wrinkling smell of sweat and urine. The young girl fought back her tears; seemed more diminutive than ever, a pathetic looking creature who lay down on the hard bunk and sobbed.

Emilio too, sat mutely in his basement cell. He was told of his transfer to the Lethbridge Gaol; it would become his home for the week before the preliminary hearing. At 5:45 pm., Saturday, September 23rd, a carload of police escorted their prisoner through stone gates towards a formidable red brick building that was the Lethbridge Gaol.

Heavily manacled, Emilio was subjected to the procedures accorded all criminals as he stood between guards and watched his property as it was turned over to the Chief Guard. There was a hostile light in the man's eyes as the guard fumbled through the bootlegger's money and papers, then filled out some forms.

Emilio was given a prisoner's number of A 4135. He was listed as age 43, with a weight of 212 pounds, at a height of 5'7" married with no alias. The guard's scratchy pen listed his occupation as hotel keeper and a Roman Catholic born in Italy. His crime was listed as murder and the term he entered the prison as remand. On another sheet of paper he listed the items taken from Emilio as one watch with the crystal cracked, one key, some letters and cash of $29.30. The guard sealed the watch in a brown envelope then put all the items in another bag and marked the name and number of the prisoner on the outside. After the guard completed his paperwork he read the charge to the man waiting before him. The jailer looked with interest at the bootlegger charged with the murder of the policeman.

In the basement of the gaol Picariello was escorted through sickly green painted corridors to a small room where he was told to remove his clothes. In humiliation he did so and naked, followed the guards to the showers.

The water was hot, the disinfectant soap strong. A wave of homesickness, the first of many, assailed him. A coarse order from the watching guard brought him back to the reality of his surroundings. He turned off the water and dried himself on a rough towel. Again naked, he was taken to the clothes room where the guard drew his allotment of articles. Emilio drew on the well laundered prison clothing that further concealed his identity.

At the heavy iron barred entrance to the cell block, the guard gave the name and number of the prisoner and turned him over to the inside guard. A key turned noisily in the lock, the heavy door swung open. This was another world, a cage of echoes and signs, a place of rebellion held in tight check, a place of loneliness and despair.

The guard walked him a short distance; the metallic ring of metal upon metal grated the stillness. The night security bar had been closed and now it was opened to admit the prisoner to his cell. Again the sounds of confinement echoed dully from the heavy walls. The step of the guard melted away and Emilio was alone. Wearily, he lay down on the straw mattress and tried to sleep.

In the week that followed Emilio had his taste of prison drabness. His cell was of gray brick, the single light dull in the stone ceiling. His bed was a slab held to the wall by two chains. There was a water basin and toilet in a solid unit, nothing else. The only way to look out was through the bars that made up the front of the 8 x 10 cell and the only thing to see was the gray wall beyond.

The next day there was only one variance in the normal day

to day prison routine. Emilio was taken from his cell to the prison administration office, where, closely guarded, he was weighed, measured and had his fingerprints taken.

The days settled into long moody hours. He ate his meals alone, had no contact with the outside world except for visitors and private talks with his counsel. Emilio's sorrow deepened on Sunday as Maria was his first visitor. During the week his counsel visited often; McAlpine, the mechanic, signed the visitor's book and yet another friend came to offer comfort. In the gloom of his cell Emilio lay on the bed and thought over the events of the day.

Once a day Emilio was taken from his cell to the exercise yard where he walked alone under close watch. One guard stood on a cement pad in the middle of the walled yard; another watched from an enclosure in the wall. The prison rule was one of silence; for Emilio it was bleak days that slipped into the black nothingness of the nights.

In a Calgary gaol, Florence, too, spent a week in heart sinking loneliness. She saw none of her family and her only visitors were the lawyers Gillis and Harris who arrived in Calgary on Wednesday, September 27 and registered at the Palliser Hotel. They both had separate interviews with Florence at the gaol. Her eyes searched their faces hoping to find reassurance that all was going to be well. It was just a matter of time she reasoned to herself, trying to hold back falling tears. Pic had promised her … he promised … he promised.[6]

---

6. From interview files with the late Charles Costanzo, in which he states that Carlo tried to tell Vincenzo and Angela that there was no capital punishment for women in Canada. He wanted Florence to take the blame and with his money Picariello would get her off. Carlo told Vincenzo not to go to Florence, not to try to change her word, that she shot Lawson. Carlo's loyalty was to Picariello as always.

XV

THEY MADE A PROMISE

THE FUNERAL FOR the slain policeman was held Monday, September 25 in the town of Macleod. At one time Lawson had been their Chief of Police and in respect, flags were flown at half mast and many business houses closed their doors for 2 hours in the afternoon.

It was a calm autumn day. At the appointed time of 2:30 pm the body of Stephen Lawson was carried from the McKenzie residence to the Presbyterian Church for the service. At the door of the church the Reverend Mr. Kennedy, assisted by Reverend D.K. Allan of Coleman and Reverend Mr. Bryan of Calgary, formerly of Taber, waited, their books of prayer in their hands. The small church overflowed with relatives and friends.

Tears blurred the eyes of the mourners as Reverend Kennedy recalled Stephen's years of service. The perfume of many flowers scented the warm fall air. The service ended with a tribute to the man whose life was given in duty It was a fitting crown for the person who strove all his life to perform his duties faithfully.

The cortege emerging from the church was a scene of quiet beauty. The brilliant scarlet tunics of the Royal Canadian Mounted Police mingled with the autumn golds and browns of the equinoctial day. Led by the Lethbridge Pipe Band, the cortege was the largest ever seen in the small town. A firing party, headed by Major Barnes and composed of Macleod men from the 93rd battery followed; behind them marched the Masons.

The coffin was borne on a gun carriage and the pallbearers, Corporals Hidson and Frewin, Constables Engle, Wilson, Taylor and McDonald, walked behind. Constable Dey led the dead constable's horse. Following close behind were family and friends. Two cars, filled with flowers and wreaths, followed.

At the cemetery, the fresh earth of the open grave was stark against the tawny grass of the sun bleached graveyard. Sobs came from the women in the crowd as the solemn tones of the minister reading the prayers floated on the soft air.

"... the Lord is my Shepherd; I shall not want. In verdant pastures he gives me repose..."

The Masonic rites were performed; the firing squad fired off three rounds into the blue vaulted sky. The sharp retort split the stillness of the day. The last Post sounded and the body of Stephen Oldacres Lawson was consigned to the earth.

"... till you return to the ground, since out of it you were taken; for dust you are and unto dust you shall return..."

Maggie Lawson turned away. It was done.

Into the General Orders book of the Alberta Provincial police a clerk penned the following terse note:

"The undermentioned constable having met his death by being shot during the execution of his duty on September 21, 1922 is hereby struck off strength effective September 30, 1922. Regiment No. 248 Constable Lawson, S.O. of D.Division."

Driving back to the Pass after the funeral a business man remarked to his passenger, "This is an awful toll for the Liquor Act. I voted for prohibition but never again will I vote for it in its present form. In the old days we had two regulated saloons and some semblance of law and order. Now we have 21 places to get liquor and you all know what we have as the aftermath of this shooting! A dead officer, a widow and fatherless children! The price, in my opinion, is too high. This murder will be the death knell to bootlegging in the Pass."[1]

---

1. Quotation from the Lethbridge Daily Herald, 1922.

After the funeral, life in the small Pass towns returned to a form of normality. It was a quiet time of year, the time of a season change as the frost burned spots on the leaves and their colours blurred pointillistically together. The harvest was done, the fields denuded of their bounty, their rape complete. But underneath the calm beauty of the near winter days, tension was felt as people waited for the next scene in the drama. Wherever people gathered, the murder and the coming hearing, was the subject on their lips. Rumour and speculation passed from group to group and in some cases was taken as fact. Many expected a reduction in the crime from murder to manslaughter. Of the many rumours there was one that was true; the defence would try for a change of venue in view of strong feelings running throughout the southern Alberta population.

A waning October sun caught the glitter of mica in the stone gates of the Lethbridge Gaol as the cars escorting Picariello and his detail of guards passed through. It was 4:45 pm in the evening. Exhaust plumed the cooling night air as the cars moved quickly down the road. Emilio would spend the night in a cell in Frank prior to the start of the October 2 preliminary hearing scheduled for 10 am the next morning.

As the cars passed over the road towards his home Emilio looked with longing at the bench of mountains he knew so well. The setting sun, wan and frail, cast light towards the bleak prairies. It caught on the peaks, holding a reflection of newly fallen snow. The saw toothed bench was bathed in an ever changing pattern of moody blue and white.

The man riding in the car wanted so much to go home. His confinement was more than he could bear as he waited, pondered, thought about the charges laid against him.

Florence arrived the next morning, coming by train accompanied by a matron and Constable Moriarity. From the window of the day coach she saw the orange, red and mustard shades of the bushes intermingled with the sombre dark green of the pines. The mountains she loved, so serenely old, were littered with fresh snow patches. She was coming home and she both wanted and feared its approach. After the train ground to a stop, her escort hurried her to a waiting car for the short drive to Coleman.

In Coleman, throngs of people waited for the hearing to start. They clustered together on the worn wooden walks, hoping to catch a glimpse of the prisoners. When 500 people tried to get seats in the Town Hall, a hurried consultation was held and the hearing was moved to the Opera house. Even there, many were unable to get seats, and they peered through doorways and windows, jostling each other for room. There was a heavy detail of police in attendance, some of them sprinkled throughout the crowded house.

A stir went through the crowd as Maggie Lawson and her children arrived. The woman was serene; she did not look around but went directly to the seats reserved for them. The people in the room watched closely and were strangely quiet as they waited for the drama that was about to unfold.

The hearing was late in starting. At 10:15 there was a sudden lull in the quiet murmur of the crowd as Emilio Picariello was brought into the room.

Picariello was collarless. His head, closely cropped, was held high and he displayed little emotion as he took his place at the middle table facing the magistrate's chair. His usually lively face was subdued and he did not glance around but kept his eyes forward. He was manacled and guarded by seven armed policemen. None of his family appeared in the crowd; his wife was not in the room.

When Florence appeared a short time later she displayed the same nonchalant attitude she had during court in Lethbridge. It was an act learned at great expense over the years. She walked in, dressed in an expensive coat; cool, confident. She was chewing gum. Her eyes sought and found friends in the crowd and she waved to them. Her act hid her apprehension and the nagging feelings of doubt that were becoming stronger day by day. Picariello had promised her; it would only be a short time before she was released. Maybe later today she thought as she settled down in her seat and sighed.

221

Then the girl leaned forward, tried to catch Emilio's eye, and looked for some assurance, however small, that everything would be alright. He would fix everything, he always did. But Picariello did not acknowledge her presence; he stared straight ahead. Florence's matron caught hold of her arm, motioned her back. In the crowd, women nudged each other, whispered behind gloved hands and spread tales about 'that hussy'.

The hearing was scheduled for 2 days. The magistrate was J. W. Gresham; Herbert W.T. Sydenham-Maisey was again the reporter. A.A. McGillivray, Esq. K.C. and J.W. McDonald, Esq. K .C. appeared for the Crown. C. F. Harris, Esq. acted for the defence.

Both prisoners were unconcerned during the first of the hearing. They sat quietly, showing no emotion through the early technical evidence. Picariello yawned repeatedly and in the face of his friends and neighbours, managed to keep up an act of bravado. The crowd was strangely unsupportive of the prisoners. During the noon lunch break the prisoners were escorted to and from their cells and passing through the crowds outside, received no signs of friendship or encouragement from the watching people. There was instead an aloof silence from the crowd, a detachment shown by the people; they were afraid of the worst and wanted no part of their former friends and drew back less the taint touch them.

"The Crown calls Charles Losandro to the stand."

At the mention of his name, the short, stocky Italian took the stand. His swagger was all but gone, he appeared very earnest. Florence raised her head in disbelief, wondering why he should be called.

Mr. Harris for the defence, was instantly on his feet. He lodged an immediate objection to this testimony but his objection was overruled.

The questions posed to Carlo were incidental. He was asked to identify his wife. He then told of their marriage in the Fernie church. At the mention of her marriage and remembering bitterly her cage of white and where it had got her, Florence broke into audible weeping. Carlo gave her a hard look as he left the stand, willing her to look at him but she did not and he was ushered from the room.

Sergeant Scott was one of the first witnesses to be called. His evidence was given in a tone of formality. He testified that Florence claimed Picariello could not have fired any of the shots as he was being held by Lawson. All the events of the day were gone over, culminating with the search of the prisoner's rooms and finding the ammunition. Scott detailed the finding of the 38 calibre gun at the Gibeau residence, the fact that bullets for a 32 automatic were found in the car and told the court one gun was missing. He pointed out the ammunition found in the girl's room would not fit the gun found at the Gibeau home, but the bullets found in Picariello's bureau would fit the gun found.

Florence twisted and retwisted a white handkerchief in her hands as Scott recalled for the court the scene in the police quarter's kitchen.

At this point the defence counsel rose to question the man. In answer to a rain of questions Scott stated he did not ask Florence any questions in the kitchen nor did he encourage her to talk.

"Was she hysterical at the time?" Harris asked.

"Absolutely not!" was the answer.

Then Harris asked the man if any threat was used against the girl. "You did not tell her she would be hanged before Christmas?"

"Never!"

"Did you tell her that she could save her life if she put the blame on Picariello?"

"No, sir!"

The relentless questioning went on and on. As the day drew to an end, the full force of her plight dawned on the girl. Now the gravity of the charge was being brought into force. Still, she clung to the promise made by Picariello. He would get her out of it, but hour by hour, he too was being drawn into the web. How could he get her out if he could not help himself? She grew afraid. Back in her cell at Frank she paced the small area, coming to stop at the cell door. She clasped the bars with white knuckled hands. The eyes that stared through the barrier were fatigued with fear.

On the second day the witnesses implicated Emilio and Florence in the shooting. It was sworn the prisoners were the occupants of the death car. It was sworn Lawson was shot in the back with a notched bullet.

Maggie Lawson was then called to the stand. When she passed in front of Picariello, the man's ruddy face paled; his eyes grew small and he dropped his head as he swallowed nervously. Then, as Maggie quietly repeated the events of the night of September 21st, Florence broke down. Her gulping sobs could be heard throughout the room. Women in the crowd shifted nervously in their seats and fumbled through handbags for a handkerchief. Men stared at their boots and fingered their hats.

Maggie was asked if the man who drove the car the night of the murder was in the room. Picariello did not look up when Maggie, struggling with sobs, pointed to him and said simply, "That is the man!"

By late Tuesday, the hearing was ready to adjourn. But prior to the adjournment, Mr. Harris asked, "Your honour, the defence seriously and strenuously objects to any evidence being introduced at the trial that was not produced at this preliminary." At the utterance of this statement, Crown counsel McDonald was immediately on his feet.

"Your Honour, there is one witness, a Steve Dorenzo, who we anticipate calling. He was the driver of the car after it was deserted by the accused." He looked up at the Judge and continued.

"The Crown has not concealed or withheld any evidence that has a bearing on the case. If further investigation reveals any facts of value, then we feel we must present these facts to the court."

By 4 o'clock the hearing was over and Florence and Emilio were charged with murder and committed to stand trial at the first sitting of the Supreme Court in Macleod. Mr. Harris asked that the two be tried jointly.

Sydenham-Maisey transcribed the evidence of the hearing and presented the Attorney General with his billing of $253.45.

Picariello was kept in his cell until Wednesday, then taken back to the Lethbridge Gaol. He would remain there until Friday, November 24. At 4 pm on that day he was taken to the Calgary gaol. Florence was sent by train back to the Fort Saskatchewan penitentiary.

The young girl remembered very little of the trip back to the gaol. The last she remembered of her home was a small field on the outskirts of town, where the skimpy trodden down snow of last night showed the marks of a game of fox and geese. The pie cut circle was marked by the running feet of children, who, being the geese, laughed, called and teased the fox who strived to catch the fleet footed geese so he too could become one of them, leaving the caught one to don the mantle of the fox.

For days, the girl sat on her bunk in her austere cell, held her head in her hands and rocked back and forth. She could not even cry, her thoughts spun her around and around. Her world was crashing down around her, falling past her ears in grinding, crunching sounds as it pressed in upon her temples and forehead. She found her eyes couldn't move without causing exquisite pain. Her skin shone white against the gloom of the day. Her cry was the cry of all confined. She knew she was again in a prison, not just in the cell in which she stood, but in a prison of her own making. She thought of her dreams; she had been so sure there would come a time when she would be safe, snug in an impenetrable place. There would come a time when the chains that held her to Carlo would be broken and she would be free. Now she was chained even further, against her will, and this time the chains would not be broken. She shuddered and sat back against the wall of the cell. The cold of the rough surface seeped through to the marrow of her back and she shivered uncontrollably. She felt abandoned, so very much alone. But Picariello had promised... Carlo had promised, and she clung to this slender thread of hope.

After the preliminary trial the newspapers in Alberta went rampant with reports that dramatically tried and hung the accused. They vied with each other, searching out information to make the front pages with stories about the bootleggers. They glamourized Emilio, calling him an Emperor of a gang of rum runners, making untold amounts of money. Newsmen searched for colour on the man and in doing so, included Florence as his adopted daughter, his daughter-in-law or as discreetly suggested, his paramour.

The reports had a strong effect on the people of southern Alberta. The case was discussed and hashed over and rumours soon got out of hand. The murder was said to be deliberate, some said the bootlegger had often bragged about putting those in opposition to his business out of the way if they got too particular. And while the prisoners sat in moody isolation, both the defence and the prosecution were poring over every detail of the case for the trial scheduled to come up on October 16th.[2]

Well before the date of the trial, a change of venue was requested by S.B. Wood. K.C. acting on behalf of the accused. The trial was to be heard in the southern Alberta town of Macleod and it was because of feelings running through the southern part of the province that a change of venue was requested.

In court, Mr. Wood produced a large number of affidavits which were prepared and presented to the presiding Judge when Mr. McGillivray, acting for the crown, interrupted. He addressed the presiding Judge respectfully.

"Your Honour, a change of venue will undoubtedly bring much additional expense to the Crown. We are not entirely satisfied with this application." He paused, turned ever so slightly, his black robe swung in neat folds from its finely tucked top.

---

2. Picariello enlarged his counsel. His main defense counsel would be A. McKinley Cameron, K.C. of Calgary. Assisting him would be Mr. Herchmer of Fernie and McGillis and McKenzie of Blairmore. He wrote of this to Florence on October 18, 1922. McKinley Cameron Papers, Glenbow Alberta Institute.

"However," he continued gravely, "if your Lordship feels, after examining the affidavits filed, the accused will not get a fair trial, we are willing that a change of venue be made..." he paused and again pivoted on his heel, "with this provision." He let the full force of his words sink in as he proceeded slowly, "A cruel murder has been committed and it is expedient that the persons charged be tried as early as possible and practicable. ... in order to determine their guilt or otherwise."

The distinguished man had the full weight of the court in his hands as they sat quietly, waiting to hear him reveal his proposal.

"If your Lordship decides on a change of venue, I would urge that Calgary be considered as being the place least embarrassing and least expensive to all parties in due regard to the giving of a fair trial."

He added that there might be some difficulty for the court in keeping 45 witnesses together and he proposed a special sitting of the court be considered.

Mr. Wood was quick to agree with the Crown Counsel.

"I agree the trial should be ordered as speedily as is consistent with the proper serving of justice."

He then read from the affidavits. They came from Granum, Macleod, Blairmore, Coleman, Lundbreck, Nanton, Stavely, Claresholm, Bellevue and other places and towns in the south country. All stated the signatories felt local feelings were too strong and the fairness of the trial would be prejudiced should it be held in Macleod. Mr. Wood opted for a change of venue to Edmonton and added that Picariello was willing to post a bond for additional expenses incurred if the trial was held in Edmonton.

To this the Judge ponderously replied, "My impressions, Sir, are that the Edmonton papers did not differ in their treatment of this case; the name of Picariello does not convey anything to the people of Edmonton except in this case."

"But your Lordship, in Calgary he is well known!" was the quick reply.

The Judge was adamant. He folded his arms and leaned

forward, "Picariello's name has appeared on court records before this case and he appears to be a fairly well known character everywhere." The man was not being swayed by the arguments. McGillivray again entered the fray.

"The Crown will neither accept the bond or money from the accused." His voice had an edge of indignation to it. "If he is entitled to a change of venue, then he should have it without the penalty of bonds or otherwise." He was firm on this point, not about to back down. He added the final deciding note. "There is no agreement to show that Picariello would not get a fair trial at Calgary. If the court decides on a change of venue then the Crown is quite willing to agree that Calgary be the place." He then went on to say that the Edmonton papers were not far behind the south newspapers in their reports of the case.

"Your Honour, everyone has read the papers. In Edmonton, as elsewhere the papers are as lurid as in the south." He stopped to shuffle through some papers, picking up several to hold up.

"Here they are. 'Picariello kissed gun and swore to get Lawson' and another, Picariello and woman sought revenge', and there's more.

The Judge spoke. "Mr. Wood, at what time would the case for the defense be ready to go to trial in the event that a change of venue is granted?"

"Mr. Harris will not be ready for six weeks or more, your Honour."

This statement immediately drew a protest from McGillivray.

"Your Honour, this incident happened September 21st. This trial should not be delayed. We want to be fair but I protest strongly the extension suggested by my learned colleague." His protest was marked by strong disapproval which showed in his manner and in the frown on his face.

The court was silent. The Judge pondered as he looked over his papers. Finally after what seemed to be a very long time he spoke.

"I deem a change of venue to be desirable but do not agree

with the learned defense to the place of the trial being Edmonton. All arguments against the place of Calgary would apply equally as well to Edmonton and it would seem that Calgary would be the least inconvenient and least expensive place to hold the trial. I am sure a jury can be found that will not be prejudiced by any newspaper reports. I order the change of venue from Macleod to Calgary."

Mr. Wood was immediately on his feet. "Your Lordship, if we produce additional evidence to show the prejudice against the accused in the city of Calgary can we then renew our application for a change of venue to Edmonton?"

To this request the Judge replied, "I doubt, Sir, you would have the right without a preliminary application to the courts to decide this." His tone had a note of finality to it. At this Mr. Wood took his chair. The Judge then continued.

"I think the date of October 24th might be a reasonable date and surely the defence could be ready by that date but I will leave it to the Attorney General to decide whether a special sitting of the court will be held. Case dismissed."

He rose from his chair and the court was on its feet as he moved to his chambers.

Before October 24th Attorney General Brownlee decided on a special sitting of the Alberta Supreme Court to be held November 27th. All that was needed was approval from the Lieutenant Governor. The sittings would take in two murder charges, a joint one for Picariello and Losandro and another one for accused murderer, Sam Joy.

Now the Pass towns settled into uneasy quiet. McKinley Cameron of Calgary and Mr. Herchmer of Fernie met in Lethbridge during the week of November 8 on business with the case at hand.[3] By November 15th Maggie Lawson and her children had moved to Macleod and Constable Wells was established in the Coleman barracks. The Pass was again reminded of the murder when Maggie visited her friend, Mrs.

---

3. The Lethbridge Herald, November 8, 1922.

Paterson in Coleman on November 23rd. When she returned to her mother's house in Macleod, the sad and lonely woman sat down to pen a note to Mr. Bryan, Commissioner of the Alberta Provincial Police in Edmonton. ".... I have today received Government Certificates to the amount of $1615.00 forwarded by you. I wish you to accept my sincere thanks also conveying some to all members of your force. I would also like to thank the gentleman in Calgary on my behalf.

Words cannot express how much I appreciate the kindness yourself and all members of the Alberta Provincial police have bestowed on me since the loss of my dear husband. I would like you to know that if I ever have to use the money it will be used to good advantage for educating my four girls and fitting them for what they would like to be.

Thank you on behalf of my family and myself, I am,

(signed) Maggie Rae Lawson[4]

The date for the trial was drawing close. On November 17th an announcement came that caught everyone by surprise. The Crown Prosecutor for the Judicial District of Macleod withdrew from the case. The press speculated J.W. McDonald withdrew because of differences of opinion between himself, McGillivray and Attorney General Brownlee. Questioned as to his reasons, McDonald declined to make a statement.

From her prison cell, a lonely Florence asked to see a priest.[5]

---

4. From Alberta Provincial Police files, Provincial Archives, Edmonton, Alberta.

5. General footnote for whole chapter, taken from Trial records, Glenbow Alberta Institute; Provincial Archives, Edmonton, Alberta; and Alberta newspapers as listed in earlier footnotes.

XVI

A LUST FOR
REVENGE

It was the 27th day of November. There was a westerly wind blowing as crowds of people gathered at the Calgary Provincial Court House for the special sitting of the Supreme Court.

It was a dull and darkening day. The wintry wind whipped and tangled the Union Jack on the flag pole. It blew through the denuded trees, blew across dirt encrusted snow patches and made the day austere.

In the sombre stone building, lighted blocks of yellow shone against the grayness of the day. Staid lawyers with brief cases and official looking people were the only ones being let into the building. They came and went; gray haired and bespeckled, carrying cases of leather, fat with papers. They stopped to converse with one another at length and those closest to the front of the line waiting to get seats, strained to hear their conversations, hoping to hear something of the trial to come. Then they could importantly turn back to pass the tidbit to the crowd behind them.

When the attendants finally opened the doors to the court, the crowd literally fought its way inside, pushing and shoving with little respect for one another as they elbowed their way through the big doors, down corridors and into court room seats. They were all there; people seeking sensationalism, others looking towards the spectacle of a tense legal battle, the morbid, the righteous wanting to see justice done, the law students. Some were perplexed, they wanted nothing to do with the feared outcome but curiosity got the better of them and they too, stood long hours in line hoping to get a seat. The students of the law schools were there to learn, to adopt the manners and stance of their peers.

Old men with meditative expressions came in droves. They saw in the court a better place to be entertained than a lonesome afternoon in their dreary rooms. Also in attendance were complacent middle aged women. They carried knitting bags; dug furtively to the bottom for cookies and sweets hidden under the wool. Later in the evening, still knitting, they would rehash the day's events over tea cups.

When the court room seats were filled, the doors were closed and locked. The halls filled with disappointed spectators. Some of the crowd outside dispersed to go back home, others went to a nearby picture show where Earle Williams and Rudolph Valentino played in another drama of the upper and lower world of Paris, 'A Rogue's Romance'. Others stood huddled on the street outside, their breath rising in frosty mantle, hoping to get a seat when recess was called.

In the court room, heads swivelled back and forth as the official preparations of the Court were conducted. The Clerk of the Court checked off the exhibits, looking closely at the tags. Some of the smaller ones were wrapped in paper. McKinley Cameron, the senior counsel for the defence, came into the room, his black robes moved and fluttered behind him as he deposited his brief case on the desk. His collar with its small tie was pristine against the sombre black of the robe he wore to court. The man had alert, inquiring eyes set in a lively face. Behind him came his assistants, Sherwood Herchmer and D.G. MacKenzie.

At the appearance of the prosecution, there were waves of head movements and whisperings from the crowd. McGillivray appeared along with James Matheson, the representative of the Attorney General for Macleod. Together they would represent the Crown. The tall distinguished looking gentleman with the regal bearing was the Attorney General of Alberta, the Honourable John E. Brownlee. Several reporters slipped from their seats to make hasty telephone calls to their newspapers to report Brownlee's presence in the court.

The tautness of the room was overwhelming; and as if this

were a play, and split second timing was the mode, the heavy doors of the court opened and Emilio Picariello, flanked by his guards, walked calmly into the room. There was an immediate stir in the crowd followed by yet another as the doors opened again and Florence, with her matron and guard, walked in and crossed the floor to their seats.

The girl looked calm and detached; this time she made no effort to look at Picariello. McGillivray looked at his watch, checked it with the pendulum swinging clock. An anxious hush fell over the room, a tinge of expectancy as the scarlet coated policeman stood. One of them asked the assembled to rise as he said loudly:

"Order in the Court!"

The chamber doors swung wide to admit the Judge, the Honourable Mr. William Justice Walsh.

"I declare this court open in the name of his Majesty the King!"

There was a rustling as the crowd took their seats after the Judge had settled into his chair. The Clerk of the Court rose after a minute to proclaim:

"Case 1141: The King versus Picariello and Losandro."

Then the Honourable Brownlee was on his feet. He addressed the Judge.

"Your Honour, as Attorney General of the Province of Alberta I will not be taking an active part in this trial but to avoid any technical objection that might be taken, I am preferring the charge against the two accused and further, I am filing a written authorization to have Mr. McGillivray act for me in this trial."

The authorization was duly filed. Both lawyers, acting for the prosecution and the defense rose to face the Judge.

"Gentlemen," he asked, "are you ready to proceed?"

Receiving their affirmative response he nodded to the clerk of the Court who loudly read the charge to the now standing Picariello.

"Emilio Picariello, you are charged with the murder of Stephen Oldacres Lawson, how do you plead?"

"Not guilty!" came the instant reply in firm tones.

The man, in contrast to the abject air he had about him at the preliminary, appeared almost jaunty. His old peremptory air was back. He was clean shaven; his moustache was freshly trimmed. He wore a white collar and blue tie; his blue serge suit was sharply pressed and his boots were shined.

The same charge was read to Florence and again came the no guilty plea. The girl was pale and she showed signs of imprisonment. It was hard to believe the youthful face once held a soft ripe glow. Now the deep dark eyes were limpid, ringed with shadowy circles from worry and lack of sleep. For her first day in court, Florence was soberly but stylishly dressed in a black suit.

The greater part of the morning was taken up with the jury selection. But before this started the Judge made a statement reprimanding certain newspapers for publishing a review of the case on the eve of the trial. The Judge's voice was brusque as he looked at the court and sternly admonished the publishing of the preliminary hearing events.

"This," he said with concealed annoyance, "is a serious breach of the customs and privileges of the press. It is contrary to the regulations of the British Court of Law. The press has the right to report evidence when it is adduced at a trial. It is the property of the press and this is right. But," and here his voice raised in volume, "reports on the eve of a trial of this importance, especially have a tendency to prejudice witnesses. I sincerely regret the publication of these stories at this time although I suspect the newspapers did not do this with a wilful intent but rather through ignorance of their rights in the matter. The responsibility of presiding over this most serious and important trial is sufficiently grave in itself without it being added to by further responsibilities and I, therefore, do not intend to concern myself any further with the matter but I felt that I owed a duty to the court and a responsibility to the jurors to express myself in the terms in which I have and having done that I content myself."

The defense, having obtained permission to speak, noted

the lurid story of the <u>Christian Guardian</u> which told of the bootlegging operations of the accused. The story carried a prejudiced account against Picariello.

The Judge nodded his head in agreement, cleared his throat and looked down at his papers. "Let us proceed then."

Before the jury selection could begin, the chief counsel for the defense was out of his seat and had permission to address the bench. He objected to the addition of 10 names to the original jury panel.

"The original panel, my Lordship, was 50 names! And to this 10 more names are being added. I question the legality of this. The sheriff, your Honour, has no authority to do so. I request therefore that the 10 names be dropped, sir."

"Mr. Cameron," came the measured reply, "unless the mutual consent of the opposing counsel is obtained I must assume that Sheriff Graham acted within his discretion. Does the prosecution object?"

"No, your Honour."

With finality, the Judge then stated, "I do not like to absolutely excuse any of these who have made application to be excused, because there are so many of them that the possibility of our not being able to get a jury from those that are left may become an important factor. When a juror is called who has asked to be excused I will be glad to let him go but I will not dispose of any of these applications until then."

During the long morning there were many and varied reasons given by prospective jurymen as to why they should be exempted from duty. When asked to state their reasons the excuses were in some cases humourous; abscessed teeth, deafness, family affairs and even, cows to be milked! Others gave reasons of business interests, vacations and various responsibilities such as being a Justice of the Peace and clergyman as reasons for exemption. The first two called had affidavits, one for a grave hardship if he had to stand for jury duty and the other was suffering from tuberculosis and a nervous breakdown. Both were excused.

It was well into the morning before the first two members

were selected and sworn. The first men to which no challenge was made by Cameron or McGillivray were W.H. Edge and W. L. Lockhardt.

The next man to come before the Judge said his hearing was bad. He therefore could not serve on a jury.

"What is your name?" asked the Judge.

The man quickly gave his name. To this the Judge said dryly, "Your hearing appears to be all right!"

A prospective juror was challenged for cause by Cameron. His reasons being the juror did not stand impartial between the crown and the prisoners. Under Section 931 of the Code the two jurors who were previously sworn would not be sworn to try the challenge as to cause. The judge looked at the sworn jurors and explained the procedure.

"The juror called has been challenged and objected to on the grounds that he is not indifferent between the crown and the accused. It is up to you, as sworn jurors to determine whether or not the challenge is good. You will have to be put under oath. The evidence on this charge will be given under oath."

The Judge motioned to the Clerk of the Court who rose to take the Bible to the first juror.

"You shall well and truly try whether Cecil H. Addshead, one of the jurors, stands indifferent between our Sovereign Lord the King and the prisoners at the bar and a true verdict give according to the evidence. So help you God."

The other juror was so sworn and both were asked to sit to hear the evidence. The challenge juror was also sworn.

In evidence Mr. Cameron drew out the man's resident town, his occupation and the fact that he was acquainted with the slain constable. He was asked by Mr. Cameron what he had discussed about the case. He drew out of the man an observation that it would not be fair to be on a jury because he knew Lawson.

The two jurymen without hesitation replied, when questioned by the Judge that the man should not be on the jury. Addshead was excused.

The selection continued and three more jurors were added

and sworn; George Barker, W.H. Bagley and Leslie H. Irwin.

Then another man came along and pleaded deafness. He was asked the same question by the Judge. This man was quicker in his thinking and replied, "Beg your pardon, my Lord?" he cupped his hand to his ear as he spoke.

The Judge suppressed a wry grin. The onlookers smiled and a small chortle went through the room relieving the tension. Even a bare wisp of a smile crossed Picariello's face.

To the waiting juror, the Judge observed, "We will look into your case."

When H. S. Jones came before the bench, he was challenged by Cameron for cause and asked if he was not indifferent to the case. After his evidence he was dismissed.

Again another man, challenged for cause as to why he should not serve and accept his duty, stated that he knew the dead policeman and his deliberations might be unfair to the accused. The Judge quickly agreed with him and the man was excused.

Another man challenged as to being indifferent freely admitted to having had his opinions formed by reading the newspaper reports. He also discussed the case with his friends and had strongly expressed views to the detriment of the accused. He too was excused from duty.

J.E. Bull was tried for cause. He too had read the reports of the killing in the *Guardian*. McGillivray asked him, "Did you object to the *Guardian* printing the story?"

"No," he replied, "they were not my views but I have expressed my opinion that the police should be upheld with regard to all this bootlegging."

"You have given people your opinions then?"

"Well, I have spoken about bootleggers in general but not ever in regards to this case."

"Well, sir, " replied McGillivray, "did you not say that crazy Italians should not be allowed to run around shooting people?"

The man twisted in his chair, he did not like the questioning and he did not want to serve on this jury.

"Yes sir, I did!"

"Do you think you could be fair to the accused in the deliberations of this case?"

"Yes sir, I think I could be but it would be hard to do."

The sworn jurors concluded that the man should be excused. The man looked relieved and left the stand.

And yet another man, J.W.Templeton was challenged by the defense. He, too, admitted that he expressed an opinion as to what should be done to the accused. He was quickly excused.

Of the next 6 men called, W. Wills, was challenged for cause when he admitted having unfavourable opinions of the accused. The 6th juror, G. Coggan was sworn in.

Constable A. Holton was sworn to take charge and guard the jury. W.H. Bagley was made foreman of the jury. At 12:00 the court adjourned for the lunch break.

When court resumed after lunch there was the same crush for seats. Hundreds were turned away and it was evident many people passed up lunch to get front positions in the lineup. The first 15 minutes of the afternoon session was taken by the Crown prosecutor McGillivray as he gave his opening address.

"When I say to you the penalty of murder is death, the accused as well as the court have the right to ask for your most serious consideration of the evidence you are presented with."

He then read the definition of murder from the Criminal Code of Canada. Then continuing, he said, "The trial will be a long one and I do not intend to address you at any length at this time. The crown will submit evidence to attempt to prove that the accused murdered Stephen Lawson, shooting him in the back in front of his own child. When the evidence has been submitted and you are convinced there is any doubt as to the guilt of the accused, I desire they be given the benefit of the doubt. But," he paused and looked hard at the jury, "on the other hand if you are satisfied that Stephen Lawson was murdered by the accused, then you owe it, as honest men, to bring in the verdict accordingly."

All the witnesses who were to give evidence were cleared from the courtroom. Only then was the first witness called to the stand.

Emilio followed every word spoken and watched with keen interest every movement of the court. Florence on the other hand, seemed lost in thought as she stared at the floor and did not raise her head. Cameron, as chief counsel for the defense, sat in his seat of prestige nearest the bench and rifled through his papers. He frowned and made cryptic notes in the margins.

The court called M.H. Congdon. The man took the bible in his right hand as the Clerk of the Court read the oath to him.

"Do you swear the evidence you shall give in this court between our sovereign Majesty the King and the accused shall be the truth, the whole truth and nothing but the truth, so help you God?"

"I do." He kissed the bible.

As the man was taking his oath, Justice Walsh lifted his head and looked with annoyance towards the rear doors of the court. He held up his hand, interrupted the proceedings and ordered the corridor cleared of all spectators who were unable to gain admittance to the room. The babble of voices, muted by the heavy doors, but still plainly heard in the quiet room, was a constant distraction to the events taking place. His request was quickly complied with and there followed a silence in which a person's breathing could be heard.

The witness was a mining engineer in the town of Blairmore. McGillivray produced Crown Exhibit "1" which was a tracing of part of the plan of Coleman. Congdon admitted supplying these tracings along with blueprints showing the location of principal buildings designated at the preliminary hearing. Congdon was followed by O. Brindley, a photographer from Coleman. All Crown Exhibits 2,3,4,5,6, and 7 were photographs of various buildings and streets which had a bearing on the shooting. The defense made a cursory examination of the witnesses.

Witness number 3 was James Houghton, Chief of Police at Coleman. The man was a star witness for the prosecution and he told his story in a clear concise manner, ending with the incident when the doctor handed the bullet, taken from the body of Lawson, over to him.

"What condition was Lawson in?"

"He was dead." The voice was instantly bitter.

"Could you see if a weapon was lying on the ground?"

"I could have seen it if a weapon was there. There was no weapon in sight."

"Did you see how the lady was dressed?"

"She had something red on her head. I can't say whether a red hat or a toque or what it was."

At a motion by the prosecutor, Crown exhibit 8 and 10 were brought forward. Houghton looked at the red tam and the green coat and identified them. Just then, the jury had questions to ask the witness.

"Are you acquainted with Mrs. Losandro? Do you think it was her?"

Florence heard the man identify her. "Yes, I saw her three or four times a week as she rode through town." He did not need to add that she rode with Picariello.

Still the jury wanted to make sure, "Did you get a good view and are you sure it was her?"

"Yes." The answer was simple.

Before McKinley Cameron was to examine the witness Crown Exhibit 9 was viewed. A small procession made its way to the garage under the court house where the McLaughlin was stored. The Judge and the Clerk of the Court led the way followed by Houghton, the jury members and the accused with their guards. The members of the jury walked cautiously around the car, the tread of their feet echoed hollowly in the closed garage. They looked closely at the bullet shattered windshield, at the door handles of the car, peered inside to see the broken dashboard. The car gleamed dully in the artificial lights of the garage. It was sinister looking. It carried the aura of death.

Standing well back from the others inspecting the car were Florence and Emilio. Picariello had been following the trial with keen interest but now, seeing the car, he grew morose and withdrew into himself. For Florence the viewing was painful.

Here in front of her was the vehicle of her nightmares. She looked wildly around her. The gloom of the afternoon hung darkly in all the corners of the low ceiling garage. As in her life, there was no ribbon of light in the blackness crowding down on her. Bitterness rose in her throat as she was led back to the court room.

For the next three hours Houghton coolly answered questions peppered at him by the defense. He stated he had been Coleman's Chief of Police for 3 years and had grown to know Lawson quite well.

"As Chief of Police at Coleman do you regard it as your duty to suppress the liquor traffic?"

"No."

The man was asked if he got instructions of the town council on the liquor traffic and the answer was negative. But the answer was affirmative when he was asked if he worked with the Alberta Provincial Police in this respect. He then spoke of his uniform, the gun issued to him and the 38 calibre revolver issued to Lawson.

"You know that because you saw him fire at the car?"

"I saw him fire at the right back tire." The witness was quick to correct the questioner.

"You were with him?"

"I was in the front seat of the car, yes."

"What car was he firing at?"

"Steve Picariello's car. We were approaching Crow's Nest Lake."

"Is not this place, where Lawson is alleged to have fired at Steve's car, a dangerous place where there is a possibility of a car going over an embankment?"

"No. Not at the place where Lawson fired."

"Is that the only shot fired west of Coleman at Steve's car?"

"The only one I heard." The witness was defensive.

The defense then asked the witness if he carried his gun with him during this chase. The answer was firm. He carried his gun in the morning but left it in his office in the afternoon. A slight frown crossed the face of the witness. He wondered where all the questioning was leading.

"You said at the preliminary hearing that you and Lawson were watching for Picariello. When did you get word to watch?"

"About ten o'clock on the 21 of September."

"At that time you had your gun?"

"Yes."

"Were any plans laid?"

"Lawson had orders to report when he saw Steve Picariello but he was not to try to stop him."

The voice of the defense was incredulous. "Your instructions were to let Steve go through with a load of whiskey?"

"Yes."

McKinley Cameron drew the information skilfully from the man. He had kept watch from ten in the morning until four in the afternoon. He knew that a large load of whiskey was coming through but did nothing to stop it.

"What were your instructions?"

"Lawson said Steve was coming back with the load and we were to get a car and chase him.

"Why did you go into the Grand Union Hotel?"

"Because the first car I saw was in front of the hotel."

The witness told of the Picariello car roaring past him as he went into the hotel.

"You ran across the street?"

"Yes."

"You heard the shots?"

"Yes . I understand it was Lawson who fired."

"Fired at the tires?"

"No." The man was uncomfortable now. "Lawson said he fired in the air."

"Did he tell you he hit Steve in the hand, firing into the air?" The defense turned and calmly surveyed the jury members to see if the question had taken effect.

"No. I asked him if he fired at the car. He said he fired in the air."

Mr. McKinley Cameron's remarks carried accusation in

them. "You were not so free with your evidence at the preliminary hearing. Mr. Harris questioned you for twenty minutes and could not get anything out of you. At the preliminary hearing in answer to a similar question you answered, 'I cannot say'. Cameron lifted his eyebrows at the witness.

There was a short, uncomfortable silence in the courtroom.

McKinley Cameron continued his questions. "Was that the only discussion you had with Lawson?"

"Yes."

"As Chief of Police at Coleman I don't suppose you allow the town to be shot up. You would investigate such shootings?" Cameron was slightly sarcastic.

"Yes."

"There have been substantial shootings in the past?"

"Yes. "The man went on to explain that he and his constable had fired on a car though it developed the car was not being used for whiskey running. McKinley Cameron then changed his line of questioning to the meeting of Lawson and Picariello after the chase.

The witness declared Picariello was driving one of the cars running west and when Lawson met Picariello he did not draw his gun.

"Lawson put his gun in his holster. I did not see him draw it out."

"Well, he held a conversation with Picariello. How far away from you would they be?"

"About twenty feet and at an angle."

"What did you hear?"

"Well, Lawson said, 'You might as well bring the kid back, cause if you don't I will', or words to that effect."

"Did he say something about getting the boy?"

"No."

Again McKinley Cameron turned to the hushed court and read from the excerpt of the preliminary hearing. The witness said on this occasion that Lawson would go and get Steve.

"I suppose it would be quite possible for Lawson to have invited Picariello to the barracks that night without your hearing?"

"No, sir. I heard every word Lawson spoke." He was definite and very firm in his answer .

"Will you swear to this?"

"Yes."

"How far away was he from you?"

"About twenty feet and at an angle." The witness repeated himself .

"As a matter of fact you did not hear anything further?"

"That's right."

"So you will take back your statement that you heard every word?" The question was put very quietly, so softly. "Picariello was facing Lawson at the time?"

"Yes."

"You claimed that you could not hear what Picariello said?"

"Yes." The man was uncomfortable. The defence had made their point.

At McKinley Cameron's prompting, the witness retraced his steps from when he went home until he heard the shots. He told of seeing Picariello driving up Central Avenue in Coleman with Florence beside him. Again the night of the murder was re-acted and Florence thought she would scream if she heard yet another telling of the nightmare. During the next four days she was to hear it over and over again. The defense asked the witness when Sergeant Scott arrived at the scene of the shooting.

"About 8:30 in the evening."

"And so you were the only policeman on the job until then?"

"Yes."

Houghton swore the constable was unarmed and there were no weapons found near his body.

"Do you know anything about guns?"

"I think so. I looked over Lawson's guns with Constable Dey."

"At the time you got to the barracks how was the visibility. Was the light artificial or was it daylight?"

"It was not dark. " The question was not answered directly.

The witness looked wearily at the clock. It was striking five. "You may step down. No further questions."

Court was adjourned until 10 o'clock the following morning. At the tables the lawyers shuffled their papers and buckled leather straps on their cases. Before leaving the court room Emilio, again in good spirits, conversed briefly with his counsel. There was no trace of flippancy in the young girl who moved uncertainly to her feet. She hunched thin shoulder blades in an effort to relieve tension in them. She looked exhausted and there was a long time to go.

The jury members were taken to their rooms and supper was sent to them on trays. They were made comfortable but denied newspapers or radios. Some played cards, others read or shined their shoes. All opted for an early bed time.

On Tuesday, November 28, Picariello entered the court room in a relaxed mood. He smiled and nodded to the newsmen. Florence too, though wan and pale, smiled tremulously at a group of Pass residents. There was roll call for the jury members; all were present and the day's events started.

"The Crown calls Andrew Petrie."

The man called was a miner in the Pass area. The car used on the night of the murder belonged to him. He told the court how McAlpine, Picariello's mechanic, had taken it away for repairs on the morning of September 21. Cameron declined to cross examine.

Mrs. Catherine Petrie was called. In her testimony she told the court of her visit to the Lethbridge Gaol. She asked Picariello to have her car returned to her. Picariello offered to buy her a new car or give her the money. She took the new car, giving Picariello a cheque for $300.00 for the difference.

Donald McAlpine, the mechanic, was the next witness called. He identified the car as the one taken from the Petrie residence. When he received instructions from Picariello to find Steve in Michel and bring him back to Blairmore, McAlpine had taken one of Picariello's cars and left the Petrie car in the garage under the hotel. The windshield was intact and there were no bullets or buttons in the car when he left it. McKinley

Cameron rose to question the witness, asking how long he had been employed by Picariello.

"From April 17 until 2 weeks ago." was the answer.

"Do you sir, believe in enforcement of the law?"

"Yes."

"If you knew Picariello was going to break the law would you be a party to it?"

"No, sir, I wouldn't."

"That is why Picariello trusted you?" The question was loaded with incredulity. "What time was this conversation with Picariello?" He was referring to the instructions the man had given him.

"About six o 'clock." was the reply.

"Do you think his instructions had any importance to the case?"

"No sir."

"Being an honest boy you might have told the police." The statement was sourly put. "You had a job with Picariello?"

"Yes."

"And afterwards there was a difference?" The lawyer seemed to know something of a disagreement. "Was this directly with Picariello?"

"No, with his solicitor."

"You felt they were not using you right?"

"Not as I figured."

"You were in Coleman at the time of the preliminary hearing and you were not called to testify?"

"No."

Then McKinley Cameron put forth facts that the witness had in fact told Sergeant Scott of the conversation before the preliminary hearing and still he had not been asked to appear at the hearing.

The defence slowly pivoted on his heel, looked over at the jury members and said slowly, "So... Scott knew about this conversation... at the time of the preliminary hearing... well!" There was a sudden stillness in the courtroom, with bated breath, the witness answered slowly, "Yes."

"No further questions. You may step down."

In quick succession several witnesses for the Crown were called. Taxi driver A. Dorenzo identified the McLaughlin car as the one he found deserted on the night of the murder. At 3 o'clock in the morning he drove it to Picariello's hotel where the car was taken from him. He had not put anything into the car nor had he taken anything out. Another witness swore he saw Picariello and a lady going west between 6:45 and 7 o'clock on the night of the murder.

At this point another witness for the prosecution was called, the 13 year old daughter of Lawson. The Judge spoke kindly to the girl, asking and ascertaining as to whether the child could be sworn as a witness.

"If you promise with your hand on the bible, to tell the truth, will you do so?"

"Yes, your honour." The voice was firm, full of conviction. The judge leaned back, convinced. "She may be so sworn."

McGillivray approached the witness. Skilfully he drew from the girl the events of the evening of the 21st until she heard the shots. At this point the child's lips trembled and she put her head down. Quickly she was given a drink of water. Picariello leaned forward, listening intently. The girl continued with the events of the evening as she had seen them until she went home.

Taking a different course McGillivray questioned the child about the guns her father owned. He asked her what her father did with his gun when he came home.

"He broke open his gun and emptied it. He put it on the bureau, there weren't any shells left in it."

"Was there anyone in the back seat of the car?"

"No sir."

"How was the girl dressed?"

"She wore a red tammie." The answer was simple and soft. He then asked her about her play about the barracks after school and whether or not there were any empty cartridges about after the shooting. The answer was negative.

When McKinley Cameron rose to question the girl, he failed

to shake her evidence, only drawing from her the fact that she knew nothing about guns, how to load them or whether they were empty or loaded. Her only confusion came when he asked her the colour of the coat the woman was wearing. She said the coat was blue, but the coat was in fact green. There was an instant buzz in the courtroom. The girl looked puzzled. There were no further questions.

The last witness before the court adjourned before 12:25 was F. Oswald, a 16 year old friend of Lawson's family. He could not identify the woman in the car but remembered she wore a red tammie. Florence nervously picked at her handkerchief.

The court adjourned until 2 pm, then F. Cole was called to the stand. He had been visiting his mother in the hospital at the time of the shooting. This witness could shed no light as to the occupants of the car. A nurse at the hospital, L. Thorpe, gave contradictory evidence on the number of shots heard. She told the court she heard 3 shots, a pause, then 3 more shots. The woman was cross examined briefly by McKinley Cameron.

The 14th witness was the doctor. Dr. Charles V. Scott. He identified Exhibit 11, the underclothes worn by Lawson and Exhibit 12, a bullet taken from the man's body.

Dr. Scott's testimony bore evidence that Lawson was unarmed. The doctor told of finding the man lying on the ground and of his attempts to save him. His autopsy report was read.

"Did you notice anything peculiar about the bullet?"

"The bullet was notched on one side near the apex. It looked as if some sharp instrument was used to notch it."

On questions asked by McGillivray, the doctor told the court the wound was enough to cause instant death. A person so shot could have made several convulsive lunges forward but not many. He was sure the bullet could not be marked or notched just by passing through the body.

The next witness identified Picariello as the man driving the car. F. Patterson was a janitor at the Central school in Coleman. He called Emilio by the familiar 'Pic'.

"Who do you mean by 'Pic'? What is his full name?" McGillivray asked.

"I can't tell you what his full name is. I have known him for over 10 years as 'Pic'." Patterson rubbed his head reflectively. He said it was Pic in the car. He got a good view of him as Pic was leaning over the side of the car out the open window.

Picariello mopped his face with his handkerchief. At the table for the defense Herchmer turned up the lead on his gold eversharp pencil and made a few elliptical notes on his docket.

McGillivray persisted with his questions. "Do you mean the man you saw was the accused Emilio Picariello, the one sitting in the prisoner's box?"

The court was quiet, expectant, still.

"Yes sir, he's the one!" There was a stir, a ripple of assent in the room. "Can you identify the woman? Is the accused Florence Losandro the woman in the car?"

"I can't identify her as the woman." Again a murmur came from the spectators.

The last witness of the day was called and sworn. M. J. Yates was briefly examined by McGillivray before the court was adjourned at 5:10 pm.

The prisoners were urged to their feet, Picariello appeared strong but a closer look revealed despondency in his eyes, weariness about his mouth.

Back in her cell Florence rested on her cot. She was exhausted from days of listening, days of questioning and requestioning, the same story gone over and over until she felt she would scream. What would they think, the girl pondered, if I stood up and screamed and screamed, shattering the politeness and formality of the court. Her supper tray came and was pushed through the small opening in the cell door.

From somewhere down the corridor there was a ringing, then an answering sound and the scraping of a heavy door opening. She went to the cell door waiting hopefully for someone to come down the corridor to rescue her from this nightmare. The young girl listened intently but all she could hear were murmurs and whispers of a harsh voice. Dejectedly Florence sat back on her cot, picked up the coverings from the supper tray and looked at the food. She pushed the cold meat and soggy potatoes around the plate and tried to eat. She knew she should eat; her clothes had an unaccustomed looseness about them. She sipped her tea; ate half the bread and left the rest. Tomorrow, she promised herself, tomorrow, when some of this mess is straightened away, then I'll eat. She took off her clothes, hung them up and slipped into a long nightgown the family sent to her. The tired girl tried to blot out her thoughts by sleep but the lights and mutterings from the cells down the corridor kept her mind in consciousness. She covered her head with her pillow and soon, mercifully, sleep claimed the young body.

When court resumed on Wednesday morning Mrs. Yates was cross examined by McKinley Cameron.

She told the court of the car standing in front of the barracks when she arrived at the hospital. She was in the hospital for two or three minutes before she heard the shots. First of all, she said she heard four shots.

"Is that all?" inquired the defense lawyer.

Then the witness changed her mind. "No. I think I heard five or six shots."

"Oh," said McKinley Cameron, "then there were shots fired after you left the hospital and reached the veranda. "

"Yes. " The witness nodded agreement to this fact.

He asked her if the shots were all together, or was there a pause between them. Carefully he asked if she had seen the flashes.

"No, " she said, "I think the shooting lasted a minute. I did not see any of the flashes. "

"What did the car do?"

"It swerved into the middle of the road. "

"You spoke of Miss Thorpe pushing you. Why did she do this?"

"I don't know."

Mrs. Yates left the stand. Before the next witness was called the jury asked that she be recalled. To their questions the witness explained she heard firing when the car was backing up and before it swerved into the middle of the road. Mrs.

Yates did not see Lawson at this time.

Three witnesses came up in quick succession; the manager of the Coleman Hardware Company, G. H. Snoad told his story but had little to add to the evidence already given. When a Nelson, British Columbia man came to the bench he testified to a chance remark made by Picariello that further implicated the unfortunate man. The witness, G. Allen, was in Blairmore the night of the shooting. He saw Picariello in front of the Alberta Hotel and swore that Picariello said, "I do not like this shooting business, if they start shooting, I can shoot too!" Emilio's face twitched and his large hands tightened on the arms of the chair.

After the next witness, N. Snoad of Coleman, the conflict over the number of shots fired was still not resolved. She heard 5 shots. Her testimony was short and she was not cross examined by McKinley Cameron.

By the time the 9 year old daughter of Lawson was called to the stand, the strain and tension in the room was showing on the faces of the accused. Even the spectators, who had so frankly gawked at all the proceedings and at every little stir in the room, seemed to have hooded their eyes and averted them. No one wanted to see the fear mirrored there.

The young girl was a principal witness for the prosecution. McGillivray addressed the court, pointing out the child in his opinion was too young to be sworn but it was his duty, he felt, to call the girl. He left the matter entirely in the hands of the Judge. Under section 16 of the Canada Evidence Act, a certain discretion was allowed the presiding Judge.

The Chief Justice addressed the child and ascertaining her responses, made his decision. "We will take her unsworn testimony. She appears to be an intelligent child."

With this, the crown prosecutor started his questioning. The child's responses brought the court spectators to the edges of their seats.

"Do you remember the night your daddy was killed?"

'Yes." was the small reply.

"Did a car come to the barracks?"

"I did not see it come. My daddy went out and I followed."

"What did you see?"

"The girl shot and daddy let go." There was a swift intake of breath by the spectators and a stir rippled the tense court room.

The child continued thoughtfully, "then more shots and at the last shot daddy fell down and I ran in to my Mama."

"Which side of the car were you on?"

"On the side near the house."

"Did you see anyone else? Do you know who fired the last shot?"

"No."

Gently the prosecutor traced the events of the evening with the child. She remembered they were to go to the show that evening and told of the car standing in front of the house pointing towards the bridge. She was standing at the corner of the house, having come out the back door. She watched her father standing at the car, his foot on the running board. There were two people in the car.

"Now, did you stand at the corner of the house until all the shooting was over?"

"I went back further but I could see the car all the time. The car was backing up when some shots were fired."

McGillivray asked her if she knew what the fight started about. Her response was negative; she thought her father was about to make an arrest.

"When the car started, daddy put both feet on the running board. I am not sure whether daddy had his arms around the man's neck when the car started, but when daddy saw the gun he put his arms around the man's neck."

"You could see your daddy and the car at all times? It wasn't very dark?

"Yes, I could see them. It wasn't dark."

"I don't suppose you could tell who was shooting."

"I just saw the girl shoot."

"Did the girl shoot your daddy?"

Florence leaned forward, gripping the sides of the seat. The memories of that night, drawn out so plainly in this grey courtroom, evoked a pain so sharp that her breathing was ragged. The words seemed to come to her in waves, engulfing and drowning her. They sucked at her, pulled her down into the inky deep and she fought for sanity, for reason, and stifled the urge to get up and run.

The child's next words seemed to vindicate Florence. "I don't know. Daddy didn't fall when she shot." There was dead silence after this last statement.

Then it was McKinley Cameron's turn to examine the girl. His first questions to her were about school.

"You go to school, make figures, read, write and have a good memory?"

The child nodded, yes.

"Were you in school the day your daddy was killed?"

"Yes."

He then took her with his questioning through the events of the night, edging closer and closer to the exact moment of the shooting.

"You saw your daddy fall?" He asked the question softly, aware of the trauma the child had been through.

"Yes!"

"How far would you be away?"

"I was just past the side door."

"The last thing you saw of your daddy before he fell was when he had his foot on the running board of the car?"

"Yes."

"You were some distance away so you did not see who fired the shot that killed your daddy?"

"I only saw the woman shoot."

McKinley Cameron, at this point, read from evidence given by the child at the inquest. She was reported to have said that Picariello also fired a shot. Again the child insisted the lady shot and her daddy let go and she did not hear any more shots.

"You didn't see the man shoot?"

"No."

"As your daddy put his arms around the man's neck the

lady shot?"

"Yes."

"The last shot you heard was the one fired by the lady?"

"No. I don't know who fired the last shot. The lady shot once and I didn't see any more."

"How many shots were fired?"

"Four."

"You don't know who fired the others?"

"No," said the child.

After her testimony 3 more witnesses were heard before court adjourned for lunch. Ernest Hines, a drayman from Blairmore, saw the accused about 7 o'clock the night of the murder. He swore Picariello and Florence were in the front seat with Picariello driving. Crown witness 23, E. Wood was not sworn. He was 11 years old. His testimony too, placed the accused at the scene of the shooting.

The last witness of the morning, J. Allen of Coleman, was confused about the number of shots coming from the car. He thought 4 or 5 shots were fired. The defense subjected this witness to a stiff cross examination.

"Who did you discuss this case with?"

"Inspector Nicholson."

"Did you see who fired the shots in the afternoon?"

"Yes."

"Well, who fired them?"

"Lawson."

"How far away were you?"

"About 150 feet."

How many shots did you hear?"

"Two, both fired by Lawson."

"Tell us exactly what you saw Lawson do."

"He held up his hand and called 'Halt!' When the car did not stop he fired two shots."

The man was questioned until court adjourned for the lunch break.

J. Emerson was the first witness called in the afternoon. She had seen the shooting from the window of her home.

McGillivray asked her if Lawson had used a gun and if he had, could she have seen it. As far as she was concerned, the witness replied, Lawson did not use a gun, he was unarmed.

Before the defense subjected the witness to an exhaustive examination, McKinley Cameron recalled witness Oscar Brindley.

With Brindley on the stand, Crown Exhibit fourteen, a photograph was produced. The photograph showed a motor car standing in front of the barracks. The picture had been taken from the veranda of Mrs. Emerson. In an instant, McGillivray was on his feet, wanting to know who had placed the motor car in the picture.

Brindley replied gravely, "Mr. Gillies, acting for the defense, asked me to get a motor car and place it in the picture. It was done under his direction."

"Well, sir," asked McGillivray, "is it just a coincidence that the motor car shown in the picture has all its curtains up and fastened?"

"I don't know. "The man was confused, not sure what the prosecutor was aiming at.

When McKinley Cameron brought Mrs. Emerson again to the stand she declared the photograph produced was taken from approximately the same line of vision she would have had on the night of the murder.

"What time of day was the picture taken then?"

"I suspect about one or two in the afternoon.

"The light was better then, than it was during the happening you are testifying on.

"Yes of course."

"Did you see Lawson's figure and features when he left the barracks?"

"Yes, I recognized him by the light shining from the door of the barracks .

There followed considerable questioning about the witness being able to ascertain features of a man with daylight failing.

"Were the tail lights of the car burning?"

"Yes." Her admittance of the lights of the car being on was

sufficient to indicate dusk was falling about the time of the shooting.

The defense went back to her testimony at the time of the inquest and the preliminary hearing and pointed out that she was not certain as to the number of shots fired and had made no mention of the fact that Lawson ducked when certain shots were fired. To this the witness maintained that while she had not sworn the man had ducked, she did demonstrate this to the questioner, Mr. MacKenzie.

"Would you swear you said at that time that Lawson had ducked?"

"I think I said so."

'Will you swear to it?" The man was persistent on this point.

"Yes, I certainly will." The woman had made up her mind.

McKinley Cameron had found contradictory evidence and he hammered her with questions again and again causing confusion and fright in the witness.

He read evidence given by the witness at the time of the inquest in which she did not say Lawson had ducked. He read excerpts from the evidence given at the time of the preliminary hearing that outlined her testimony that four or five shots had been heard by her.

He questioned her about seeing Lawson fall. His questioning was severe and when she was describing how the man fell, the woman abruptly broke down and cried. Her hands covered her face and her shoulders shook. McKinley Cameron turned to walk back to his table.

He said, "I will cease my questions for a time. I do not want to examine a weeping woman." He had found a chink in her evidence and was making the most of it. When the woman was able to contain herself and wiped the tears from her eyes, the defense continued.

"Did Lawson stoop much when you saw him conversing with the occupants of the car?"

"Not much."

"How tall was Lawson?"

"About 5 or 6 feet."

Again and again he questioned the woman about the shooting, drawing from her an admission that running boys had taken her attention away from the incident. The defense lawyer read quotes from her earlier evidence given in the other courts, then dismissed the witness. She had been on the stand over an hour and was exhausted and unsteady when she left the witness chair.

The rest of the afternoon drew nothing of great importance. Fifteen year old R. Ash adduced the lights were shining on the front of the motor car which reinforced the claim by the defense that the light was not good.

Before adjournment the Judge announced that night sessions would be held so the trial could be completed before Saturday. There were at least 10 more witnesses to be heard. Part of Friday was being reserved for the addresses by the prosecution and the defense to the jury.

During the night, the mercury dropped to 9 below zero and in the coldness of her cell Florence tossed and turned in fitful sleep. During the long nights the girl tried to forget the torment of the trial hours, replacing her thoughts with memories drawn from the sunny corners of her mind, corners now filled with dust and cobwebs, corners visited such a long time ago. She spent long hours with these memories, taking walks in the forest of her mind where warblers harvested grubs among the pines, where she walked and gathered wild flowers, delicate and fragrant. She felt the texture of the petals against her fingers, smelt their perfume. Then she woke to the grey dullness of her cell and cried.

Starting Thursday's testimony was witness thirty one, Robert McGillivray Dey. He told of the search for the slain man's guns. All guns were empty. One gun, a 32 calibre colt automatic was found in a cupboard along with police effects. The other two, a 38 calibre revolver and a 38 calibre pistol were found in a drawer, the magazine was out of the colt.

This constable claimed he was stationed at Coleman from midnight on September 21 and had searched outside the barracks for shells in the morning. He found four empty shells from an automatic. They were made by the Dominion Cartridge Company and were produced under Exhibit sixteen.

"Did Lawson have any 32 calibre shells in the house?"

"Yes sir. They were Savage shells."

"Where else did you search?"

"In the vacant lot where I found some broken glass which I thought might have come from the windshield of the car.

"What did you do with the ammunition?"

"I gave it to Mr. Lawson's brother-in-law, along with the guns all except the service gun which belongs to the government."

The witness stated that Houghton had been with him during the search for the guns. He stated that a mistake had been made on his part at the preliminary hearing as he gave evidence that one of the guns was a 32 calibre revolver. It should have been a 38 calibre but he was mistaken by its size.

At that point McKinley Cameron drew himself up and stated the witness had made another mistake. "Did you say you did not look for the ammunition at the preliminary hearing?"

"I don't think I did, I certainly looked for it."

Again the defense lawyer read from the evidence showing the witness had made such a statement.

"Did you take any notes of your search?"

"No, sir none."

With the next witness a shuffle of the guns was evident. A. Dunn testified the guns and ammunition were turned over to him. He, in turn, gave the guns back to Constable Dey at the time of the preliminary. The ammunition was given to Mrs. Lawson. Dey was called back to the stand. He testified the guns were given to Sergeant Scott.

Witness 33, G.L. Stephens, testified finding the car. He found a bullet hole in the right hand side of the speedometer. The angle of the hole was downwards and the size appeared to be from a 32 calibre. His testimony reinforced the theory that two guns were used in the shooting.

When James W. Gresham came before the bench he admitted giving Picariello a permit for 2 guns.

"Did you ever issue a permit to Mrs. Losandro?"

"No." came the firm reply.

Three police officers, E. Clarke, E. Tutin, and J. Bradner, told of their part in the capture of the accused.

The defense dealt with the fact that no notes were taken at the time of arrest even though the police had notebooks with them. He drew admissions the accused was reasonable and not erratic.

"You told him you were arresting him for the murder of Constable Lawson."

"Yes ."

"And then you say one of the first questions he asked was 'How is he?'"

"Yes."

"Well, do you think this was a reasonable question?"

"I do under the circumstances." was the reply.

"You might have been a little ruffled by the hard climb", suggested Cameron, "Did you take any notes?"

"No. Not until I returned to the police station." The man was uncomfortable with this fact; none of the 3 arresting officers had taken written notes at the time. Bradner then said he clearly recalled the incident, however.

McKinley Cameron then pointed out the differences in testimony between the 3 officers. Bradner had quoted Picariello as saying 'Lawson had a gun on him.', while Tutin said, 'Picariello said, He tried to shoot me.'.

"Do you think you might have been mistaken?" he asked the man in the witness chair.

"No," came the reply, "I think I am right and Tutin is wrong."

McKinley Cameron looked hard at the jury. He turned to go back to his table, his robes swung with the movement of his body. He had clearly made his point. There was no written evidence.

The November light was starting to fade as Crown witness Michael Moriarity took his oath.

He told of finding the girl at the home of Mrs. Gibeau. She had a red tam on.

"Would you examine the contents of this bag?"

He took the bag into his hands, looked inside.

"Do you recognize this?"

"It's the red tam taken from the accused after her arrest."

Moriarity identified Florence's coat and the gun found at the Gibeau residence.

He was asked, "What were Mrs. Losandro's exact words regarding the gun being at Mrs. Gibeau's?[2] Did she say her gun?"

" I cannot say."

"Did she make use of the word 'My'?"

"No. She said the gun."

"Did you say that if you opened your mouth Picariello would not be in jail for long?"

"No."

"Did you discuss this aspect of the case with any other men at the time." The defense gave three names in quick succession.

"Yes."

The lawyer nodded affably, "And so, Mr. Moriarity, have you talked to any of these 3 men in Calgary since the trial opened?"

"Yes." The man was uncomfortable. "One of them told me Mr. Gillies went to him and asked if I had said such a thing."

"You have been removed from the Pass since the shooting?"

"Yes, I am now at Big Valley."

"You do not wish to retract anything?"

"Certainly not. I have told the truth."

"You never made any admission to the guilt or the innocence of the accused to any person?"

"No. I did not."

The defense said abruptly, "No further questions."

The last witness for Thursday was Sergeant J. O. Scott. He

---

2. It was strange that Mrs. Gibeau at whose house Florence and the gun were found, was not called to testify either at the preliminary or the main trial.

traced his part in the events of the fateful day. He ended his dialogue with the capture of Florence and the finding of the gun.

"Are you sure the gun belonged to Mrs. Losandro?"

"Yes."

"Did she admit it was hers?"

"Yes."

He told of his experience with guns during his 6 years as a police officer. The gun found was loaded but one chamber was dirty and showed powder lines.

"Did you go back and see Mrs. Losandro?" he was asked.

"When I came back she asked, 'Did you get the gun?' and I said, 'Yes' and showed it to her. She said, 'That's mine'."

Scott said the girl described the shooting and told him they heard Steve was shot. "She asked me about Steve. I told her he wasn't badly hurt. I was wondering why she was worried about Steve. Then she said, 'I like Steve' and made some remark to the effect that I need not tell Charlie."

Scott made this remark in reference to Carlo Losandro. At this point Florence blinked her eyes as she steadfastly looked at the floor. Tears brimmed over and ran down her cheeks.

Scott declared Florence described the events leading up to the shooting saying 2 shots were fired at them, one broke the windshield, one went past her foot. Then she pulled her gun and fired hitting Lawson in the stomach and he fell back. She told Scott Picariello didn't fire any of the shots because Lawson was holding him and she didn't fire until she saw a gun pointing at her. Florence stated at first she fired 2 shots and later said she fired them all.

Scott then told the court of the search of the rooms of the accused. He found clothing and letters addressed to Mrs. Losandro in her room. He told of finding the shells, their calibre and make.

"You have seen the four empty cartridge shells found in front of the barracks in Coleman following the shooting?"

The man nodded affirmatively.

"Do these cartridges correspond with any of the cartridges

found in Mrs. Losandro's room?"

"Yes."

There was an instant murmur from the crowd and the judge tapped his gavel for order.

McGillivray continued his line of questions drawing from the man details of the search of Picariello's room. In the room Scott found documents and clothing belonging to the man. Also in the drawers of a bureau were ammunition for a 38 calibre revolver and some 30-30 ammunition. Again came the question as the man sought to drive his point home.

"The ammunition found in Mrs. Losandro's room would be capable of being used in a 32 automatic.[3] We have heard of a permit being granted to Picariello for a 32 automatic revolver. Did you search every conceivable place for such a gun? Have you found it?"

"No, sir, we have not."

The contents and damage to the vehicle were discussed. Scott found a button from a coat, a spent bullet, a piece of nickel and broken glass in the car.

"Have you compared the button with the buttons on the coat worn by the Losandro woman?"

"Yes I have."

He was shown Florence's coat. He told the court the button was identical to those on the coat and the coat was a button short. The people in the court room wondered at the violence that caused the tear.

With skilful questions the lawyer made his point with regard to ammunition used by Picariello which was Dominion Cartridge in comparison to the ammunition used by Lawson which was Savage. The point was well taken.

Scott examined and identified exhibits during his testimony. Exhibits 18, 19 and 20 were the revolver and loaded cartridges. Exhibits 21 and 22 were materials from the preliminary hearing and consisted of more cartridges. Exhibit 23 was one 32

3. There was no 38 calibre ammunition found in Florence's room which could be used in the gun Florence claimed was hers.

cartridge, exhibit 24 was a spent bullet and a small chip of vehicle; exhibit 25 was the button.

After the direct examination of Scott, Mr. Justice Walsh motioned McGillivray and McKinley Cameron to the bench. After they consulted in low tones; the jury was asked if they were in agreement to a night session of two hours duration. At their agreement the session was ordered for eight o'clock in the evening. The court adjourned at four fifty .

When court resumed it was the defense attorney's turn to question the witness. Again Scott was returned to the witness stand. The first part of the questioning concerned his examination of the car and the direction of the bullet that smashed the speedometer. Carefully the defense lawyer went through all the minute details of the shooting which finally came to the arrest of Florence.

He drew admission from Scott that no warning was given the girl at the time they found her at the Gibeau house. She was brought to the barracks but instead of being put into a cell, was taken to Scott's private residence. The defence lit upon the fact that Florence's confession was not put down in writing.

"On the way from the Gibeau house, were any questions asked about how Lawson was shot, and the number of bullets in him?"

"Never."

"Did you tell her that four or five shots were heard ?"

"No."

"She was not adverse to talking; you couldn't keep her quiet?"

"That's about right."

"Up to the time she got to your kitchen she was not told she was not obliged to answer any questions?"

"No."

"When you warned her, you were not alone?"

"Someone was with me, but I cannot recall the name."

"Whoever was with you has not been called?" The tone was incredulous.

Scott then testified that he was alone with the girl when she made her statement. He had, in fact, read the warning to Florence from a small sheet of paper, but did not take any notes of the conversation.

"You had a notebook and were alone with her. Would it not have been a good thing to take notes of what she said. She wanted to talk."

"I remember what she said," the witness was suddenly defensive. He shifted slightly in his seat.

"Did you deem her confession to be of importance."

"Yes."

"And still you believed it preferable to rely more on your memory than on a written confession."

"I remember the story."

McKinley Cameron harped on this point. He drew an admission from Scott the first time Florence's confession was committed to writing was at the preliminary hearing. Suddenly McKinley Cameron switched his line of questions to the gun found at the Gibeau residence. Scott would not swear, however, he had shown the gun to Mrs. Gibeau. Although the woman had been subpoenaed to appear at the inquest she had not been called. The defense thought it strange the woman was not a witness at the trial. Again he came around to the question of the gun.

"You said you showed the gun to Mrs. Losandro?"

"Yes," said the man, "a short time after my return. She said, 'Did you get the gun?' I asked her what kind of gun was hers. She said, 'an automatic'. When I showed her the gun she said, 'yes, that's it'."

"You will not swear you are trying to put an automatic in the hands of the girl and the 38 calibre revolver in the hands of Picariello. Isn't it a fact that you tortured the facts to put an automatic into the hands of the girl and not the 38 calibre revolver?" The man's voice rose with the insistence of the question. But the answer came back to him with a dull 'no'.

Cameron then started off on another track, the scene with Picariello as he sat in the car waiting to go to Lethbridge.

McKinley Cameron wanted to know what Picariello said to

Scott at that time. Scott replied that Picariello called him over and asked if anything could be done to get Steve back from Michel. Scott told him he thought Steve was all right and may be better off than Picariello. Then Picariello said, 'They told me Steve was shot and I don't remember anything after that'.

"He might have said, I don't remember anything else," said the defense.

"I don't think so," said Scott.

"Do you think that would have any bearing on the case."

"Yes."

"And that it might supply a motive as to why he would have shot Lawson. Why didn't you ask Picariello to sign a statement for the man's own protection, and for the protection of the crown. Can you offer any reasonable explanation as to why you did not do this?" The voice was accusing, probing, angry.

"I was busy walking and..." the words trailed off helplessly.

"Walking!" The words were explosive, they fairly flew from the defence attorney's lips. "Was there anything more fundamental to both justice and the accused than this?"

"No."

"Do you realize that a man's and woman's life hangs on those few words?"

Stubbornly came the response, "I didn't take them down."

During this man's testimony the full plight of the evidence given closed around the girl. She sat with her head sunk down to her chest, a throbbing pain shot up her right arm into her neck and head. She wanted to shout at them, wanted to know where this would all end. The gun had been traced to her, they had her confession she shot Lawson and still, they went over and over it. Picariello promised to take care of her but he could not even take care of himself. Day by day he was pulled into the morass. Florence's head hurt from trying hard not to cry.

McKinley Cameron's questions of Scott continued for nearly two hours and when he was finally finished, McGillivray asked for the floor. He questioned Scott about the telephone conversation presumed to have taken place between Steve Picariello and someone in Blairmore on the afternoon of the chase. Turning to Scott, he asked him, "You did not hear about it?"

"No. Later someone told me about it."

"Who?"

"A Police officer."

It was 10 o'clock when court adjourned and a weary Florence was led back to her cell.

The Friday session began with Corporal Hidson testifying he was present when Scott read the warning to Picariello. Two more police officers were called, Corporal Drummond and Superintendent Nicholson, then Maggie Lawson was called to the stand.

The woman came in to the court room accompanied by a relative. She took the oath and made her way to the witness box.

In quiet tones she told the court of the peaceful events prior to the shooting, her words painting the warmth of the close family scene of that night.

McGillivray urged her on. She shuddered and her words took on the sharpness of the destructive scene. When she came to the shooting and told of finding her husband, she struggled for composure and wetness traced her cheeks. Women sobbed audibly in the courtroom and McKinley Cameron observed quietly, "There will be no cross examination."

Of the 3 last witnesses called, T.J. Brown, a civil engineer working in a CPR tunnel gave damning evidence as he reported, "He was talking (meaning Picariello) with a number of foreigners and I heard him say if he shot my boy, I will kill him tonight by God and he kissed the automatic gun he held in his hand!"[4]

Witness G.T. Freeman, station agent at Crow's Nest quoted Picariello as saying, 'If they have shot my boy I will kill every

---

4. Book of Evidence, Volume 4, Trial records, McKinley Cameron papers, Glenbow Alberta Institute.

policeman in the Pass. He then pulled out his gun and held it to his face.'

Witness G.E. Menning said, "He made a remark to the effect that if his son Steve had been hit through the shootings that occurred in Coleman that afternoon, he would get every policeman in the Pass." He too said Picariello put his gun to his lips.[5]

By 12:30 the case for the crown was closed. No evidence was offered by the defense and the court adjourned until 2 o'clock.

McGillivray's address to the jury on the afternoon of December 1 took 3 hours. It was eloquent, logical, impressive, with the concluding contention the Crown left the 6 men to decide the guilt or innocence of the prisoners.

Looking at the jury members he continued, "If you are convinced of the guilt of the accused, then you should say to the people of this land that crime shall not ride rampant among any class and our officers of the law, who, by day and by night protect our homes and children, shall not be shot down like dogs."

He proceeded, step by step, to trace the various incidents culminating in the killing of Lawson. He pointed out the occupants of the death car had been positively established as the defendants. He contended there was no hostility shown by Lawson when he went out to meet the defendants at the barrack door. The number of shots did not matter, what mattered was that Lawson was shot down in cold blood, in the back, and the bullet that killed him, issued from the car occupied by the defendants. The fact that Lawson was shot in the back indicated that Lawson was not attacking but seeking shelter from the rain of bullets.

"Now," said McGillivray, "the defense has expressed wonderment that Mrs. Gibeau, in whose house Florence Losandro had taken refuge, was not called to the stand. It was the privilege of the defense to put the woman on the stand if they

---

5. Ibid.

thought she could shed any light on the issue. But they did not do this.

"At any rate," he went on, "what material bearing can the testimony of one Italian woman have on this case, in the light of the great amount of evidence produced by the Crown?"

At this point, McKinley Cameron interrupted. "As a matter of fact the woman is Irish." The comment was dry, tinged with veiled sarcasm. The court however burst into tension relieving laughter.

"I appreciate the wit and cleverness of my learned friend," McGillivray said witheringly. His eyes narrowed to slits and he looked intently at the courtroom. "It is always a pleasure to be opposed by one whose ability never fails to produce everything in his power in favour of his client but I hold that the points involved in the trial, a trial involving life and death, should not be brushed aside like a joke!"

The faces of the participants in the courtroom sobered quickly on hearing this sombre statement and expectancy and uncertainty crowded in again. The people dropped their eyes, some shuddered not wanting to be there to hear the awful events leading up to the final decision but unable to tear themselves away from the dread fascination of the case. The crowd had an atavistic fascination with robbery and murder and were deeply interested in the crime but were also interested in the punishments meted out. They wanted justice to triumph in the end.

McGillivray continued his presentation. He ridiculed the claim of self defence. There was evidence to show that while Picariello and the girl were in hiding they framed up between themselves the best possible story to shield themselves. This apparently was that the girl would shoulder the blame, saying she shot in self defence. It had been said that Sergeant Scott, one of the Crown's chief witnesses, struck the Chief of Police in Blairmore. "But I ask you,' said McGillivray, "was Scott asked by my learned friend why he struck the Chief of Police?

"In a British court of justice the sex of a prisoner must not be considered. The girl went for her gun in order to accompany

Picariello to Coleman to get Lawson, and her interest in the young Steve Picariello probably supplied the motive." All eyes fastened on Florence at the utterance of this statement but she did not move, did not flinch. She remained immobile, her eyes cast down and only those very near would have been able to see the tightening of the soft mouth, the fire that lit briefly in the dark eyes.

"In the days of chivalry even murder by women was not tolerated!" He paused, then presented his summarizing arguments:

"Firstly, that on September 21 Constable Stephen O. Lawson was killed with a 38 calibre bullet. Secondly, the bullet was the cause of death, thirdly, that it mattered not that one bullet only entered his body. He was killed and both parties in the shooting are jointly guilty." He ticked off the points on his fingers, "fourth, the shots issued from the car in front of the barracks on the night of the murder. Fifth, both accused and they only, were in the car and from that car came the bullet that killed Lawson. Sixth, two guns were used, one a 38 calibre produced as an exhibit and acknowledged by Florence Losandro as her gun and another, a 32 automatic, not yet found, but which belonged to Picariello. He was seen with an automatic on the day of the murder," he paused to let his words sink in, "he was issued a permit to carry the gun along with the 38 calibre, the two guns in use in the slaying of the constable. Seventh, having regard for the evidence, the guns were the only ones capable of shooting the kind of bullets produced. Eighth, from the various statements made by Picariello it can be inferred that the crime was deliberate cold blooded murder. "

McGillivray moved to his table, turned and faced the jury. "Ninth, the motive was either revenge or the terrorizing of the police, impressing upon them that it was a dangerous thing indeed to touch the family of Emilio Picariello. Then tenth, at the time of his death, Lawson was unarmed. Eleventh, Lawson was shot in the back while moving away from bullets fired by these people and certainly these defendants could not have been defending themselves as Lawson was shot in the back, not in the stomach, as Mrs. Losandro stated in her confession to Scott."

The prosecution's methodical step by step summarization came to an end. Court was adjourned until 7:30 in the evening.

When McKinley Cameron started in on his address to the jury, a plea of self defense or justifiable homicide was the theory he advanced. In his adroit arguments he contended that Picariello's state of mind the evening of the shooting was one of triumph over saving the load and outwitting the police. He was not agitated but apparently went to the barracks to square things up with the officer and see if he couldn't get Steve back from Michel. A scuffle followed Lawson's arrival at the side of the car and Lawson grabbed Picariello around the neck. This, he said, was related to the court by Lawson's 9 year old daughter.

The defense lawyer continued, "It appears from the evidence given to this court that Lawson leaned down into the car, probably to get the automatic which we have made no attempt to show was not in the possession of the accused. Then there was the discharge of a gun from somewhere, one bullet came close to Mrs. Losandro's foot. She considered her own life in peril and thereupon shot, as she confessed to Scott, using the 38 calibre gun, the shot of which was found in Lawson. The 32 calibre bullets went wild in the melee that followed, smashing the speedometer and windshield. Lawson was shot while stooping over the car and not as he attempted to beat a retreat." McKinley Cameron's voice rose on the following points, "It was in this stooping position that the frightened woman fired, striking him in the shoulder and felling him. She said the bullet struck him in the stomach, but this was probably due to her excitement.

"Therefore," he continued, "the contention is that Picariello did not shoot Lawson or fire any shots wilfully or deliberately but that Lawson appears to have grappled the man around the neck probably choking him. Then, shots were fired from somewhere, followed by the firing of the woman in obedience to nature's first law, that of self defense."

McKinley Cameron argued the Crown had produced evidence which fitted into his theories with far more consistency than it did into any of their theories which he said arose and vanished as the case proceeded from day to day.

He then explained to the jury that the prisoners were being tried separately unless a common design on the life of Lawson had been proved and this he denied. He ridiculed the efforts of the Crown to prove that Lawson was unarmed. There was no suggestion made by the defence that he was armed. Picariello's conduct the evening of the shooting was not of bitterness or revenge. He felt proud that he had outwitted the officers and that even Scott had said his threats were a joke .

The lawyer made reference to rum running in the Pass. He observed dryly, "It was dangerous when the police did not want you to go through, but quite safe when they approved of your going through."

Cameron then dealt with Sergeant Scott. He gave the man severe censure, for his not taking down the confessions of the accused. If it was not for Scott's confession, tucked away in the corners of his mind but not on paper, where would the case for the crown be anyway?

The defense lawyer asked the jury, "If Picariello had been in a rage and wanted to get Lawson, don't you think he would have shot him on sight as he appeared in the doorway of the barracks. There was no trace of a design to kill Lawson. Again there appears to have been no provisions for protecting themselves after a shooting. They could have gone east or west in Picariello's high powered car and probably reached the border. But, there was no trace of a plan. There was no evidence shown of a common design to kill on the part of the accused."

The man thumped his hand on the table, "All through the trial the Crown has attempted to put the 38 calibre gun into Picariello's hands. This was due to their keenness to get a conviction. Their theories were like their witnesses — funny. It is unkind to a gallant officer like Lawson to be accused of retreating and to be shot in the back. I say that Lawson had hold of the automatic and never let go until he received his wound in the back."

McKinley Cameron concluded his address with an impassioned plea that race prejudice not be allowed in any way to influence the jury. Neither should they be influenced by the vicious propaganda that had been circulating since the trial opened or of any reports that have appeared in the press. Finally, McKinley Cameron wound up his address. He stirred the jammed court room with his concluding statement.

"Gentlemen, do not be bullied or influenced by the presence here of the Attorney General or of public sentiment, or of the dramatic appeals of my learned friend in an attempt to vindicate the virtues of the Alberta Liquor Act. Such a mess has been created down there that some victim must be found. Give this man the same consideration as you would your neighbour or friend." He turned and stalked back to his seat. It was twenty five minutes after eleven.

There was a dead silence and finally the Judge spoke.

"I feel the task before me to be a weighty one. I do not feel I would be able to properly charge the jury before two o'clock on Saturday," He continued gravely, "however, if the jury desires, I will fix the hour for eleven o'clock." The man's strong, intelligent face was saddened by the events of the testimony.

The jury foreman talked quietly to his fellow members. There was a nodding and shaking of heads. He arose to confirm agreement to the two o'clock session.

As the trial drew to an end, evening papers outlining the case were eagerly snapped up by the public. They gathered to listen to the radio, waiting through the dance hits on CJCA until the reports of the market, news and sports were given at nine forty-five. They listened to the waltz, 'Lovely Lucerne' by Matt's Orchestra and the popular, 'Thru the Night'. Some rose to dance to the fox trot music of 'Sweet Indiana Home', 'No Wonder I'm Lonesome' by Bailey's Lucky Seven and were glad they were not in the defendant's shoes.

On Saturday, standing room in the court room was at a

premium. The room overflowed with grave looking people. In order to hold back the crowds the police placed a rope across the corridor leading to the Supreme Court chambers and only a limited number of people were allowed to pass through.

The Honourable J.E. Brownlee was seated beside Crown Prosecutor McGillivray and the rest of the principals in the case were in their seats when Mr. Justice Walsh strode into the room to give his charge to the jury. The room was very quiet. The Judge started to speak.

"This is a case of absorbing interest and great responsibility. This is true of all murder trials. There are some circumstances in this case which increase the responsibility. The victim of this tragedy was an officer of the law, whose duty was to detect and assist in the punishment of crime. It is not suggested he met his death in the execution of his duty, but following events that led from it. Another matter which increases the responsibility is the fact that a man and woman are charged. It is a case of murder, a charge arising out of the death of one man and a charge by the Crown that both are responsible for this one man's death. You all have a general idea of what murder is. Murder in its broadest general sense is the unlawful and intentional taking of life . It is not always necessary to prove the intention to kill. If the killing of a human being takes place and there is no explanation of the circumstances, the intent to kill may be implied. If there is no excuse to justify this, the law will assume that the killing was intended and therefore he was murdered. Manslaughter is a lesser crime because there is not intent. There are killings of human beings which are justifiable. An officer of the law who carries out the execution of a criminal is excused of this. The Crown has charged both with the murder of Lawson, that is the charge which it is its duty to prove to the last degree before you would be justified to bring in a verdict of guilty.

"These two people came into this court last Monday as innocent people in the eyes of the law. That is as it should be. The evidence of the Crown has tried to prove them guilty. If the

Crown has not succeeded, then your verdict must be 'not guilty'. But, if on the other hand, the charge has been proven, you cannot escape the responsibility of bringing in a verdict of guilty. There is practically no evidence as to how Lawson was killed. He was shot behind the right shoulder by a 38 calibre revolver, which caused his death. Near the place where he was shot, he fell, practically in front of his home and in the presence of his wife and two children. These things are proven conclusively. You cannot escape the conclusion as to how he came to his death. The person who fired the shot committed murder, unless the shooting took place under excusable circumstances. If so, that is manslaughter. The remaining question is, does the evidence of the Crown satisfy you that the accused committed this act or does the evidence satisfy you that they are guilty of the lesser crime of manslaughter. The Crown has called many witnesses who clearly prove, if you believe them, that the two went to the barracks that night of the shooting. You are not under obligation to believe a witness who goes into the witness box under oath. Your duty is to take what you believe is the truth. You have the evidence of a number of witnesses some identifying the man and some the woman. Mr. Cameron admitted last night that these two defendants were in the car. Now, if you believe the witnesses, you will be perfectly right to find that they were in the car. There is no doubt that Lawson went out and engaged in conversation. After a time, firing began. Either the last or the second last shot is the one that lodged in Lawson's body. Now you are satisfied that one of the occupants fired that shot. If you are not, the Crown has failed in its case. If you concluded that the shot that killed Lawson was fired by one of these accused you should try to find who fired the shot. The person who fired that shot is the person who must be held responsible. If that person fired without acting in concert with the other, that is the person who is guilty. On the other hand, if they were acting in concert, then both are guilty."

The Chief Justice stopped to explain the law on this point.

After a short pause he continued.

"So if these two people went together for a purpose, each is responsible. With that view, it is immaterial who fired the shot. But you may not agree, so it is essential that your endeavour is to find who fired the shot. The evidence on this point is not very clear and conclusive. Lawson's 9 year old daughter's unsworn statement was to the effect that the lady fired the shot. There is the woman's statement, if you accept it, that she fired the shot. You are not bound to accept Sergeant Scott's statement in this connection, if you think that Scott made his story out of 'whole cloth' you must disregard it. On the other hand, if you think Scott's evidence was truthful, you may believe it. Another point which leads to the belief that she fired the shot is the hole in the front of the car. She was on the right and Picariello on the left. There is the gun, a 38 calibre corresponding to the bullet found in Lawson's body. If she is right in saying she carried a 38 revolver on the night of the murder, it is obvious she fired the shot. There is some suggestion that Picariello carried the 38 calibre revolver and the woman the automatic. This was brought out by Sergeant Scott in finding the ammunition in the rooms of the accused. There is no evidence except Scott's that he searched the two rooms of the accused. He gave reasons for his expressions and you can judge the same as Scott and decide whether Scott was in the right rooms.

"You are supreme Judges when it comes to a decision of facts. I am not going to impose my opinion on you. You will be judged entirely by your appreciation of the facts. If you are able to decide from evidence which one fired the shot then you may fix the responsibility in connection with this tragedy. Then again you must decide whether the other one is equally responsible."

The Judge shifted in his chair, read to the jury the section from the Criminal Code dealing with the question of aiding and abetting. He paused and looked thoughtfully at the jury members:

"What is the evidence from which the Crown relies that these two went to Lawson's home for a common purpose? There is the woman's own statement, the statement she gave to Scott is against herself and herself alone. She made some references to Picariello but you must not connect him on that account. The same applies to Picariello's statement. As to Picariello, what is there to justify the conclusion that he and the woman were acting in concert. That brings us to the story of the chase in the afternoon and the shots fired by Lawson at Steve. Picariello followed the constables in the chase and got into British Columbia. He was at the Crow's Nest Pass station and Picariello it seems, learned of the shooting of Steve. You have heard a witness, Brown, say that Picariello had at that time, said, "If he has shot my boy, I will kill him tonight by God. " He then kissed his gun. Freeman and Menning also made similar statements though the wording was different. Picariello then returned to Blairmore where he met a George Allen. Picariello had said, "I don't like this shooting but if they can shoot I can shoot too." He later met Sergeant Scott and said, "It is lucky that Lawson did not shoot my boy, else I would kill him." Picariello, it is suggested, had a telephone conversation with someone in Michel about six forty-five with reference to Steve, therefore he knew that Steve was alive. In consequence to the affair in the afternoon and in view to give an effect to those threats, he started out to give effect to those threats. Regarding Picariello having a revolver, three witnesses have sworn he had an automatic revolver earlier in the day. The condition of the car indicates that an automatic was used that night. There is a hole through the speedometer board; now if those two people left Blairmore with the girl having a 38 gun and the man an automatic, what was the object of this mission? So far as the girl is concerned, we have her statement to Scott. Regarding Picariello, we have no such statement. After all, we have the conduct of the two after the crime. They went back to Blairmore, deserted the automobile and disappeared. The next afternoon Picariello was taken climbing a hill back of the town. He disregarded the command to halt. He was found crouching down on the top. That may be excusable thinking perhaps that some harm had come to Lawson. It may have been prompted by a guilty conscience or by a degree to escape arrest. In answer to statements that he had not given Lawson a chance to defend himself, he said to Constable Tutin, 'he tried to shoot me'. To Bradner he said, 'Lawson had a gun'. There is a significance in the difference in the words used. I don't know what you think of discrepancies of that sort but I am generally inclined to think little of a slight disagreement in a minor point. If Picariello made a statement what inference would either of these statements have on your mind. It has been proven and admitted that Lawson was unarmed. There is no suggestion in the evidence that Picariello ever denied that he was concerned in it but rather that he had taken a part and had made a statement which was not borne out in fact. If you think this was not a prearranged affair then there was no common design to commit the act. If, on the other hand, that it was prearranged with both taking guns, and went with the purpose of doing bodily harm, then you have to hold both equally guilty. If they went for that purpose and shot Lawson, what defence is there to this charge? In my opinion there is only one around which could be set up as absolute defence, and that is, this shooting was done in self defence. The burden of proving this lies with the accused. It is not the duty of the crown."

Here Mr. Justice Walsh again paused, referred to his books and read the law on self defence.

"There is no evidence that assault was committed upon the Losandro woman. Picariello was not under her protection. If, because of the fact that as she says, the gun was pointed towards her, she would be justified in shooting the man who held the gun. It is a very difficult section of the code to explain to you. If Picariello started trouble which provoked an attack he would be justified in killing Lawson afterward if he believed his life was in danger. This only applies if he had not provoked the assault. What are the facts we have? Lawson's 9 year old daughter saw her father's arm around Picariello's neck. We have Scott's statement that Mrs. Losandro had fired when the gun was pointing towards her. It is quite obvious that there was a struggle in the car. The broken windshield and bullet holes speak for it. As against these statements we have Mrs. Emmerson's evidence. She said she saw Lawson with his feet on the car. She said she had seen Lawson stagger back and fall."

The man again searched through his papers, outlined to the jury the evidence of the 9 year old daughter which was unsworn.

"The evidence of the Losandro woman relating to the part she took in the shooting was very damaging to her, if you wish to believe Scott's story. If you think she made that statement, how far does it get you, with respect to the plea of self defense? You must bear in mind that Lawson was unarmed. It is quite true as Mr. Cameron pointed out, that they could not know that Lawson was unarmed, in view of the shooting in the afternoon. You saw Mrs. Emmerson break down on the witness stand. You are entitled to consider the location of the wound. Do you think that the wound was such as would bear out the plea of self defence? What inference do you draw from the meagre information on the subject? The shots in the windshield and the hole in the footboard? Is that consistent with the theory that Picariello, having drawn his gun, was seized by Lawson and in the struggle Picariello's hand was deflected and the shots went through the board and glass? If that is so, can you say that Lawson should be shot? Proof of this kind should be strong and conclusive. Can you find it in the evidence? If you can, you should give effect to it in your verdict. Regarding the plea of self defence it must be established as facts before you that the lives of the accused were threatened. If these people went to kill Lawson in cold blood there would have been less risk killing him when he came down. Mr. Cameron argued this and I again give it to you for what it is worth. What is there in the evidence that up to the time the arms of Lawson were seen around Picariello's neck to show that Lawson was belligerent? I don't think I have anything more to say. I have tried to confine my remarks to the evidence in dispute."

The Justice then paid tribute to counsel for both the Crown and the Defence. Further, he said, "It is my duty to say to you that there are two grounds, either of which you may reduce murder to manslaughter."

Adjusting his glasses, he read from the criminal code. He outlined the reasons why a manslaughter verdict might be returned against Picariello. It could only be done if Picariello had taken his part in the heat of passion. Going on he stated:

"This could not apply to the woman. She could not get in a heat of passion over what happened to Steve Picariello. She was nothing to him." At his words, Florence shrank miserably further down in her chair. She wanted to scream at them all, 'Get this over with, enough.... Oh, I have had enough..." But she remained impassive, only her hands in her lap clenched and unclenched. "There was the other ground, the occurrences in the car. If you think that what took place there was not self defence you may think perhaps that in the heat of the argument there might he sufficient evidence to conclude that the intent to kill was not there. That is for you to decide. If you find that only one was concerned in the murder, the other one should be acquitted. If you find it was a common design, then they can be both held responsible. If you find a plea of self defence established then you can acquit that one. If you find the crime was committed in the heat of passion, then you must bring in a verdict of manslaughter. I am confident you want to give a true verdict according to the evidence."

It was eighteen minutes to four when the Justice left the room. The jury was retired to a special room to make its decision and the prisoners were escorted back to their cells.

On the city streets the trial was on everyone's lips. Rumours were rampant. When the crowds realized a verdict might be expected when the court reconvened at eight o'clock that night, hundreds of spectators gathered. The court house doors were locked however and only those who had given evidence, court officials, lawyers and newspapermen were allowed into the building. A silent crowd waited.

In the courtroom, there was an air of apprehension in the room. People were on edge, there was a hesitancy in the talk, a dread.

A few minutes before eight the prisoners were brought in. Picariello was sullen, he came first and took his position on the right hand side of the dock. A pale and weak looking woman followed; Florence was on the verge of collapse.

As if in a play, at the stroke of eight counsel for the Crown and defense filed into the room and took their places. His Lordship Mr. Justice Walsh followed.

Immediately after his Lordship was seated the sheriff opened the door and the jury walked to their places. Their faces were drawn, pale; their eyes downcast.

The Clerk of the Court, Lawrence J. Clarke, took a formal jury check and they answered to their names. Before asking the jury for its verdict, the Judge issued a stern warning to those assembled. "I wish to state before this verdict is given that no matter what kind of verdict it is, I will not tolerate a demonstration of any kind. This is a court of justice and if any person starts a demonstration, I will see that he is brought before me and properly punished."

He asked for the verdict. The Clerk of the Court rose and addressed the jury: "Gentlemen of the jury, have you agreed on a verdict? If so, make it known through your foreman."

Bagley, the foreman, slowly rose to his feet. He faced the Judge. "We have, your Honour."

"What is your verdict then?"

There was the pause of only a moment but it seemed an eternity. Only the ticking of the clock was heard. It seemed that the world stopped, all breath abated, the courtroom and its people were suspended in time.

"We find both the accused, Emilio Picariello and Florence Losandro, guilty of murder!"

The words sounded through the silence, resounded and echoed around the room. Guilty......guilty....... People bowed their heads and shut their eyes but the sounds were still there.......Guilty.....Guilty!

Then his Lordship spoke.

"Gentlemen of the jury, I must express concurrence with your verdict. If any other decision had been reached it would have been, in my opinion, a grave miscarriage of justice. I felt at the close of the trial that the Crown had clearly proven the charge against these two people. During my address to you I endeavoured to instruct you as was my duty..." he paused and looked intently at the two rows of men on whose shoulders the decision rested, "and I endeavoured to withhold my own thoughts upon the matter after hearing the evidence. And you have reached the only possible verdict under the evidence given."

He turned towards the prisoner's box and asked Emilio if he had anything to say before sentence of the court was imposed upon him.

McKinley Cameron rose and went to his client and they conversed in low tones. The lawyer turned to the Judge and said, "Nothing, my Lord."

"Emilio Picariello, stand up." commanded the Judge.

Picariello stood. His shoulders were well back. He looked directly at the Judge. Mr. Justice Walsh continued, "You no doubt heard my remarks to the jury and I will not repeat them at this time. The laws of Canada leave no discretion to the Judge as to the sentence he can impose upon anyone found guilty as you have been, on the charge of murder. Every word spoken in this case will be transcribed and sent to his excellency, the Governor General of Canada, together with my report. I am not holding out any hope to you that he may commute this sentence. I am merely telling you what will be done."

He motioned and the Clerk of the Court crossed the courtroom, took a calendar from the wall and passed it up to the Judge.

Picariello retained his poise but his face was gray, the prison pallor heightened by the doom he was about to receive. He watched intently as the Judge counted the days to follow, counted the days of his life span.

In the deadly quiet the dreaded words came.

"I therefore order that you be removed from here and taken to the Fort Saskatchewan gaol. You will be taken from your place of confinement on February 21, 1923 and on that day you will be hanged by the neck until you are dead. And may God have mercy on your soul."

The man's legs buckled as the worded blow hit him. He dropped heavily into his seat and stared unseeingly into the floor before him.

The Judge asked the same question of Florence. "Do you have anything to say before the sentence of the court is imposed upon you?"

In a daze Florence slowly shook her head and McKinley Cameron again stood. "Nothing, my Lord."

"Florence Losandro, stand up."

With an effort Florence rose, looking smaller and thinner than ever before. Her matron supported her. "I have no alternative but to sentence you to the same fate. In view of the fact that you are a woman, it might be possible that some clemency will be extended to you. I am merely telling you of this possibility but you should prepare yourself to meet your fate. I therefore order that you be removed from here and taken to the Fort Saskatchewan gaol. You will be taken from your place of confinement on February 21, 1923 and on that day you will be hanged by the neck until you are dead and may God have mercy on your soul."

Florence bent slightly forward as she strained to catch each word. She recoiled in terror and shock as the final words came from his lips. Her lips moved as she sought to speak but the "no... no..." was soundless. With a small moan she closed her eyes and in a half faint dropped into her seat.

The tension in the room snapped. People moved in their seats, sought each other's hands, felt empathy for the two condemned and moved to seek comfort in one another.

The Judge rose and in accord the court rose too. It was over.

The news flashed over the wires at 8:20 p.m.. Concerts and the theatre were interrupted while the news was announced. It was told that justice was satisfied, law and order vindicated and a blow dealt to crime.[6]

---

6. General footnote for chapter, verbatim evidence and speeches taken from Book of Evidence, volumes 1 to 4, Trial records, McKinley Cameron papers, Glenbow Alberta Institute.

XVII

WATCH WITH ME

THE GIRL WAS led back to her cell and left alone. Her racking sobs echoed down the hall as she shook in convulsive spasms. The culmination of the week of dread and terror loosened the gates of emotion and her anguished cries escaped the pillow into which she thrust her head. The words of the Judge came back to her, searing themselves into her brain. She writhed on her bunk, trying to get away, to escape, but the words stung her, causing excruciating pain to the young body.

A matron came into the cell, hesitantly put her hand on the girl's shoulder and told her an escort had arrived. Florence was going back to Fort Saskatchewan on the evening train. The matron busied herself, gathered the girl's few possessions. She stuffed them into a canvas bag belonging to the gaol. The woman looked around the cell, satisfied herself that nothing was left and again put her hand on the girl's shoulder. There was no response. The matron bent forward, strained to hear the words, mingled with the cries, coming from the tortured girl. Wringing her hands in despair she fled.

At the railway station a few Saturday travellers, reporters and morbid curiosity seekers braved the bitter cold. A brisk wind slid over the frozen ground, rawing the temperature of 10 degrees below zero.

The station building was dingy, its siding faded to a dull red. A black and white sign proclaiming 'Calgary' swung from each end of the roof. A wooden planked walk, a foot or so higher than the rails, was gouged and rough, worn by repeated trips of the iron banded wheels of the baggage wagons.

In the waiting room a pot bellied stove glowed futilely in the high ceilinged room. A naked bulb cast shadows on garish green walls lined with hard wooden benches. Sooty windows were finger smudged by anxious travellers who rubbed a hole in the frosty pane to get a glimpse of an approaching train.

A station agent, in his small ticket window, looked with interest at the prisoners before turning to close a dull metal safe neatly inscribed 'Dominion Express Company, J.J. Taylor Safeworks, Toronto'.

The train was waiting. Picariello carried a small tan club bag, a quiet Florence carried nothing. She shivered as their party of guards crossed the rough walk. Looking up before she boarded the train, she saw Carlo and Steve standing to one side. She tried to greet them, to smile but no smile would come to the pale countenance; her eyes filled with tears and she stumbled up the few stairs into the day coach. Seeing them was too much for her and she turned her head away in pain. She was going back, back to the greyness of the gaol that had become her home.

The train started to move, rocking gently. The movement was almost soothing or could have been had the young girl been receptive to its motion. The coach was deserted except for the prisoners and their guards. Picariello and two guards sat at one end of the coach. Florence, her matron and one guard were seated in the middle. Sergeant Scott and Constable Bradner were in the party. The guards read newspapers, smoked and talked in subdued tones; the matron knitted endless stitches on an endless garment. Florence stared out the window.

The train glided past a jumble of buildings on the outskirts of Calgary and was soon into the countryside. It slid past rich, dark fields in corduroy furrows, neatly hem-stitched with gray wired posts. Here and there cream coloured fields appeared, with straw rows lying like grosgrain silk. Some fields had piles of straw rising like dumpy loaves of bread. The fields where interspersed with clumps of purple gray bushes and trees denuded of leaves. Sometimes a pond lay close to the tracks, its frozen surface caught with moon silver. The land was silent, spent, and the girl felt akin to it.

As the train moved into the night, small farm houses appeared among the trees, tucked like tiny boxes into the earthen patchwork. Orange rectangles of light shone from their depths. Against the blur of silver the russet tangles were etched against a heavy sky. A thin seam of moon was crowded by the moving clouds and was gone. Florence closed her eyes.

It was 8 o'clock Sunday morning before the small party of prisoners and guards arrived at the police barracks in Edmonton.

The man and girl were put into cells and breakfast trays brought in. Under the metal covers were porridge, toast and strong black coffee. The girl cupped the tin mug and felt its warmth in the cradle of her hands. She looked with no interest at the thick porridge, the white of the thin milk filling its coulee edges. She bit into the toast but it went around and around in her mouth and she could not swallow. She was suddenly sick.

Florence had hoped to be free after the trial. She believed with blind faith Picariello would somehow save them both. Now she was faced with more weeks of fear and loneliness with the spectre of death at the end. Again she would have to cope with the cacophony of jail noises, the distressing metal upon metal sounds that grated and rang in her ears. She would be subjected to bold stares, appraising glances and a knowledge of her own anonymity. As she contemplated her own private purgatory a cold sweat broke out on her face and she strove to control a nervous tic. Panic rushed at her but she had nowhere to turn.

Footsteps echoed down the corridor. The matron was at the cell door telling her to get her coat and hat on.

"Did you eat your breakfast?" The older woman peered under the metal covers, saw the one bite from the toast. "You have to eat, girl, you'll make yourself sick." As if it matters thought Florence. She slipped into her coat and was ready.

The drive to Fort Saskatchewan was over too quickly. A warm sun broke through the muddy dawn and its warmth drew moisture from the hoary crystals of the night that clung to dead roadside brush. From this rose misty wisps, floating gently, undisturbed until the car's passage caused the vapour to mix and swirl around, mingling and intermingling. Florence saw her last glimpse of countryside before the cars turned into the forbidding gaol yard at noon.

Again the prisoners went through the indignity and demoralizing recording of their persons on admission to the gaol. On a long ledger sheet the Chief Guard inscribed the details. The only sound was the scratch of pen nib against the paper and his infrequent questions.

Picariello's entry number was 3283 and they wrote he was married, age 43, weight 210 pounds, height 5 feet 6 1/2 inches, ruddy complexion, brown eyes and dark hair, turning grey. Of his special marks they noted a Union Jack and Italian flag tattooed on his right forearm. His occupation was listed as merchant, his creed Roman Catholic. He was sent from the Calgary District for the crime of murder. The date of the sentence was December 2, 1922 and the term, sentenced to hang February 21, 1923.

For Florence they assigned the number of 488 and noted she was married, age 22, weight 115 pounds, height 5 feet, 1 inch, complexion dark, eyes brown, hair dark brown and bobbed. Under special marks was listed an operation scar on her abdomen. Her occupation was listed as housewife, her creed Roman Catholic. The details of her sentence were the same as Picariello's with the exception she was handed over to matron Osgood. On both forms the date of discharge was noticeably left blank. There was to be no discharge for this pair.

The news of the trial soon faded from public view. The cost of the trial, purported to $15,000.00 was reported in 3 inches of newspaper space compared to the blaring headlines and columns of reports taken at the trial which filled several pages. Cold weather, heightened by a keening wind, turned newspaper space to advertisements for flannels and wools and Christmas ads started to appear.

In the gaol, both prisoners slipped into the routine with ease. With Christmas approaching, Emilio was acutely conscious of his loss and yearned for his family, remembering other warm advent days in the big house. The shock of his sentence did not culminate in tears. Instead he grew morose, ate nothing and stared into space. The prison doctor was called on Tuesday, December 5 and Emilio was treated for depression.

Prisoners under sentence of death did not have contact with the main body of prisoners. Emilio occupied an isolated cell in the main prison while Florence was held in a similar cell in the women's section.

The night guard book showed no great fluctuation of prisoners. On an average there were 105 male prisoners of which 69 were in cells, 35 in dormitories and 1 trustee lodged in the boiler room. Females on the same date showed 34 in dormitories, 6 in cells. Prison routine was dreary and monotonous. Both Emilio and Florence were forced into its routines; there was nothing else to do but submit. As with all male prisoners, Emilio's hair was clipped short by an inmate with a slight tendency to barbering. He spent his time alone in his cell, reading and writing letters, eating very little. He took his exercise alone, ate alone, seeing on a daily basis only the guard assigned to him for the day. Often they played long games of checkers through the opening in the cell door where the food trays passed through.

For Florence, her life each day started with the shrill ringing of the bell. She was to wash and dress, make her bunk and be ready for her breakfast tray. She spent her days writing letters, reading and doing embroidery and crocheting lace. Her cell, although segregated from the others, was the same and contained a bunk, toilet bowl and wash basin. There was a small bench and very little else. It was clean and neat.[1]

The young girl settled into the prison fabric of life with the same docile quietness marked by her other episodes with

---

1. Letter of Father Choicoine to the author dated July 31, 1978 — "Florence's cell was a regular one in line with the others provided with a bed, toilet bowl, and a bench and little else, if any. It was neat and sanitary."

authority. She passed a pensive Christmas reflecting on her plight. The point of her full maturity came quietly, almost unnoticed by the girl. She passed through dark days, her sanity saved by a few threads of hope. She was calm, seemingly to have accepted the reality of death. Other days however were filled with tears of self pity, thoughts of hatred and anger towards those who put her there. It was a common idea of the day that justice would deal lightly with her, being a woman and so young, but in this case it was not so and the sentence of death was a shock that came back to haunt her every move.

She passed through spasms of remorse and her days became unbearable. Then she wildly considered taking her own life but found herself unable to attempt it. The bewildered girl searched for a hand she could take in her time of need.

From the window sills of her mind she took down her dreams; watered them, nurtured them, allowed them to flower. She gathered all her lovely memories and lived the golden hours of her yesterdays and turned, fortified, to prepare herself for a long journey. Her searching need, for solace and peace, for the hand she sought, took her to a renewed relationship with her God. In her mind a childhood echo of prayer came to her and she asked to see a priest.

On January 7, and every week thereafter, except one, Florence was visited by Father Fidelis Chicoine.[2]

A small brick church of the Roman Catholic faith was located near the provincial Gaol. Called Our Lady of Angels, the parish was under the care of the Franciscan Fathers of north Edmonton. Assigned to this post was the 27 year old monk from St. Charles, Quebec.

Father Fidelis entered the order of the Franciscan Fathers in 1916 as a postulant. As the Catholic population of the town of Fort Saskatchewan was very small and amounted to less than

---

2. Details of prison life of Florence and Emilio were provided to the author by Father Fidelis Chicoine in numerous written reports, telephone conversations and a meeting with him in Montreal, Quebec.

25 families, there was no resident parish priest. The young monk was in charge of the Catholic inmate population of the gaol, visiting them on Sunday afternoons and holding a service for both men and women once a month. Father Fidelis would arrive on a Saturday, administer to the needs of the parish and the gaol, then leave the following Monday.

On January 7, the young priest brought the mass to an end in the women's prison. Turning, he blessed the inmates then left the public hall to remove his religious garments. In the main administration office there was a list left for him with the names of inmates wishing to speak to him during the afternoon. All the inmates, except one, were brought to the public hall under the watchful eyes of a guard. Their requests were many; some wanted families found, illiterates needed help writing letters, some merely wanted support, someone to talk to, a person to care. The eyes of the monk flickered over the last name on the list. He would attend the woman in her cell and her name caught and held his interest. She was the young woman under sentence of death and the young monk's heart went out to the person carrying this heavy load.

His surprise was great when the young girl, so delicately small, came to the cell door to greet him. Her greeting was slightly shy but as the monk talked to the girl, a strength of spirit emerged and took over. During the remaining months left to Florence the monk met with her each week. Her sentence of death was set for February 21 and she had very little time left to accomplish what she felt was necessary to save her soul.

She displayed no bitterness to the monk, did not mention the shooting nor did she ask about Picariello. He had failed her, could not help her and she must find her own way. Now, during the long weekdays, she had something to occupy her mind as she studied the catechism left by the monk. On each visit she had questions about her faith. Her curiosity was aroused and she wanted to know more, to understand, to believe.

As she awakened to her religion, she found she could be free, not free in body away from the prison, but free in her mind. She turned to a state of loving her God and felt Him living within her. Every morning was a true new morning, nothing in the new day allotted to her was part of her past. No lingering fogs from her yesterdays crowded into this time to claim and obliterate her. The only thing important was her preparation, and to this she gave her utmost devotion.

Her newly awakened faith was all that helped the young girl through long nights of terror. She was acutely aware of being alone, with no one to talk to, no one to comfort her in the dimly lit cell. Florence could hear the winter wind moaning as she awoke from dreams of terror and nightmares that caused a scream to catch in her throat. When this happened, as it often did, she buried her face in the pillow and pulled a blanket over her head. It was a futile gesture, there was no place to hide, no escape from the reality of approaching death. She thought of Steve but the young man was a blurring image far away in the fields of her youth and these thoughts brought about bitter-sweet memories of days that seemed to have never happened, days far away and not important. She grew afraid of the dark, it represented a void she was about to enter. Bruise coloured circles formed under eyes perpetually clouded with pain.

At times Florence was overcome by days of complete exhaustion of mind and body,[3] she ate little of the bland prison food and lost weight. Only her exercise, taken daily in the frozen yard, huddled into her coat, stirred the girl as she became aware of the drumming cold. Her luminous eyes sought the sky, searching. The silence of the prison reinforced the repressive atmosphere that clung to the girl and she spent her days hungrily learning the mysteries of her religion.

As the prisoners waited, legal efforts were being put forth by lawyers seeking an appeal. Mr. Herchmer wrote to Cameron December 26, 1922 putting forth 2 points on which to base an appeal.... 'You will no doubt remember that in talking over the

---

3. Ibid.

alleged confession of Mrs. Losandro to Scott that there was a suggestion that Scott did actually threaten Mrs. Losandro and, although I cannot remember just who told me, the information I gathered was that the matron who was in the Frank Barracks at the time of Mrs. Losandro's arrest was present when Scott made his threats to the effect that Mrs. Losandro might just as well make a clean breast of the whole affair as she had eaten the last Christmas dinner she would ever eat in this world. I further understood that the matron will be prepared to furnish this evidence and I imagine that if we could secure an affidavit from her that it would greatly strengthen our position coupled with the other two points that the Crown did not definitely prove the confessions and that they were not taken down in writing as promised.'[4]

The information given to Florence regarding the appeal by her family and Carlo were vague and distressing. McKinley Cameron had raised 32 questions of law in his appeal factum to the Appellate Court of Alberta. The application was refused by Mr. Justice Walsh who held that none of the questions were debatable. Then McKinley Cameron announced he would carry the application directly to the Appellate Division of the court. The hearing was set for January 29 in Edmonton. At this hearing McKinley Cameron would try to prove to the 3 appellate judges that Mr. Justice Walsh wrongfully refused leave to appeal. If the application was granted then the lawyer would apply for a date upon which he could appeal the verdict.

One of the questions raised by McKinley Cameron was the legality of the additional names to the jury panel. This was quashed by the Court as being quite regular. One by one the questions raised by the lawyer were dismissed by the appellate judges. As to Florence, the judges ruled there was no basis for a verdict of either manslaughter or not guilty. There was nothing that could be considered as provocation on her part.

---

4. McKinley Cameron papers, Glenbow Alberta Institute, Calgary, Alberta.

They rejected a plea of self defense for her.

Of the five appellate judges, 4 concurred. These were Justices Stuart, Simmons, Ives and Hindman. The 5th judge, Beck, dissented. He held there were insurmountable objections to the charge of the trial judge on the subject of manslaughter.

The appeal to the Appellate Division of Alberta was dismissed.

In stony silence Picariello received news of the appeal. In front of his guard he maintained his detached air, to him any open display of fear was a sign of weakness. He turned a white handkerchief over and over in his hands. He was visibly shaken and turned away to contain and conceal his thoughts.

On February 16, Florence awoke with a cold premonition. All day the feeling stayed with her and she spent most of the morning staring sullenly at the floor. A matron came into the cell and the girl jumped with a start.

"Florence, the warden's coming to see you." The matron was all crispness and neat in her uniform. The girl did not lift her head, nor did she acknowledge the remark. She continued to stare at the bare floor.

"Come on Florence, you can hear me. I know you can. That's a good girl, brush your hair now." The older woman rummaged in a canvas bag and pulled out a brush. She thrust it into the girl's hands.

Florence's heart pounded. There was a known situation, the hanging, but before there were all the unknowns; it was these small preparations, the ones before the event that Florence dreaded and was so afraid of. It was these unknowns that made her heart pound with an inner apprehension. She wondered what the warden wanted and she shrank from his call.

Footsteps were coming down the hall. The girl started slightly and her eyes fixed on the ugly metal of the door. She ran the brush through her hair and composed herself. Her face was impassive, her manner detached and cool when the warden stepped into the cell.

Without ceremony the man gently told the girl of a stay of

execution. It would be another month he said, the new date was to be March 21. The reprieve was granted waiting for a decision as to whether the appeal to the supreme Court of Canada for a new trial was allowable.

The girl's hand went to her mouth and she turned abruptly from the warden. A surge of anger welled up against those who played havoc with her life. Frustration surged from deep inside.

The warden left the cell. Florence then turned and pounded the walls furiously with her hands. The rough texture bit deeply into the soft flesh, blood oozed from cuts on her palms and ran down her wrists. She was oblivious to the blood and pain, a deeper hurt held her fast inside.

Florence paced her cell. Her matron came hurriedly along the corridor with a pan of warm water and cloths. The distraught girl allowed her hands to be taken, allowed the medication but did not feel its pinch.

"Why me?", she muttered, "why are they doing this to me? I never hurt them, why me?" There was no one to answer her questions.

The matron sat with the girl all evening. She tried to talk to her but Florence withdrew in silence. A fierce battle waged behind the dark eyes. It was late when she fell into an exhausted sleep.

The monk heard the news with relief. There was the appeal to the Supreme Court, there was hope. The next day, February 17, he hurried to the gaol to see Florence.

After the catechism had been studied and all the girl's questions answered, Florence seemed inclined to talk and she reminisced about the home country she loved. They talked about the mountains and the smell of the pines. She told him about the delicate wood violet found on the meadow floor. It grew strongly in spite of the tall, overpowering vegetation around it. As she talked, the bittersweet thought of the day lilies came to her. She remembered that day in the sun and how Steve's hands shook as he held the flower to her throat to see the reflection of the golden stamen on her skin. She spoke earnestly of the day lily,of the elegance of the slender stem crowned with a pure creamy head. The young monk told Florence about the lily and its connection with the resurrection and eternal life.

"Father," she said suddenly, turning to look at him intently, "will you do something for me?" The monk nodded and she continued softly, "If I have to go, you know... Father. Will you buy some lilies to take along with me?"[5]

Her eyes teared at the thought but she swallowed and smiled bravely. She struggled with her composure and won. "Maybe I won't have to go." This last sentence was wistful.

The monk promised.

As the winter months passed, the newspapers seemed to forget the prisoners. Now, with the dismissal by the Alberta court and the pending appeal to the Supreme Court of Canada, newspapers stirred themselves and the accused were again at the front of the news.

In Mexico City, radical groups demonstrated March 6 against the death sentence imposed on two Canadian women, Florence Losandro and another woman by the name of Irene Christensen. The appeal and the demonstration competed for newspaper space with other world events; the death of the famous Sarah Bernhardt in Paris and the approaching marriage of Albert, Duke of York to the Lady Elizabeth Bowes-Lyon in Westminister Abbey.

Again, as Florence steeled herself for the date of March 21, another reprieve came to the tormented girl. On March 13, a reprieve was ordered. The new date of execution was set for May 2. The date of the last appeal to the Supreme Court of Canada was scheduled for April 3 in Ottawa.

Told of the new reprieve the young girl collapsed. The lights blurred and the room swung crazily around her. It was cruel, cruel to keep a false new hope stirring within her. For a time she could not talk, sleep or think. She paced the small cell

5. From Father Chicoine's writings to the author.

throughout the long night till morning light filtered through the bars. Exhausted and weak, she slumped to the floor. On April 1 the monk was called to the girl 3 times as her depression deepened.

On April 3 the lawyers gathered in the court for the Supreme Court sitting. This was the highest court of the land and Emilio's and Florence's last hope.

The appeal was heard by a panel of 5 judges of which Justice Idington was the presiding Judge. A. Geoffrion of Montreal, Paul Leduc of Ottawa, McKinley Cameron and Sherwood Herchmer acted for the accused. McGillivray and S. J. Helman appeared for the Crown.

At the outset of the appeal McGillivray suggested the case would be limited to the reasons as set forth by Justice Beck. The Chief Justice concurred. Picariello's lawyers however were seeking a new trial and they put forth a motion for delay to the Supreme Court. Leduc, acting for Picariello, wanted more time to prepare for the appeal. Then, when he said he would not be ready for a month the court grew indignant. Geoffrion added his voice to the motion for a delay but the Chief Justice intimated counsel was merely trifling with the court.

McGillivray, acting for the Crown, continued arguments opposing a new trial. He stated the trial judge was right in stating a man was deemed to intend the natural consequences of any act he committed, citing a House of Lords judgment to this effect.

Idington pointed out the report of the trial was in court and he could not accept the plea the whole record was not in place. The plea for delay was denied.

The appeal was thus limited to the objections made by Justice Beck. One by one the dissenting objections were gone over by the court. The first one was the law of provocation, the second was evidence of a telephone conversation. The defense held that the trial judge was in error in drawing the attention of the jury to the alleged telephone conversation between Picariello and his son as this was only heresay evidence. It was the trial judge's responsibility to see only proper evidence went before the jury. The third point was indifference as to the acts and conduct of each of the defendants as evidence against the other and the fourth, the charge was defective on the question of common design.[6] McKinley Cameron argued strongly on the question of the charge to the jury by the trial judge in not keeping clearly in his mind Section 53 of the Criminal Code which deals with defense against assault. If, argued the lawyer, Lawson was the person who started the assault, the provision of Section 53 should be kept fairly in the Judge's mind and then put to the jury. He pointed out the trial judge did not have this section in his mind nor did he point it out to the jury but instead dealt with sections 54 and 55. Quoting from Section 53 McKinley Cameron noted the provision, 'if a person found his life to be in danger he could rebuff by force and could cause death or grievous bodily harm if he did so under the apprehension of death or grievous bodily harm'.

However the 5 judges could see little foundation for the objections. When their decision was reached, the robed men filed back into the courtroom to deliver the verdict.

Judge Idington rose at once. His words were solemn and final.

"The appeal is dismissed with costs!"

Having delivered the verdict, the Judges rose, assumed their three cornered hats and filed from the court.[7]

In Ottawa, McKinley Cameron wired the warden of Fort Saskatchewan advising him of the dismissal of the appeal. He advised the warden to tell the prisoners. The news came as a shock to both Emilio and Florence. What little hope they had left was built on the appeal and the finality of the verdict brought them one step closer to death.

On April 17, McKinley Cameron, racing against time, made efforts to secure a commutation of the sentences. The applica-

---

6. Quoted from newspaper accounts from Ottawa, April 11, 1923 and the Edmonton Journal report of information. Verbatim statements used along with Provincial Gaol Records, Fort Saskatchewan, 1920-1930. Provincial Archives, Edmonton, Alberta.

7. Ibid.

tion had been put before the Minister of Justice several weeks earlier but was being held pending the decision of the court. Now, with the denial by the court for a new trial, the only hope left to Emilio and Florence was commutation of their sentences to life imprisonment by the Minister of Justice who would be taking their case before cabinet in the form of a report. Cabinet would decide whether the law would take its course or the sentence be commuted in the case of one or both of the condemned.

On April 24, McKinley Cameron had a long interview with the Minister of Justice and urged clemency but Sir Lomer Gouin would give no indication what his recommendation to cabinet would be. For the last 20 years it had been customary to commute the capital sentence imposed upon a woman. It was Florence's last hope.

As the young girl waited out the decisions of the courts, she was claimed by nostalgic sadness on the wastefulness of her young life. Her feelings grew within, wild and irrepressible. They beat inside her until she collapsed spent and defeated. She waited for letters from home. It was her only link to her past, and she read and reread the letters and dreamed of going home. She had a feeling of dread, a feeling she would never go back to see the fields of her youth, to walk under the skies, to touch a field daisy. Her mind overflowed with memories and her day dreams took her back to hours precious. She was sickened and repelled by the approaching day but held her feelings in check until the night hours. Her skin took on a luminous shine, her voice a bare whisper of a sigh.

Florence studied her catechism, clung to the hope of a life hereafter, one that would surely be better than the time of her short stay on earth. It was getting close to the end and there was one last hope for commutation of the sentence.

In his austere cell, Emilio sat down to settle his affairs. He was distressed when he heard that the Pass Clothing Company had been closed up without notice. Emilio wrote a long letter filled with instructions. In Blairmore, Maria puzzled over the letters. She had taken no part in the conduct of his business affairs and was bewildered by the details. Picariello instructed Steve to write to all the clothing companies, informing them not to ship any further stock to the Pass Clothing Company. He told him where to find the names in his books. Then Carlo, at Emilio's request, made up hand bills advertising the sale of stock of the company. Steve and Carlo distributed the hand bills from house to house. Carlo continued to collect the rents from the hotel and turned them over to Maria. Funds from the 2% bar went to pay brewery bills.

Carefully Emilio listed all his debts. He instructed Maria to pay these from the dwindling bank accounts being drained by lawyer fees. Emilio was unconsciously clearing his slate. Maria did what she was told, paying all outstanding bills, all except those of the Pass Clothing Company.

XVIII

THE
LILY

IN THE SMALL town of Fernie, British Columbia, Angela Costanzo pulled on a wool mackintosh and stood in the shelter of a narrow porch. A cold drizzle fell from the lowering skies. She looked to the heavy sky; her eyes travelled over the glistening roof tops to a pale spot of colour in the gray day. She thought of Florence and how she loved flowers. The girl, wrapped in the dullness of the prison, would not see the splashes of colour that came suddenly to the sodden fields.

All through the long winter months Angela had contemplated her daughter's plight. What can I do? How can I help? Who do I go to? She turned her empty hands open to the dull sky. The questions were turned over and over in her mind. Tears came often to the mother's face as she struggled to raise the rest of her young family. Late at night she sat down to write her missives in Italian; the same plea was in each one, 'Philomena, you innocent. Tell truth, my daughter, tell truth before it is too late. Please, my daughter, tell the truth'.

The next day, as she rolled the pasta mixture very thin, an insurmountable urge to see her daughter came over the woman. With years of experience she deftly cut the long strips as she worried about getting money for the trip. She grimaced; there was no meat to put in the sauce, it was always Lent at their house. By the time the pasta was ready Angela had worked up the courage to speak to her husband.

Then strangely enough, Vincenzo put pride aside and borrowed money for the trip. Angela was terrified at travelling herself. She decided to take an older child with her and of course would take the baby. She spoke very little English but the older child was fluent in the language and she did have enough money to pay her fare and half fare for the older child. The baby would ride free. With trepidation she boarded the train.

The date of the executions was drawing very close. Florence slept badly, fighting against dreams and nightmares that tried to claim her. In her dreams she was again in the grassy fields of her youth, reliving the picnic near the slough. Happily she felt the sun on her face again, heard bird song from the willows. Someone was with her, a man who moved with easy grace through the quiet scene, a man who held out a lily of purest white with a stamen of glowing gold. She could not see his face, it was shrouded in mist. She turned and held out her hand but the man faded into the haze and was gone. She was lost in the haze and the nightmare started.

She woke with a start, looked around and in disappointment saw the dull walls of her prison cell. All day the dream stayed with her as she turned it over and over in her mind. Little by little her thoughts became clearer, like the ribbons of light coming over the mountains at home, ribbon bands that broadened, bit by bit, hour by hour, until the light burst in exhilaration over the top.

A high colour came to her cheeks, contrasting markedly with the palid face as she realized the significance of her dreams. There was a resurrection, the monk had said so. There was a life hereafter and she had a chance to prepare for it. She turned completely to her God.

Florence was deathly afraid but now she had something to hold onto. She had someone to go with her. The hanging was repulsive but it would be over quickly and if she must die, there was no other way open to her. Now more than ever her thoughts turned to what was beyond. This life had nothing new for her. The trip she would take to new fields, to a new life beyond filled all her waking days. There had to be a better life, once she got beyond the void. She made peace with her Lord and felt He was beside her to guide her along the way.

Now, waiting word of the decision by cabinet, the monk read daily to the girl from the Gospel of Saint John.

"Let not your heart be troubled. You believe in God, believe also in Me. In My Father's house there are many mansions. Were it not so, I should have told you because I go to prepare a place for you... "

As the words washed over the girl, she felt a lift in spiritual strength, experienced a strange peace within herself, an acceptance. She was reconciled by the love of God. And still, the girl clung to that one faint hope.

Emilio, too, as he pondered his fate, harboured a hope for commutation of his sentence. As he was a criminal condemned to death, Emilio was entitled to make his own spiritual decisions. When the court of appeal refused to hear the case, the monk went to see the man. Father Fidelis saw Picariello for the first time on Sunday, April 29.

The man who rose to greet the young religious was courtly and a faint smile came to his face. He grasped the extended hand, then gave the younger man the only seat in the cell. Picariello sat on the bunk and they discussed what had passed.

The man was morose, he wanted so desperately to talk, to make a last statement. The monk readily agreed to send a statement to the Minister of Federal Justice, Sir Lomer Gouin. Painfully, Picariello made his statement which was written out by the monk.[1]

Copy of the statement I sent to Ottawa on Monday night 30th April:

Saw Picariello for first time yesterday. He made long written statement including the following.

He made threats to shoot if his son was killed but when he learned he was only wounded in the hand he

---

1. From author's conversations with Father Chicoine, "Picariello was not a fervent Catholic and he did not call for a priest. He was depressed, moody, morose when Father Chicoine approached him. He wanted the priest to send in his confession." Also included in the chapter are Father Chicoine's writings of Florence's last days.

was quite calm and had no such intention. He asked Lawson to come with him to get his son. Lawson refused. Picariello called him a foul name. Lawson throttled him and tried to get Picariello's gun out of his pocket and there was a struggle. Believes the shot that killed Lawson came from a gun fired by someone at a distance from the car.

Picariello's statement was made without his knowing that Mrs. Lassandra had made any statement and in the main agrees with hers.

Saw him again tonight and he stated the following "Provincial Police Moriarity said if he talked Picariello would not be in any longer ..."

Meanwhile a frightened Florence was taken from her cell and led through the corridor to the public hall. A tight formation of guards flanked the girl and her matron.

"Where are you taking me?" the girl's eyes flew from face to face.

"You have a visitor." The reply was non committal.

"Who? Who is it? Is it my mother? My husband?"

"Come. You see," the matron opened the door to allow Florence and two guards into the room.

On the other side of the enclosure Florence saw her mother's tear stained face. She dug her fingers into the wood of the chair she slumped into.

"Mama, mama," she sobbed.

"Oh my bambino. I love you and want to hold you. Oh to see you again." Tears spilled down the older woman's face as she caught sight of the drawn face of her daughter. She saw, as only a mother can, the sorrow haunting the depths of the girl's eyes.

The matron handed the girl a handkerchief to wipe her face.

"Did papa come? Did my papa come?" Florence's voice rose with anxiety.

Angela's voice sounded helpless. She had so little to give the girl and even this, a small request, she had to turn down.

"No, bambino, no money. Papa. He borrow the money to send me. He loves you, Philomena, he loves you."

"How did you get here? It is so far for you to come, and all alone."

"The train, we come on train, your brother and sister and me." Florence was barely conscious of the frightened faces holding onto Angela's skirts.

"Help me, Mama. Please help me. Get someone to help me."

"You tell truth, Philomena. I get help for you. Get truth down, with words, on the paper." Her mother made motions of writing. "I take it to get help. But no can write. You get someone to write?" The voice was anxious, probing, urgent. Again her mother urged her to save herself, to confess the truth.

"You know Picariello and Carlo made me say I did it. I always had to do what they say, you know that Mama. I didn't hurt that man."

Florence made her request known and quickly prison officials gathered to hear her statement. At her side was the faithful monk.[2]

Edmonton, Alberta, April 28 — 29,1923.

Minister of Justice, Ottawa, Ont.

Following voluntary statement made in writing and signed by Florence Losandro in the presence of her spiritual advisor and provincial Government officials called at her request today, Saturday the twenty-eighth, is hereby transmitted to you at her request, quote: Mr. Picariello went to Fernie on the day of shooting with his wife, son and another girl, for liquor as he told me. He came about 4:30. I heard him say the policemen are after me. He called his son out and said when you hear

---

2. Confession in varience with other testimony but included verbatim. Alberta Provincial Archives, Edmonton, Alberta.

me whistle you beat it back to B.C. with the load. I knew that the boy had gone. About 6 p.m. I heard that the boy had been shot going through Coleman stop. About twenty to seven the boy called up through the phone from Michel. I answered the phone. Stop. He asked for his father who came to the phone and talked to the boy. Stop. I heard him say can you drive back. Stop. I don't know what the answer was but heard Mr. Picariello say he would drive up to bring him back stop He went out, got in the car and I went with him at his request in order that I might bring the boy's (Steve) car back. stop He told me to get a gun. I went to my husband's trunk and got the gun and some bullets stop We went to Coleman. He did not talk on the way stop When there, we stopped at a hotel and he had a conversation with a man, who told him his boy was shot but that he did not think he was badly hurt. stop He drove to corner of Main street and turned back toward Lawson's place stop He stopped car in front of house, door of which man open Stop I saw a man inside. Picariello called to him and he came out and said yes sir Stop Picariello said do you know that you have shot my boy? He answered "Oh do I" Mr. Picariello put one arm on back of seat and the other on steering wheel and Lawson leaned forward on door of car Stop They talked but not in an excited way. I was not paying much attention and all at once I heard two shots stop. I turned around and as I did so I saw a flash go over my legs and saw Lawson on top of Picariello with his arm around his neck and struggling for a gun, don't know in whose hand gun was stop I screamed got on my knees, got hold of someone's hands. I don't know whose stop The gun went off again stop After that I saw two flashes in the alley and next thing I saw was Lawson lying on his back in the alley stop The gun they were struggling for was not the one I brought but one that I supposed belonged to Picariello. I don't

know what became of that stop I went back to Blairmore
in the car I went to a little shack there and stayed there
with Picariello the greater part of the night stop We
discussed the matter together and I ask him how it
happened. He said I don't know stop I asked him if it
could have happened when I struck his hand up. He
said it might have for me to take the blame as women
don't hang in Canada that when he would get out he
would spend the last cent he had to get me out stop I
never touched the gun in the car stop Just after we left
Lawson Picariello said oh my God what did I do stop
After we got out of the car at Blairmore he gave me the
gun for my protection stop On our way back from
Coleman, Picariello appeared to be dazed and I had to
help him with the steering wheel he seemed helpless
stop He asked me to load the gun for him but I said I
don't know how he then loaded it while I held the
steering wheel stop I went out with Picariello and the
son for protection in order that I might say it was my
booze and I would take the blame stop. He said they
would not fire on a car with a woman in it. stop. My
husband was working for Picariello and we all lived
together as one family he treated me as a daughter.
stop. I saw Picariello arrested when I was in a house
of his friend nearby. stop. I said to the woman in the
house, I might as well give myself up. She said yes,
and we agreed that it would be best for me to take the
responsibility and say that I did it as women don't
hang in Canada and he would get off. Stop. I never
heard of Lawson before the shooting - Did not know
where he lived and on the way to Coleman we discussed him stop. I did not know until afterward that
he had shot Steve. I only cared for Steve as a brother
and had no reason for revenge stop. Lawson was shot
by a thirty eight revolver but I don't know how it
happened. I am positive that I never had a gun in my
hands. Stop. He also told me to say in case his finger

prints were shown on the thirty eight that I should say that I gave it to him to load and that he loaded it for me. I did not know how to shoot a gun and when he handed me the thirty-eight after leaving Coleman I told him I did not know how to shoot a gun. He said just pull the trigger stop. I never shot a gun in my life, was always afraid of them stop. On the way to Coleman, he was talking to himself and I heard him say I'll shoot the son of a bitch I told Father Fidelis some two months ago that I was innocent stop I told Harris, my first solicitor that I had agreed to take all the blame but I never mentioned this to Cameron stop Picariello told me to say as little as possible and he would do the talking stop While we were nearing Lawson's house noticed that man in house was policeman - could tell that by his breeches stop I said to Picariello whatever you do, do not shoot stop he made no reply. Afterwards he says you tell anyone who asks you that you did it and if anyone tells you that I have confessed tell that they are damn liars stop he was to tell the same story stop Foregoing statement is made by me voluntarily, taken down at my request to be used for transmission to Minister of Justice, Ottawa or otherwise as my spiritual advisor may see fit. Quotations stop ...

(Signed) Florence Losandro

J.E. Brownlee, Attorney General

On Monday, April 30th the communication was received by the Department of Justice in Ottawa. In Calgary, the Woman's Labour Party passed a resolution asking that the sentence be commuted to life imprisonment. Then again the Canadian Prisoners' Welfare Association made a final appeal for clemency for Florence. Their message read:

"Having for some time past protested the proposed execution of the woman, Florence Losandro, at Fort Saskatchewan, the Canadian Prisoners' Welfare Association desires to enter a final appeal that the degrading and revolting spectacle of hanging a woman in the twentieth century should not be permitted under your regime. It is twenty four years since any such occurrence in Canada. A similar event in England caused widespread horror. We are aware that local sentiment especially on the part of the woman is for hanging but suggest that the spirit of revenge should be checked rather than encouraged by a Christian state.

In any case the desire for blood would be satisfied by the execution of the man though even this is against our principle as we wish all capital punishment be abolished. We wish formally to wash our hands of the blood of this woman on Wednesday, next."

As the prisoners waited for the last final decision the arrangements for the executions were taking place.

Sheriff John Rae left his office in Edmonton and drove slowly in the direction of Fort Saskatchewan. He was to superintend the arrangements for the double executions. The work of building the open air scaffold had been started but there were other preliminary arrangements to tend to. The hangman had been alerted and the sheriff reflected on his fee... $200.00 for each person executed. Well, thought John Rae, he could have it. Rae wouldn't do the job for all the money in China.

The man turned his attention to the countryside, to the dark brown earth lying expectantly, waiting the touch of a plow. Gentle spring rains had come, bringing a lushness to the land. His mind kept going back to the haunting sad face of the young woman.

The sheriff would be one of the witnesses at the hanging along with the Jury that was required to certify the deaths. Rae knew that Section 1071 of the Criminal Code provided the body of every offender executed be buried within the walls of the prison. He knew, too, Steve Picariello and the woman's husband petitioned the Lieutenant Governor to release the bodies for a Christian burial. The chilling report was given to Rae to read: "The Executive Council has had under consideration the report of the Honourable Attorney General, dated May 1, 1923 stating that:

Whereas Florence Losandro is now confined in the Provincial Gaol at Fort Saskatchewan under sentence of death, which sentence is to be executed on Wednesday the 2 of May, 1923, and

Whereas it is provided by Section 1071 of the Criminal Code that the body of every offender executed shall be buried within the walls of the prison within which judgment of death is executed on her, unless the Lieutenant Governor in Council otherwise orders, and

Whereas Charles Losandro, the husband of the said Florence Losandro, has requested that the body of his wife may be interred otherwise than within the walls of the said prison, and

Whereas it is expedient that such request be complied with, Therefore upon the recommendation of the Honourable Attorney General, the Executive Council advises that the Sheriff of the Judicial District of Edmonton be and is hereby authorized, after the holding of the inquest directed by the Criminal Code, upon the request of the said Charles Losandro, and upon the said Charles Losandro making provision for all the expenses of the interment, to cause the body of the said Florence Losandro to be interred in the Roman Catholic Cemetery at North Edmonton and if no such request shall have been made to the sheriff and provision made for the costs of such interment by the said Charles Losandro on or before twelve o'clock noon on the second day of May 1923, the said body shall be interred within the walls of the said prison."

(signed) H. Greenfield, Chairman[3]

The same cold impersonal orders were completed for Emilio at the request of Steve.

It was 24 years since a woman was executed in Canada. A woman by the name of Emily Hilda Blake of Brandon, Manitoba paid the death penalty on December 27, 1899 and the same year, Cordelia Viau was put to death in St. Scholastique, Quebec for the murder of her husband. There had not been an execution of a woman since.[4]

Sheriff Rae was nearing the small town. Early morning sunshine gleamed on dew gathered on weed stocks rotting in the ditches. The air was heavy with moisture and the piping sounds of birds. Now the gaol buildings, strangely ugly, came into view.

There was a strange sort of quiet permeating the prison. Fear of death and the approaching certainty of his visit was seen on the faces of the inmates. They were sullenly silent; they averted their eyes in utter hopelessness. On Tuesday, newspaper reporters were given a tour of gaol facilities. The crowd of reporters followed the guard giving the tour. They saw it all, looking around curiously and counting the 18 steps up the gallows. They made morbid notes as they walked, careful not to omit anything that would draw readers to their papers. They would not be allowed in the gaol on Wednesday, the executions, if they took place, would be held in the prison yard in strict privacy with only the necessary officials present. Admission to the scaffold was through the prisoner's door at the rear of the gaol.

After the newsmen left, Florence was moved from the

---

3. Attorney General Files, Provincial Archives, Edmonton, Alberta.

4. News clippings, Canadian Press, Ottawa, April 28, 1923.

women's section of the prison to a main floor cell in the men's prison.[5]

The hangman, a short man in his fifties, arrived at the prison on this last day, carrying a satchel under his arm. His appearance was one of shabbiness. He imperturbably went about his business, checking the levers, oiling the trap, putting out the black caps. He was avoided at all costs by most people at the gaol, he carried death and despondency in his hands. When he had measured and weighed his subjects he left the gaol. No one knew, or cared, where he went.

In Ottawa, newsmen gathered around Minister of Justice, Sir Lomer Gouin, when he left his office. Questioned on the possibility of a commutation he would give no information.

"Sorry, Gentlemen, the final decision will not be available until later in the afternoon." His tone and manner offered no hope.

Newsmen speculated among themselves, with the majority feeling the original decision not to commute the death penalty would stand.

It was late in the afternoon and an early twilight wove a soft web through the bars of her cell. Florence lay curled on the bunk... waiting. Then the door opened and Father Fidelis stepped inside. Florence looked anxiously into his face, searching, trying to read hope in his eyes. She stood and he took her outstretched hands in his.

"Florence, I am most sorry. I will have to buy the lilies for you."[6]

At once she grasped the meaning and her hands went to cover her face. Long, shuddering sobs shook the slight body. The very silence seemed to echo the words...sorry...sorry...the lilies.

The monk, sick at heart, burst into weeping. Then, curiously

---

5. I remember that the very night preceding her death, she had been transferred to a different one. I am of the opinion that the condemned to death were not allowed to mingle with the other inmates. I do not think that a special guardian was assigned to her writings of Father Chicoine to author.

6. Taken from writings June 5, 1978 of Father Chicoine to author. His actual words to Florence, June 5, 1978.

the girl, heart sick and afraid as she was, turned to comfort him. The man stayed with the girl, talking, comforting her. Then he left, promising to come back soon.[7]

As the evening shadows crept into her cell, Florence was bitterly engulfed in massive waves of revulsion and fear. The feelings built inside her and hammered at her very being. The shell she built contained the feelings, enclosed the masses of horror, keeping it tightly within. On the surface she appeared calm and contained.

She called her matron into the cell. Her last requests were few; her rosary set aside to give to Father Fidelis. He would give it to her mother. She destroyed her letters, gave away her unfinished and finished embroideries and small personal possessions to her matrons. There was nothing left. She sat down to wait for the monk.

Florence was to pass through a terror stricken evening. In her half shock she had the sensation of being chased and suffered the inability to move. A sudden start brought her to reality and she lay shivering on her bunk.

Throughout the night there was the sound of rain and the drops, forming in heavy sheets, blurred the lights of the town. People looked out their windows towards the gaol, rubbed steam from the panes and wondered which lighted windows held the two unfortunate people. Extra guards were posted at all the entrances to the prison grounds and security was tight. Police, walking with dogs, moved over the grounds. One by one the lights of the houses in the town went out as people locked their doors, pulled down the blinds and went to bed.

When Emilio received the painful news, he sat down and wrote a last long letter to Maria. He spoke of each of his children, from Steve, the eldest to the baby of two years. He assured Maria of his love and asked her to take care of the children, then sealed the envelope, put down his head and

---

7. From writings of Father Chicoine to author — "Florence showed bitterness when told of having to buy the lilies. It was a common idea that justice dealt lightly with a woman, so Florence was sure she would not be hanged."

wept.

Later, when Emilio sat alone with his thoughts, a friend's conversation came back to haunt him and he heard the words, poignant and soft, as if they were spoken just yesterday.

"Mio, why don't you retire from your work?"

No mention was made of bootlegging but they both knew what the man meant.

The two men were leaving the room where the town council of Blairmore had met in session.

"Sell your property, Emilio, go back home to the old country. Live in the country like a gentleman. Get a small vineyard...." The voice trailed off. He looked closely at Emilio hoping he would listen. He tried to laugh off his next statement. "You can't run on good looks forever." The laugh which came was hollow.

Emilio shrugged and smiled.

"No, mio, this is my life, I stay."

"Yeah," said the other one sorrowfully, "but the day will come and you will not be able to go back. What is the use of it all? The bravado, the prestige here among the others will be of no good to you. You don't need to struggle anymore, you have made your living. You are the Emperor among us but back home you would be the King. Enough of the lawsuits and the dance of death with the boys in blue. Go soon, my friend, before it's too late."

Emilio rose to pace the cell. He pounded his fist against the rough walls and blood came to the deep scratches. His friend's prophecy was coming true. He would never return to his country, never. At midnight Father Fidelis came to him with Holy Communion.

Then the monk returned to the cell where Florence sat staring into nothingness. The girl looked up at his approach.

"The lilies, Father, when will the lilies come?"

The girl fretted not so much over the flower in itself, but over what its significance meant to her.

"Father, won't I get the lilies in time? You did order them, I know you did. Then why aren't they here?"

The lilies still had not arrived. The monk had ordered the flowers from a florist on Jasper Avenue opposite the Hudson's Bay Store in Edmonton. He ordered six perfect unblemished lilies for the girl.

Then Florence knelt to receive the Host and the blessing. She turned, composed, to say her prayers.

The monk read to her from the Discourse of the Lord to his disciples at the Last Supper as quoted from the Gospel of St. John. The words fell softly and simply from his lips.[8]

"He who believes in me, believes not in me but in Him who sent Me. And he who sees Me, sees him who sent me. I have come a light into the world, that whoever believes in me may not remain in the darkness....."

It was a pathetic scene in the cold dark gloom before the first light of dawn. The monk, youthful in body and stature, was aged by eyes that had seen suffering and pain. The young girl, defeated and fearful, with darkened circles under her eyes, sat listening to the words coming softly in the vast stillness of the prison night and did not seem to notice the muffled footsteps of preparation.

The words the monk spoke comforted the girl, fell with poignancy on the weighted shoulders carrying the dreadful burden. Florence listened carefully to the words uttered by Jesus before he underwent the bitter tortures of the crucifixion.

"Amen, amen. I say to you, he who believes in me, the works that I do he also shall do, and greater than these he shall do, because I am going to the Father. And whatever you ask in my name, that I will do, in order that the Father may be glorified in the Son. If you ask anything in my name, I will do it."

Gradually it came to her, a resigned submission as she heard the words of her Savior's love. The words washed over her, balmed the ugliness awaiting her.

Relentlessly the minutes ticked on towards the dawn.

---

8. Ibid.

At 4 o'clock, the officials who would be at the executions were awakened at the hotel. Before the dawn, the hangman walked alone down the gravelled road to the gaol.

In the gaol, a tight knot of Jurymen drew together. They had been subpoenaed to attend the executions and reluctantly they arrived, one by one, before the dawn. E. LaRiche was the foreman, C. Lepage, F. Hattebuhr, A. Paterson, V. Faulhafer, and J. Meyers made up the jury.[9] The coroner was Dr. Henry. Two witnesses were H. Dodge and Dr. Mooney. Dr. Henry would be paid $20.00 for his duty; the others would receive $1.00 each.

The law said an inquest will be held after each execution when the jurymen had viewed the body and were sworn in. The billing for the charges was ready to go forward to the Attorney General. In chilling impersonal language the billing read 'for services authorized and performed, charges fair and just'.

And so these men, commanded to do a job, were drawn together to support each other. They felt time converging upon them, pulling and sucking against their safe contented lives. They watched each other and hoped for bravado in their eyes. Death was too close to them now, they wanted to be done with it; and, greedy for life, wanted to get out of the shadow of the scaffold, away from the pall of death.

In the warden's office the officials charged with the executions gathered. Sheriff John Rae was there, along with Commissioner W.C. Bryant, Superintendent Nicolson, Detective Leslie and Father Chicoine. Coroner Dr. Henry was the last to arrive. As the sheriff listened to the muted talk in the room, he was asking himself which one would be first. When he turned, he voiced the question to the room.

In the silence that followed his question, Father Chicoine spoke up. The man should go first, he said, hoping in his heart that Picariello might make some kind of declaration to clear

---

9. Names vary in different files, may be shown incorrectly. Fort Saskatchewan, Provincial Archives, Edmonton, Alberta.

Florence before he passed away. To the monk's relief, Rae agreed with him.

Just then, Dr. Mooney came back to the Warden's Office. He recorded in the books the medicines administered to the prisoners in the late evening. To Picariello he had given 2 ounces of Spiritus Frumenti. To the woman, the doctor had given 1 ounce of the same and an injection of a half gram of morphine.[10]

At 5 o'clock the Sheriff, the warden and guards along with Father Chicoine went to the cell door where Emilio was being held. He was manacled and the procession marched along the hollow corridors to the gallows. The procession passed near the cell where Florence was being held. She heard their steps and sensed the ultimate destination of the march. She was a step nearer to death, a breath closer to eternity. She felt light headed, the drug was taking effect. Her young face with the dark eyes was unfathomable, strangely serene.

At 5:15 a.m., Emilio, without a word or gesture, went to his death.

When they came for Florence, the girl hesitated for just a moment at the door. Her matron looked at her, put out her hand to support the girl. Florence bit her lip, closed her eyes, steeled herself and when she opened them again, only a trace of moisture showed. Quiet and composed, she left the cell.

Then, for a very short interval of time Florence was seated on a stool in the public hall surrounded by guards. The hangman appeared in the doorway and, crossed the floor to fit the manacles on her slim wrists. He pulled at them hard; the cruel steel bit into her soft flesh and she cried out in pain. Father Chicoine stepped forward, asked him to loosen them and the hangman did so immediately without comment.[11]

The procession started off. The Warden, the Sheriff and guards, then the monk. Florence was followed by her matron,

10. Doctor's Daily Records, 1923, Fort Saskatchewan, Provincial Archives, Edmonton, Alberta.

11. From the writings of Father Chicoine to author.

the hangman was at the rear. The only voice heard was the monk's as he intoned the prayers for the dying. The girl moved with decorum, seemingly fully self possessed. Again Florence followed the path of Picariello as unwillingly as she had during her short life. She started the long walk to another life as she had as a bride, hesitant, afraid; only today she did not have her earthly father's comforting hand.

They came to a door and her eyes travelled over it. It was an omen, a passage through which she would pass, never to return. It opened. She stepped through.

At the foot of the stairs, Florence started up steadily. Her matron fell into a dead faint and was carried away. Florence never noticed what went on behind her. She saw the soft blue of a very dimly lit sky, the break of dawn through torn cobwebs of cloud. She seemed to be saying a good bye to someone; barely audible words, hopeless whispers caught against lips that trembled, "....to You do I look, and in Your name..."

The moments were slipping away. Shaking her head as if to clear her head from the daze of the drugs, she stepped to the gallows. She was determined not to break, she had held on through all these months, it was just a little bit longer, just a little bit more.

She stood quietly on the trap as the black hood was put over her head. The hangman adjusted the noose. Father Chicoine stood close to the girl, speaking softly, his voice in prayer giving her comfort and support.

"Please, father, wipe away my tears."[12]

The monk did so ever so gently.

The girl was asked if she had anything to say.

"Picariello, he lied. I didn't hurt anyone, ever. I will not forgive any of you for doing this to me."

Then the monk spoke quickly, "Florence, remember Our Lord, at the Last Judgment will render justice to everyone

---

12. Father Chicoine in an interview with the author in Montreal stated he had kept the handkerchief used to wipe away her tears for many years after.

according to their merits. Remember too, Florence, the words of Jesus Christ on the cross. In His agony, He forgave everyone for what they did."

There was a swift intake of breath, then her words came through the black fabric.

"Father, I...forgive..."[13]

Turning away sadly, the monk moved from the side of the girl and nodded to the sheriff.

Falling to her death, Florence cried out.

"Mother..."

---

13. From the writings of Father Chicoine to author.

Epilogue

Taken from writings of Father Fidelis Chicoine, O.F.M. dated June 5, 1978 to the author:

"I had scarcely come back to my office when Florence's mother rapped at my door. After expressing my condolence I handed out to her the rosary which Florence had set apart for her. Naturally enough for a mother, she complained bitterly over the whole tragedy. After her departure I said Mass for the repose of those passing and pitiable parishioners of mine.

The daily Edmonton Journal gave a moving account of that double hanging which had held the population in suspense for days and weeks principally to the singular plight of Florence Losandro whose culpability had been put in doubt by a great many although she had at first assumed the responsibility of Lawson's death. She took the blame presumably to save Picariello whose culpability, right or wrong, she took for granted, hoping that a woman would escape easier the capital punishment. Whatever opinion one may hold as to these conjectures, her stand, more heroical than wise, has deserved for her deep pity and sympathy.

Fr. Fidelis Chicoine, O.F.M."

On a warm fall day, I visited the North Edmonton cemetery and found the unmarked graves of Emilio Picariello and Florence Losandro.

Jock Carpenter

"... and again bootleggers always turn in bad end, and so fathers, take my advice, never learn your children to take your footsteps in bootlegging, never brake the laws, or they will be a day you'll pay for it.

Picariello and Florence paid dear for their good times while bootlegging together, they both got hung in Saskatchewan jail, what a life to end.

Picariello done his work mostly at night, he had two cars, one for his son and one for himself, with the money he was making he didn't want for anything, money makes the mare go ..."

from the diaries of Marie Rose Smith

The End

About The Author

Jock Carpenter, like her Metis ancestors is a prairie girl, and is intensely proud of her status as an official, card carrying Metis. A resident of Lethbridge, she won wide acclaim for her sensitive literary prowess with her first book Fifty Dollar Bride. An interest in her heritage grew from early enquiries to five years of research which resulted in the story of her grandmother, Marie Rose who was sold by her family to a trapper for fifty dollars. Fifty Dollar Bride is in its second printing and still selling after seventeen years since its first publication.

Ms. Carpenter combines a talent for the most meticulous research with a beautiful typical and sensitive writing style. She has the uncanny skill to create each of her characters with deep respect while at the same time revealing their intrinsic traits of good or evil with surgical accuracy.

Bootlegger's Bride is the product of 10 years of research and writing.

It is warm and compassionate and becomes the definitive story of one of Canada's most intriguing murders.